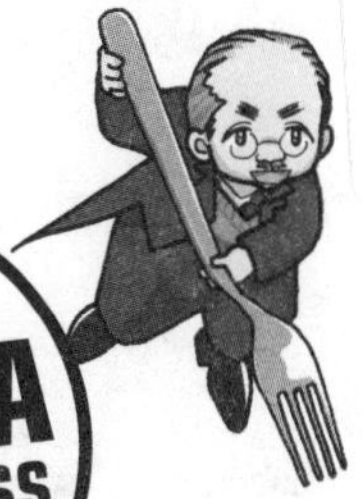

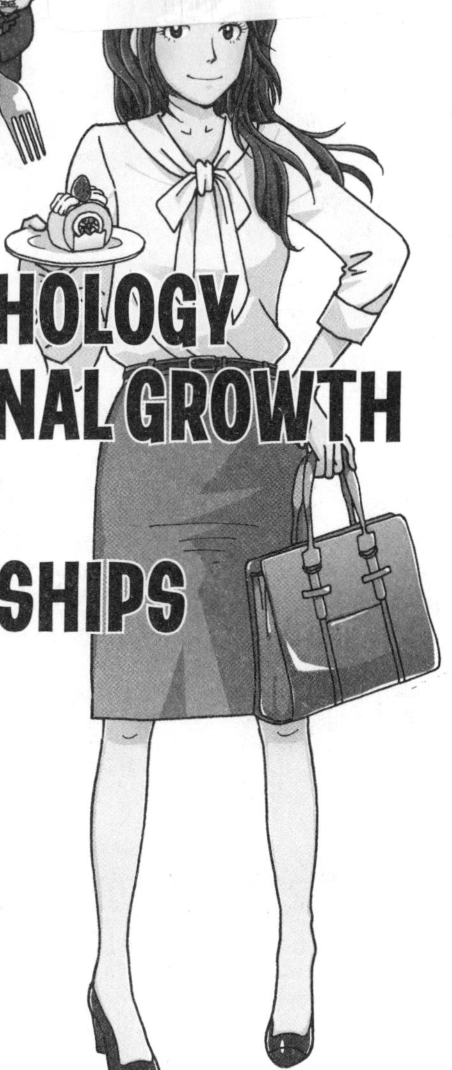

MANGA FOR SUCCESS

THE PSYCHOLOGY OF PERSONAL GROWTH & BETTER RELATIONSHIPS

WRITTEN BY
TOSHINORI IWAI

SCENARIOS BY
HIROFUMI HOSHII

ILLUSTRATED BY
AKI FUKAMORI

WILEY

Published by John Wiley & Sons, Inc., Hoboken, New Jersey.

Published simultaneously in Canada.

Original Japanese edition published by JMA Management Center Inc.

English translation rights arranged with JMA Management Center Inc. through The English Agency (Japan) Ltd.

For general information on our other products and services or for technical support, please contact our Customer Care Department within the United States at (800) 762-2974, outside the United States at (317) 572-3993 or fax (317) 572-4002.

Wiley also publishes its books in a variety of electronic formats. Some content that appears in print may not be available in electronic formats. For more information about Wiley products, visit our website at www.wiley.com.

Library of Congress Cataloging-in-Publication Data is Available:
ISBN 9781394176076 (Paperback)
ISBN 9781394176083 (ePub)
ISBN 9781394176090 (ePDF)

Cover Design: JMA Management Center Inc.
Cover Images: JMA Management Center Inc.
© ShEd Artworks/Shutterstock

SKY10042724_031023

Contents

Prologue

What Is Adlerian Psychology?

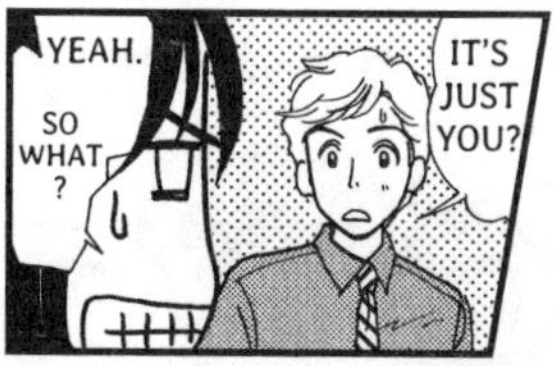
IT'S JUST YOU?
YEAH.
SO WHAT?

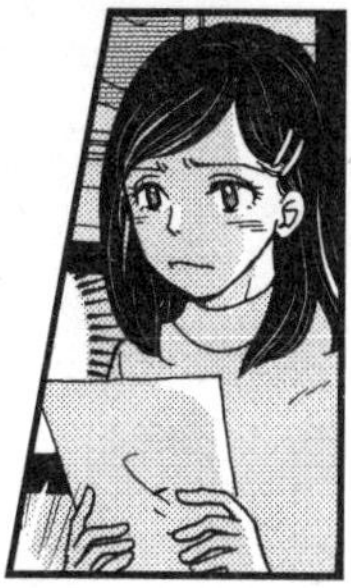

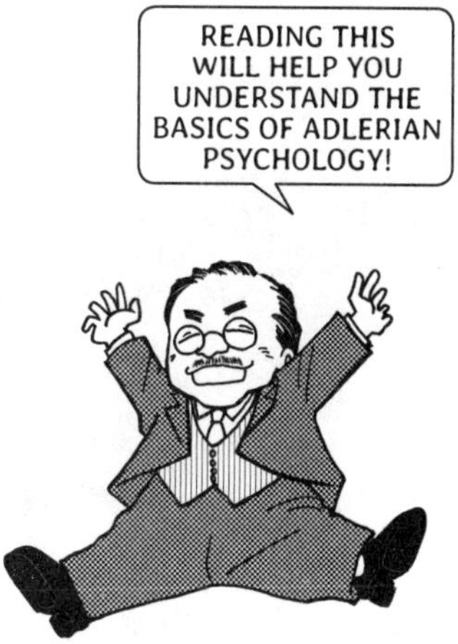
READING THIS WILL HELP YOU UNDERSTAND THE BASICS OF ADLERIAN PSYCHOLOGY!

Part 1

If You Change Your Perspective, Your Life Will Be Easier

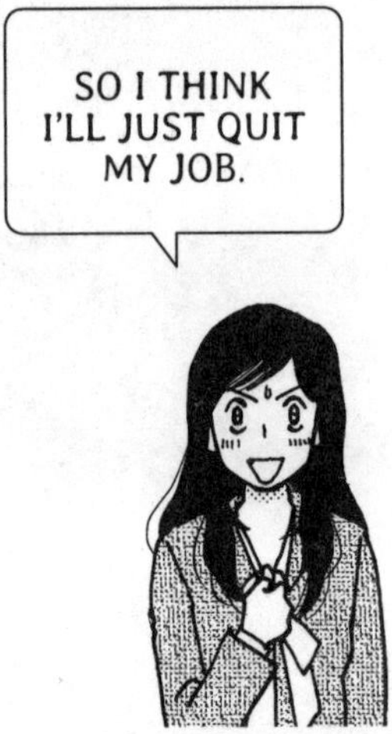

SO I THINK I'LL JUST QUIT MY JOB.

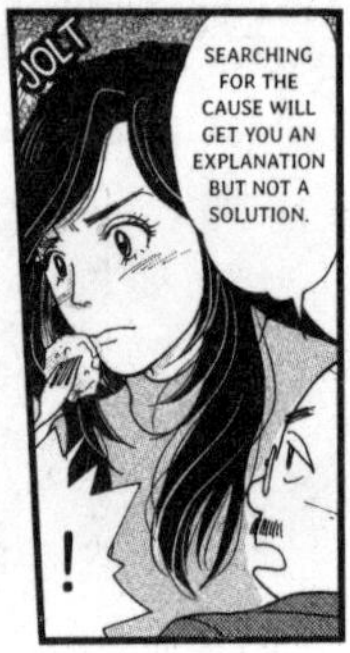

JOLT
SEARCHING FOR THE CAUSE WILL GET YOU AN EXPLANATION BUT NOT A SOLUTION.
!

Part 2

Understanding the Role of Emotion in the Formation of Lifestyle

Part 3

From the World of Assumptions to Common Sense

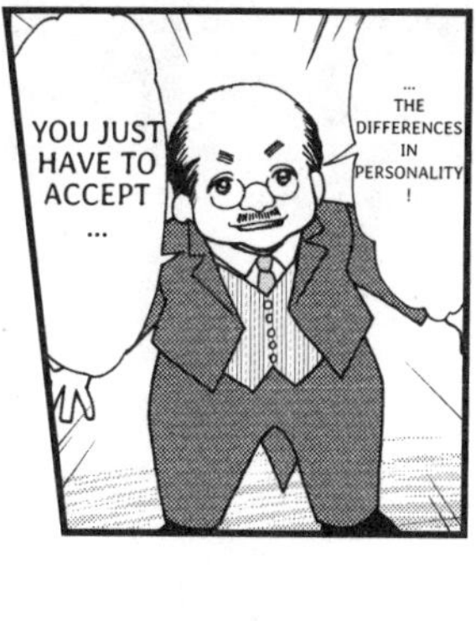
YOU JUST HAVE TO ACCEPT ...
... THE DIFFERENCES IN PERSONALITY !

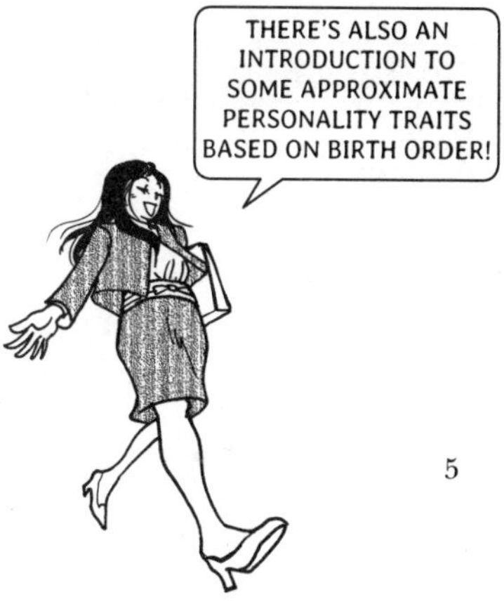
THERE'S ALSO AN INTRODUCTION TO SOME APPROXIMATE PERSONALITY TRAITS BASED ON BIRTH ORDER!

Part 4

Interpersonal Relationships and Emotions

EVERYONE LIVES IN A SPHERE OF THEIR OWN ASSUMPTIONS.

I'M GOING TOO.

WHAT

COULD IT BE THAT WHAT YOU'RE FEELING ARE FEELINGS OF INFERIORITY?

Part 5

What Is Encouragement?

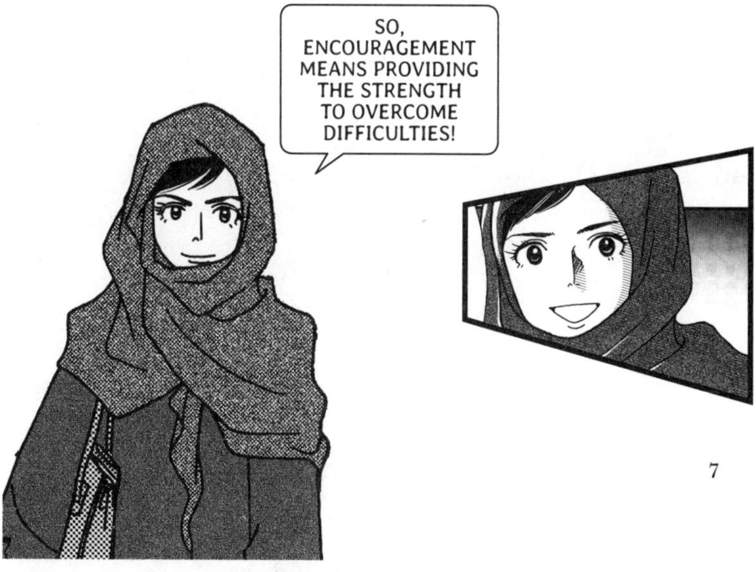
SO, ENCOURAGEMENT MEANS PROVIDING THE STRENGTH TO OVERCOME DIFFICULTIES!

Preface

Alfred Adler is one of the great psychologists of the last century, most well known for his work emphasizing the individual within their social and family environments. His work is enjoying a recent rise in popularity because of the mental health challenges people around the world are facing. This book is my attempt at making the essence of Adlerian psychology as easy as possible to understand for this growing audience.

It has been a long but short 30 years since I first began working with Adlerian psychology. I have used this experience to try and condense the essence and practical application of Adlerian psychology into the most easy-to-understand format possible in this book.

Many people whom I have met in my research and counseling have said to me that they understand the theory of Adlerian psychology but want to know how to apply it to their everyday lives.

Adlerian psychology is all about putting things into practice. Adler would probably be upset if he heard people weren't applying his teachings in the workplace, at home, or in their personal lives. This book isn't solely Adler's direct teachings but includes later developments in his psychology, as well as my own experience from study, counseling, and knowledge born from everyday life.

This book will encourage you! The manga section follows our main character Yukari and the story of her growth. You should be able to find plenty of encouragement just by empathizing with her and those around her. Afterward, in the written sections, you can further your understanding of the material and learn how to apply it to your own life in order to achieve your own personal growth as well as encourage the growth of those around you.

Finally, let's look at how to read this book. There are three patterns. The first is the normal way: just read it from start to finish. The second is to read only the manga sections. The third is to read only the typeset text.

If you feel it is difficult to read everything from start to finish, then it is fine to read only the manga section first. Then, once you are finished with that, go back and read the typeset text.

This book is designed to guide you through all the steps from understanding to capability to mastery. I hope you are able to look forward to your own progress as you turn the pages. Thank you very much for purchasing this book. I hope that when you have finished reading it, you will feel a sense of gratitude to yourself as well.

Toshinori Iwai

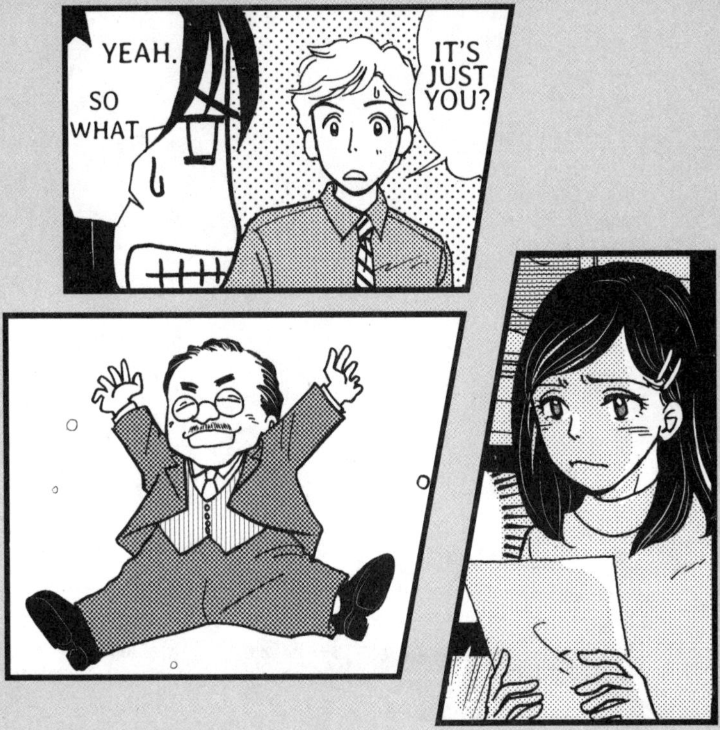
YEAH.
SO WHAT
IT'S JUST YOU?

Prologue

What Is Adlerian Psychology?

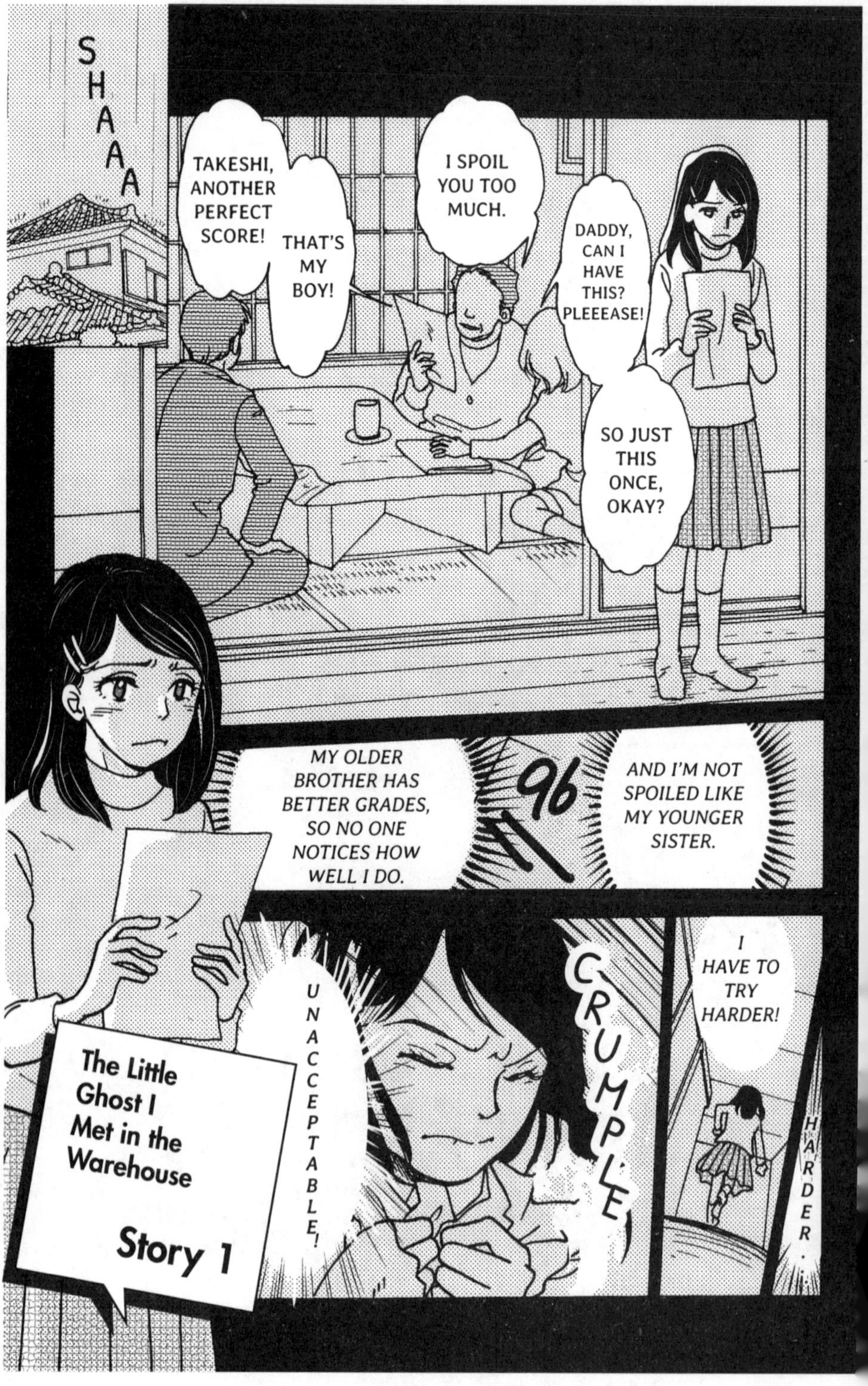
SHAAA
TAKESHI, ANOTHER PERFECT SCORE!
THAT'S MY BOY!
I SPOIL YOU TOO MUCH.
DADDY, CAN I HAVE THIS? PLEEEASE!
SO JUST THIS ONCE, OKAY?
MY OLDER BROTHER HAS BETTER GRADES, SO NO ONE NOTICES HOW WELL I DO.
96
AND I'M NOT SPOILED LIKE MY YOUNGER SISTER.
The Little Ghost I Met in the Warehouse
Story 1
UNACCEPTABLE!
CRUMPLE
I HAVE TO TRY HARDER!
HARDER...

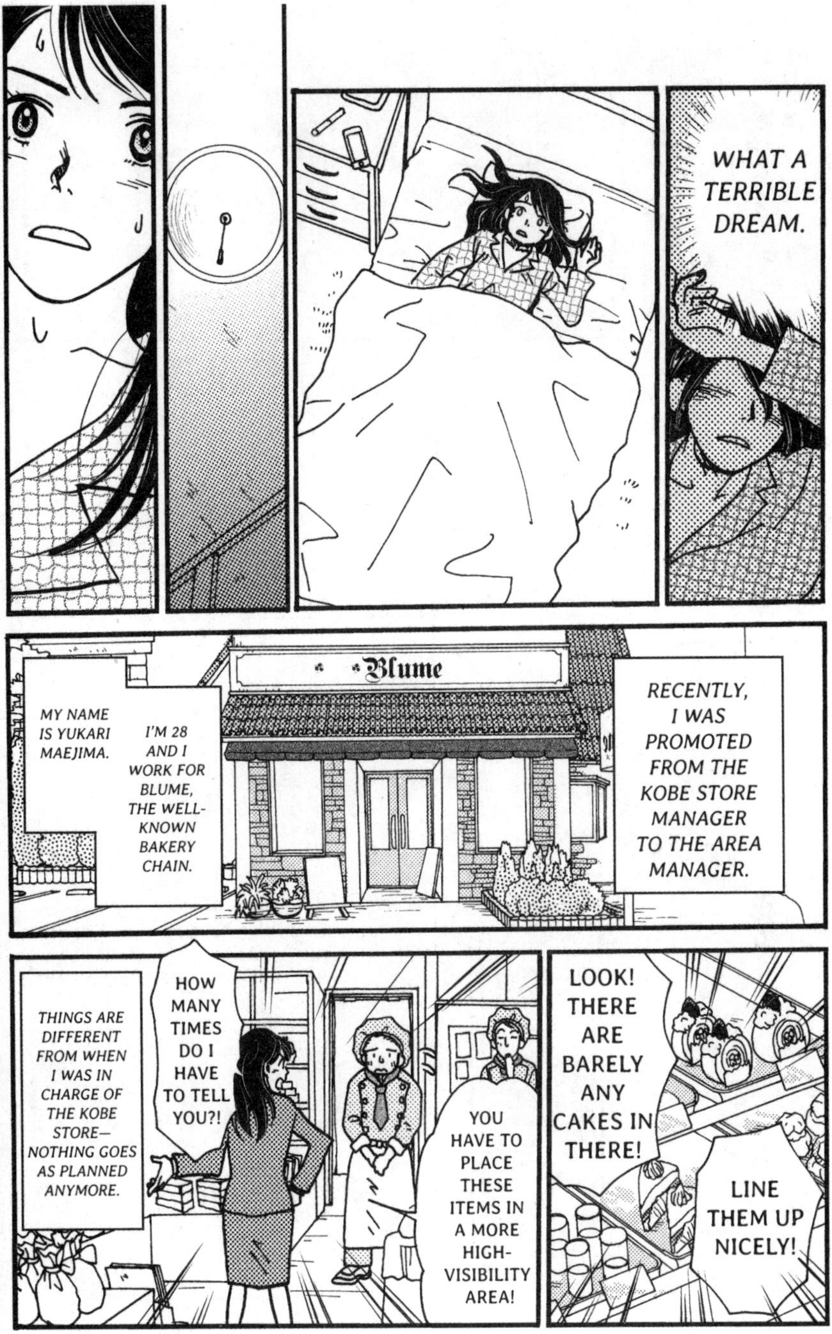
WHAT A TERRIBLE DREAM.
Blume
MY NAME IS YUKARI MAEJIMA.
I'M 28 AND I WORK FOR BLUME, THE WELL-KNOWN BAKERY CHAIN.
RECENTLY, I WAS PROMOTED FROM THE KOBE STORE MANAGER TO THE AREA MANAGER.
THINGS ARE DIFFERENT FROM WHEN I WAS IN CHARGE OF THE KOBE STORE—NOTHING GOES AS PLANNED ANYMORE.
HOW MANY TIMES DO I HAVE TO TELL YOU?!
YOU HAVE TO PLACE THESE ITEMS IN A MORE HIGH-VISIBILITY AREA!
LOOK! THERE ARE BARELY ANY CAKES IN THERE!
LINE THEM UP NICELY!

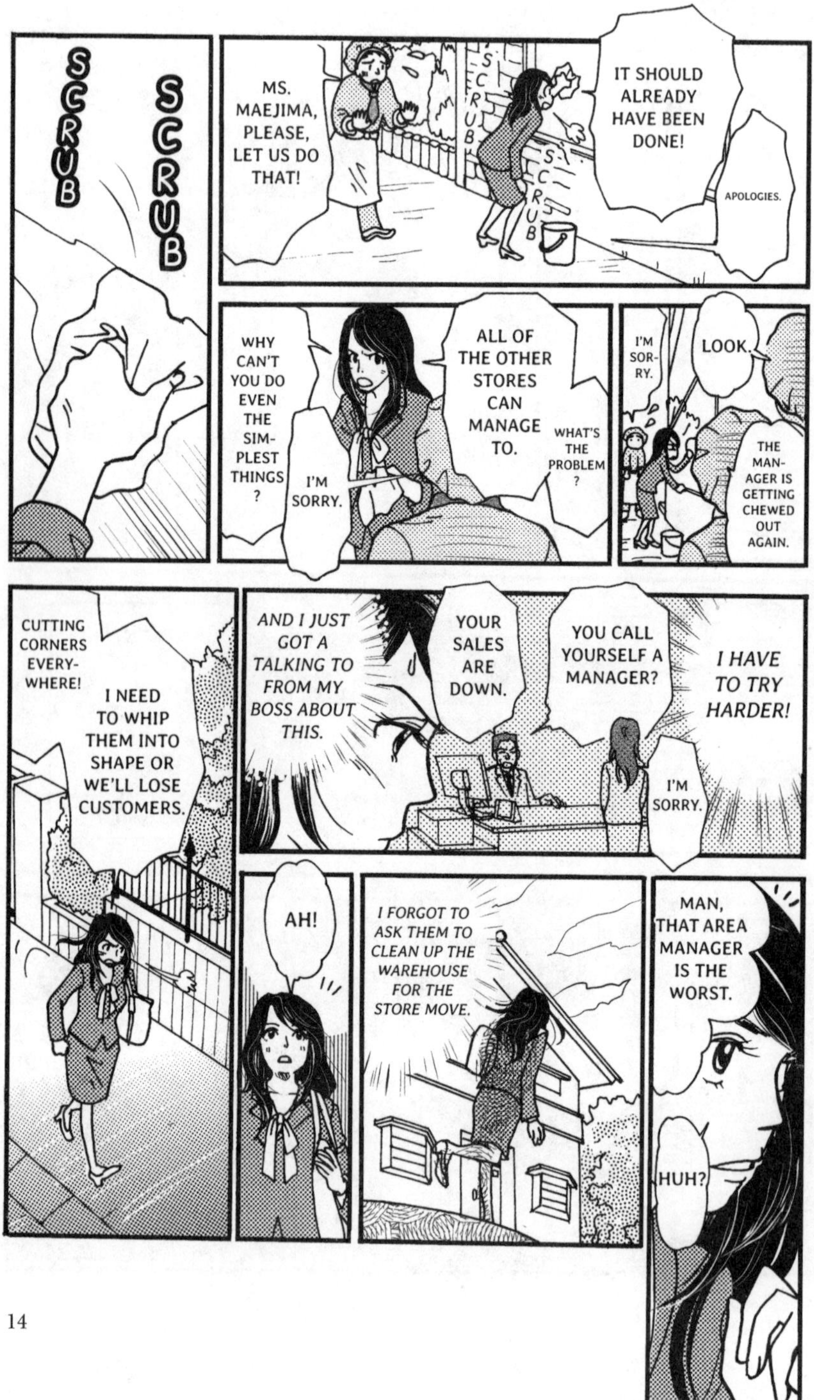
SCRUB SCRUB
MS. MAEJIMA, PLEASE, LET US DO THAT!
SCRUB SCRUB
IT SHOULD ALREADY HAVE BEEN DONE!
APOLOGIES.
WHY CAN'T YOU DO EVEN THE SIMPLEST THINGS?
I'M SORRY.
ALL OF THE OTHER STORES CAN MANAGE TO.
WHAT'S THE PROBLEM?
I'M SORRY.
LOOK.
THE MANAGER IS GETTING CHEWED OUT AGAIN.
CUTTING CORNERS EVERYWHERE!
I NEED TO WHIP THEM INTO SHAPE OR WE'LL LOSE CUSTOMERS.
AND I JUST GOT A TALKING TO FROM MY BOSS ABOUT THIS.
YOUR SALES ARE DOWN.
YOU CALL YOURSELF A MANAGER?
I HAVE TO TRY HARDER!
I'M SORRY.
AH!
I FORGOT TO ASK THEM TO CLEAN UP THE WAREHOUSE FOR THE STORE MOVE.
MAN, THAT AREA MANAGER IS THE WORST.
HUH?

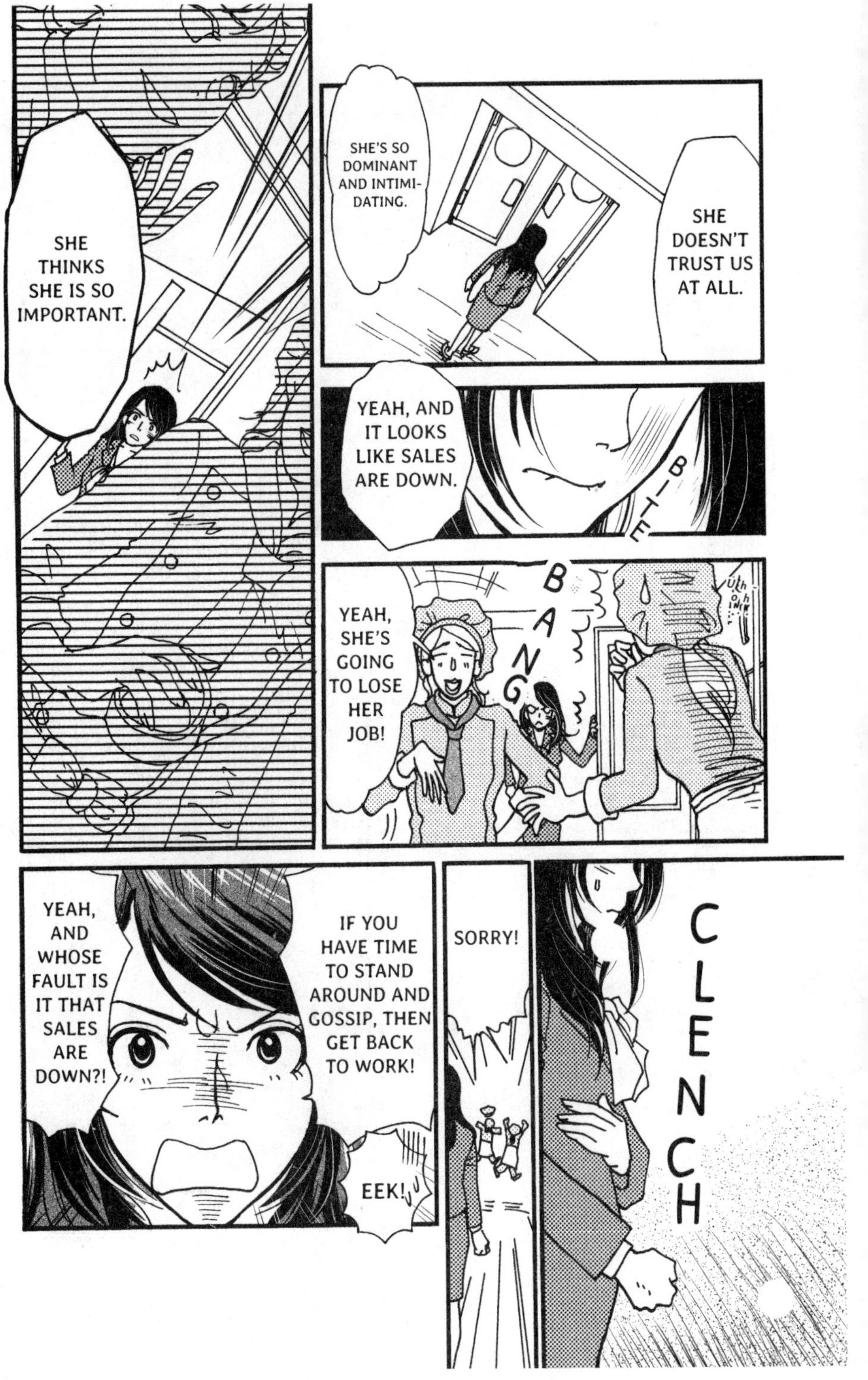
SHE THINKS SHE IS SO IMPORTANT.
SHE'S SO DOMINANT AND INTIMI-DATING.
SHE DOESN'T TRUST US AT ALL.
YEAH, AND IT LOOKS LIKE SALES ARE DOWN.
BITE
YEAH, SHE'S GOING TO LOSE HER JOB!
BANG
YEAH, AND WHOSE FAULT IS IT THAT SALES ARE DOWN?!
IF YOU HAVE TIME TO STAND AROUND AND GOSSIP, THEN GET BACK TO WORK!
EEK!
SORRY!
CLENCH

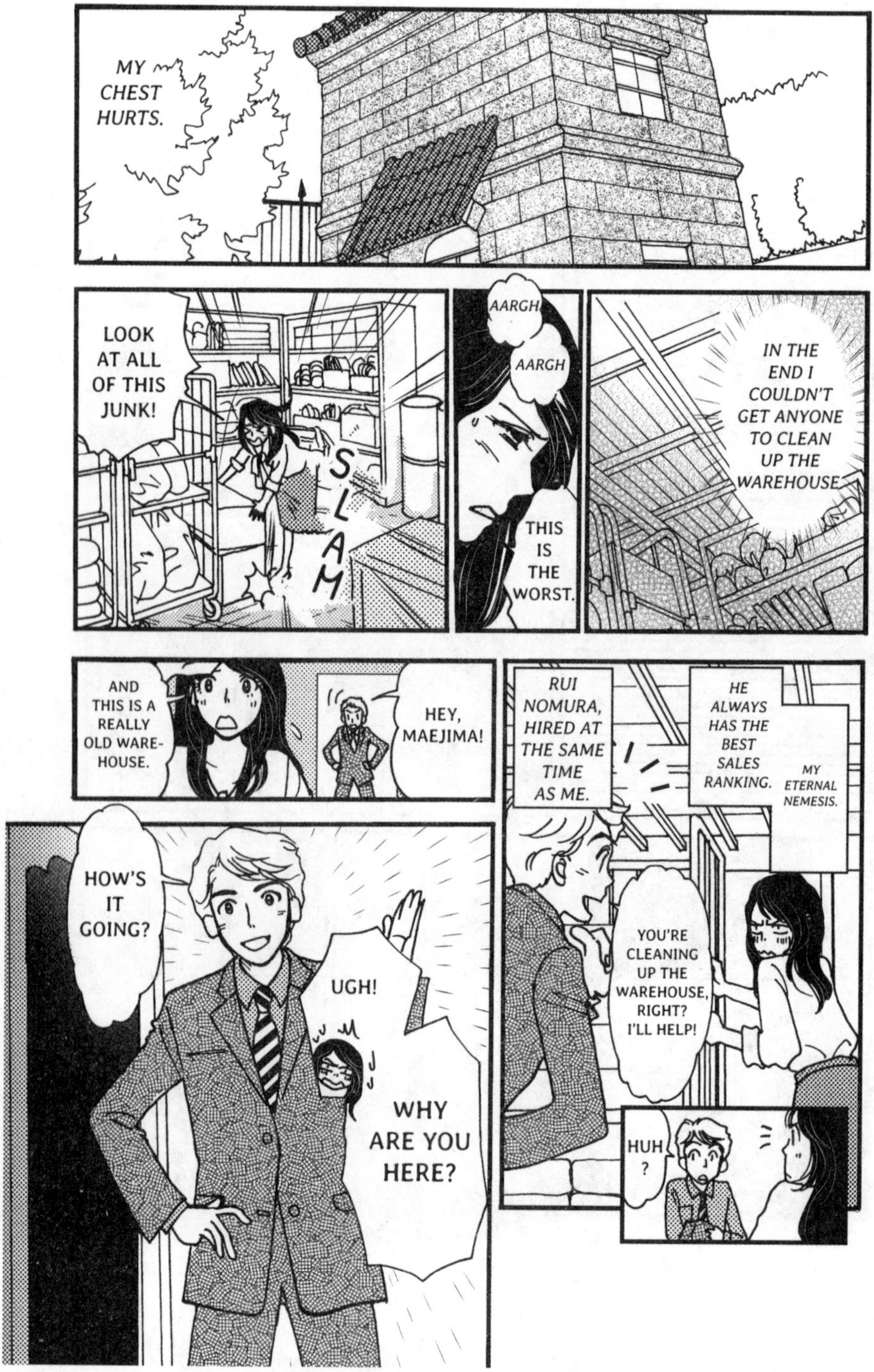

MY CHEST HURTS.
LOOK AT ALL OF THIS JUNK!
SLAM
AARGH
AARGH
THIS IS THE WORST.
IN THE END I COULDN'T GET ANYONE TO CLEAN UP THE WAREHOUSE.
AND THIS IS A REALLY OLD WARE-HOUSE.
HEY, MAEJIMA!
RUI NOMURA, HIRED AT THE SAME TIME AS ME.
HE ALWAYS HAS THE BEST SALES RANKING.
MY ETERNAL NEMESIS.
HOW'S IT GOING?
UGH!
WHY ARE YOU HERE?
YOU'RE CLEANING UP THE WAREHOUSE, RIGHT? I'LL HELP!
HUH?

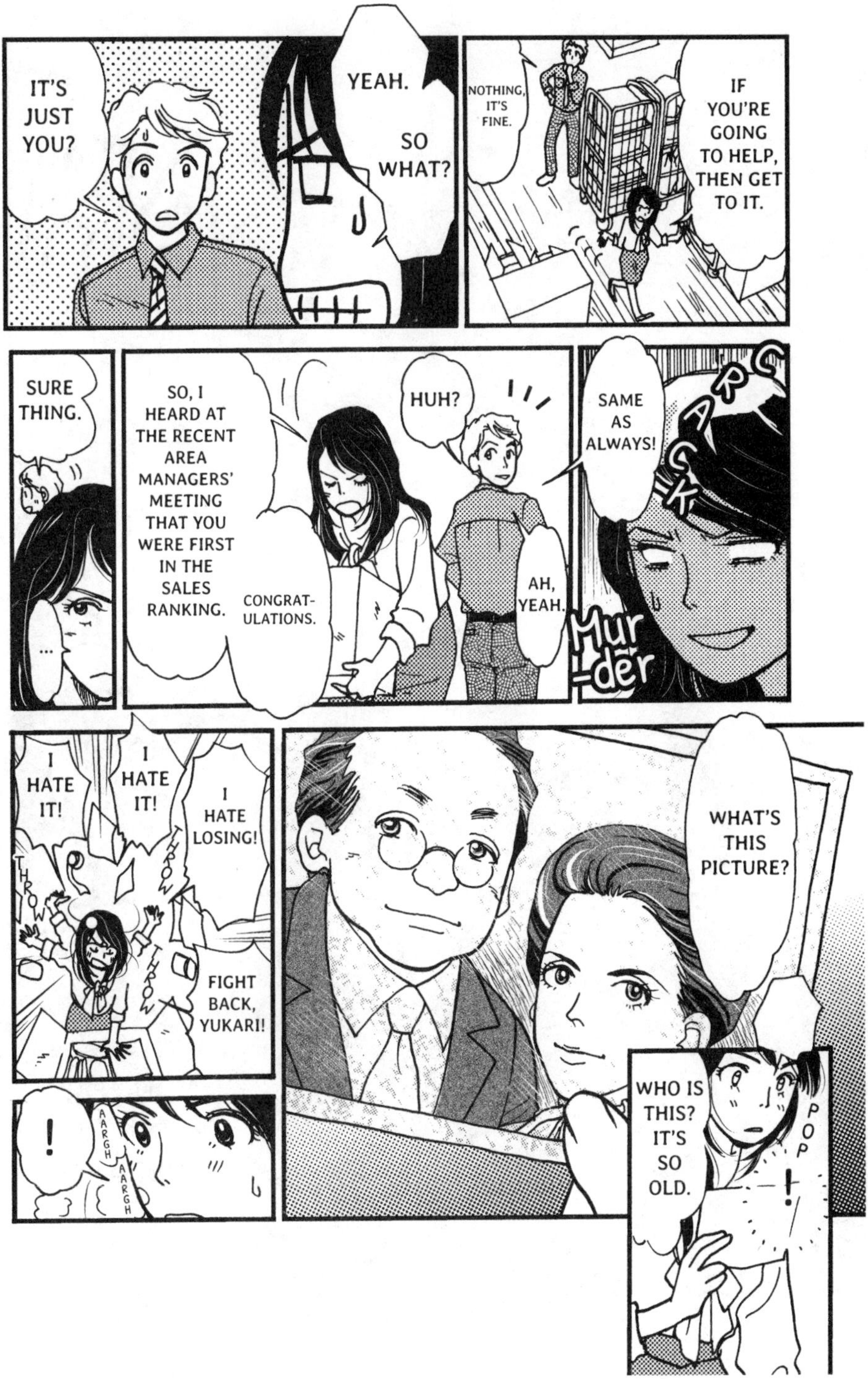
IT'S JUST YOU?
YEAH.
SO WHAT?
NOTHING, IT'S FINE.
IF YOU'RE GOING TO HELP, THEN GET TO IT.
SURE THING.
...
SO, I HEARD AT THE RECENT AREA MANAGERS' MEETING THAT YOU WERE FIRST IN THE SALES RANKING.
CONGRAT-ULATIONS.
HUH?
AH, YEAH.
SAME AS ALWAYS!
CRACK
Mur-der
I HATE IT!
I HATE IT!
I HATE LOSING!
THROW
THROW
THROW
FIGHT BACK, YUKARI!
!
AARGH
AARGH
WHAT'S THIS PICTURE?
WHO IS THIS? IT'S SO OLD.
POP
!

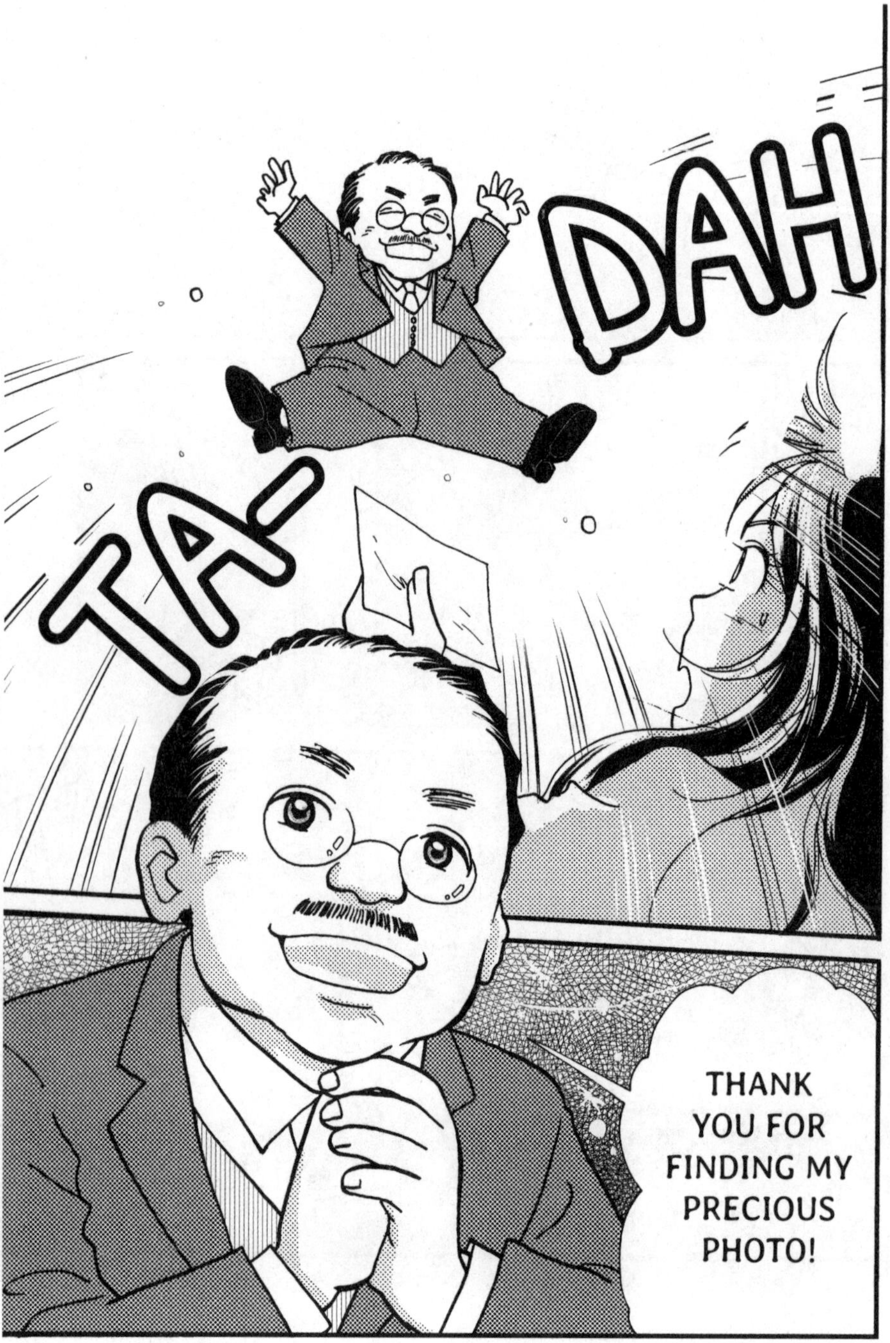
TA-
DAH
THANK YOU FOR FINDING MY PRECIOUS PHOTO!

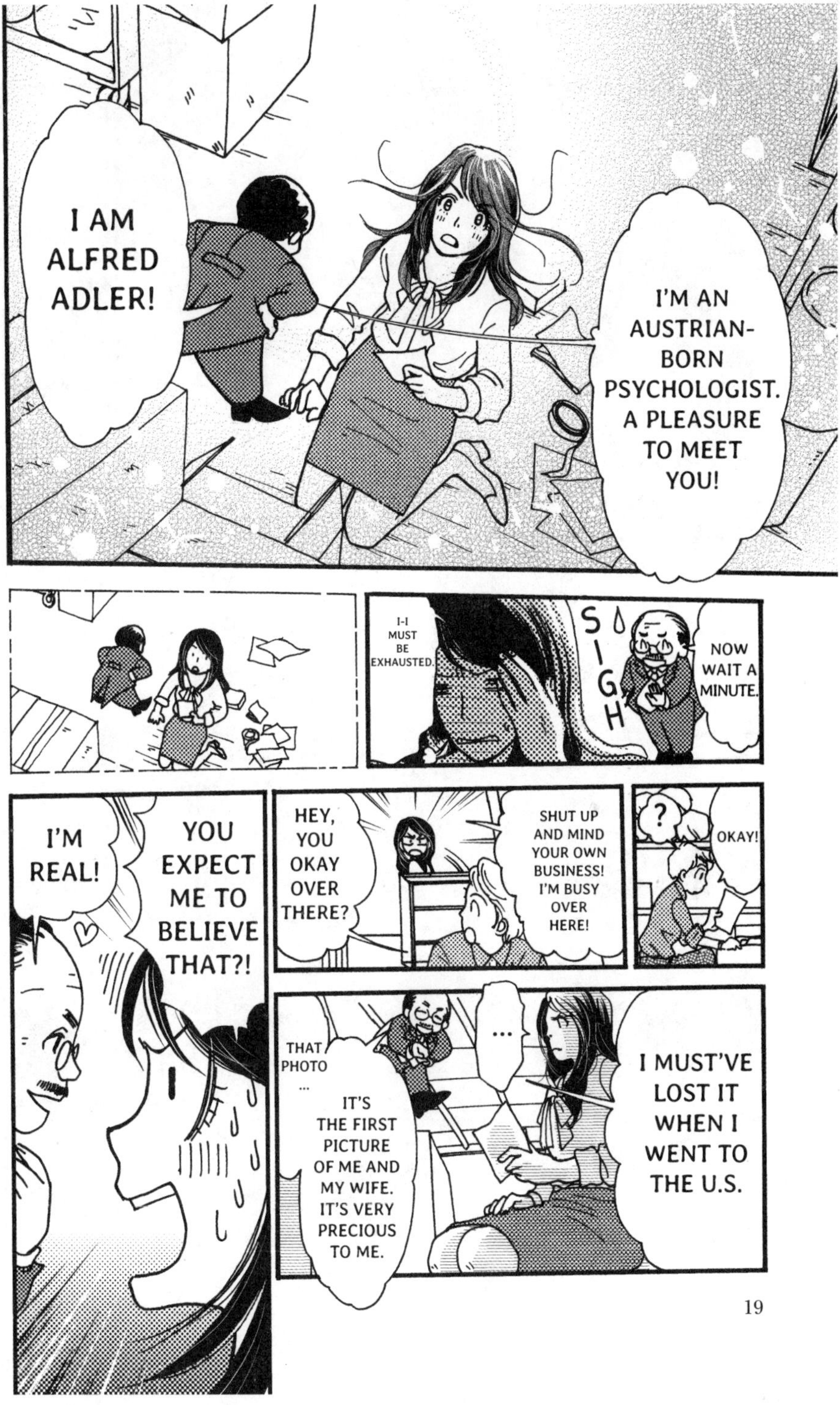
I AM ALFRED ADLER!
I'M AN AUSTRIAN-BORN PSYCHOLOGIST. A PLEASURE TO MEET YOU!
I-I MUST BE EXHAUSTED.
SIGH
NOW WAIT A MINUTE.
YOU EXPECT ME TO BELIEVE THAT?!
I'M REAL!
HEY, YOU OKAY OVER THERE?
SHUT UP AND MIND YOUR OWN BUSINESS! I'M BUSY OVER HERE!
?
OKAY!
...
I MUST'VE LOST IT WHEN I WENT TO THE U.S.
THAT PHOTO ...
IT'S THE FIRST PICTURE OF ME AND MY WIFE. IT'S VERY PRECIOUS TO ME.

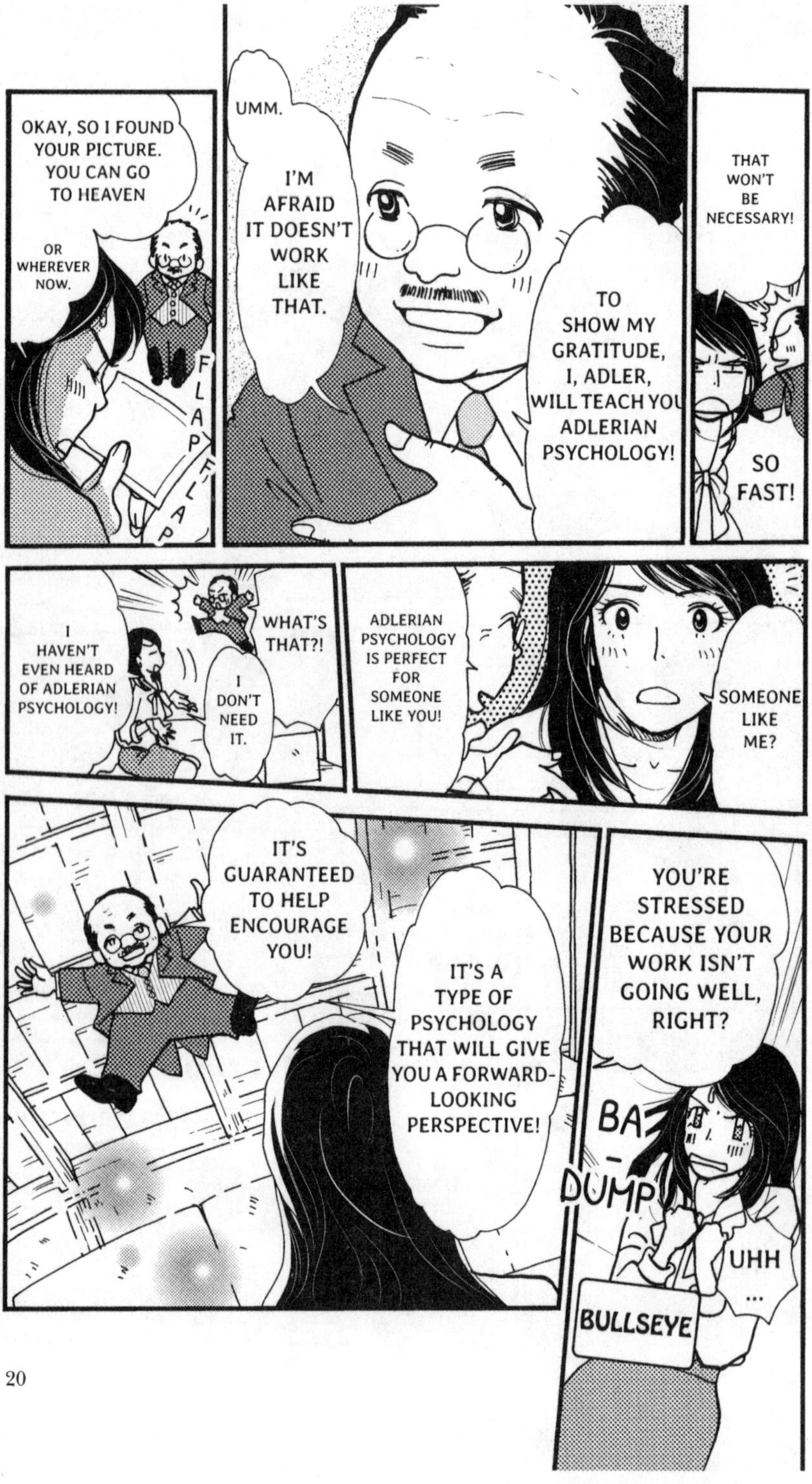
OKAY, SO I FOUND YOUR PICTURE. YOU CAN GO TO HEAVEN
OR WHEREVER NOW.
FLAP
FLAP
UMM.
I'M AFRAID IT DOESN'T WORK LIKE THAT.
TO SHOW MY GRATITUDE, I, ADLER, WILL TEACH YOU ADLERIAN PSYCHOLOGY!
THAT WON'T BE NECESSARY!
SO FAST!
WHAT'S THAT?!
I HAVEN'T EVEN HEARD OF ADLERIAN PSYCHOLOGY!
I DON'T NEED IT.
ADLERIAN PSYCHOLOGY IS PERFECT FOR SOMEONE LIKE YOU!
SOMEONE LIKE ME?
IT'S GUARANTEED TO HELP ENCOURAGE YOU!
IT'S A TYPE OF PSYCHOLOGY THAT WILL GIVE YOU A FORWARD-LOOKING PERSPECTIVE!
YOU'RE STRESSED BECAUSE YOUR WORK ISN'T GOING WELL, RIGHT?
BA-DUMP
UHH ...
BULLSEYE

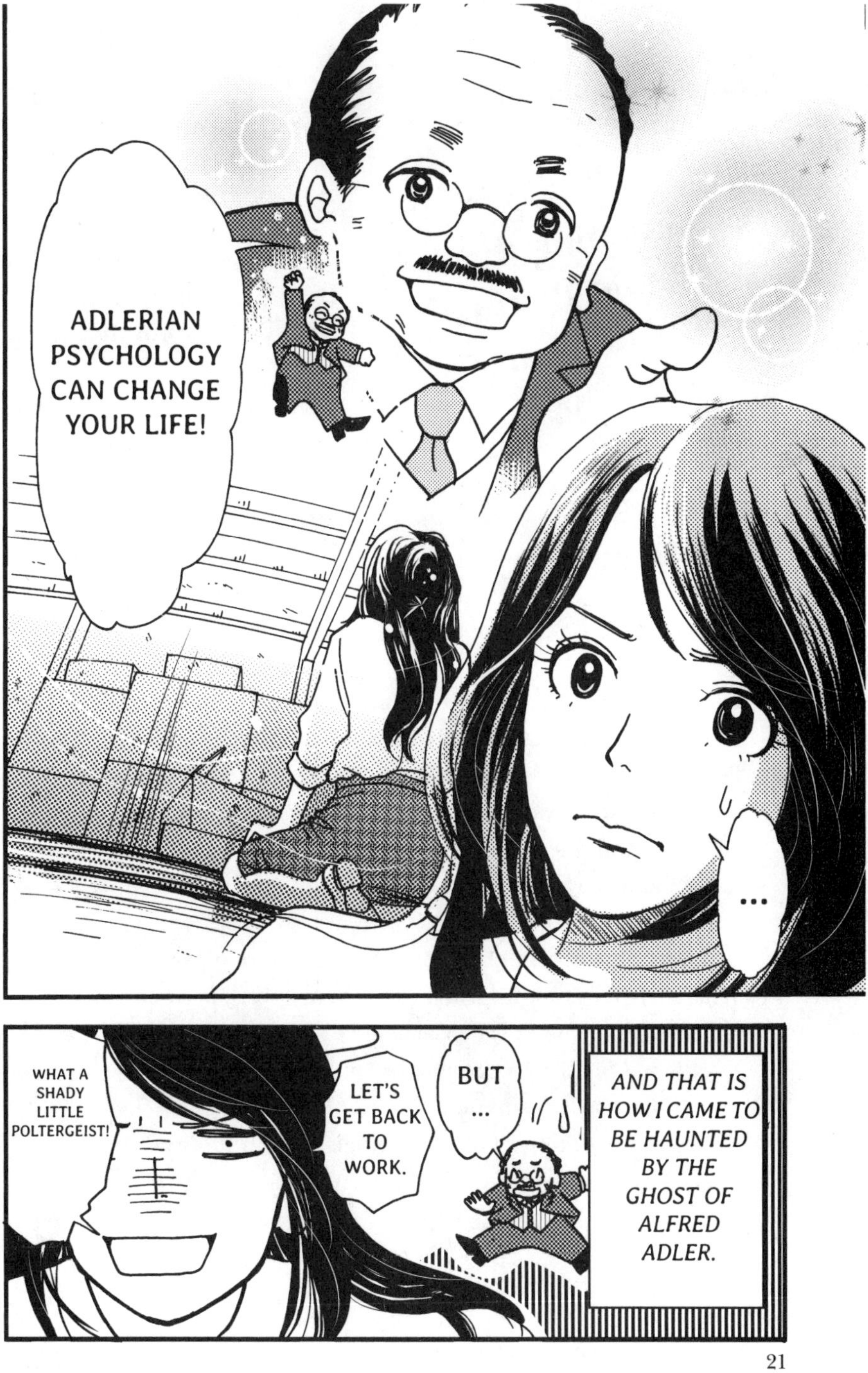
ADLERIAN PSYCHOLOGY CAN CHANGE YOUR LIFE!
...
AND THAT IS HOW I CAME TO BE HAUNTED BY THE GHOST OF ALFRED ADLER.
BUT ...
LET'S GET BACK TO WORK.
WHAT A SHADY LITTLE POLTERGEIST!

Grasping the Whole Picture of Adlerian Psychology

1

⇨ **A Forerunner to the Psychology of Self-Development**

Yukari, the newly promoted area manager of the well-established bakery chain Blume, is the middle of three siblings. She has grown up alongside her older brother, who excels at everything, and her younger sister, who can do no wrong. She loves a challenge and is quite capable, but she occasionally finds herself spinning her wheels and feeling exhausted with life. In this story, we'll follow Yukari as she discovers Adlerian psychology and learns to use it to overcome her problems by herself and stay on top of her so-called life tasks.

Some readers may be thinking, "Adler? Adlerian psychology? What are they? I've never heard of them." Well, perhaps you have heard of one of Dale Carnegie's best-sellers, *How to Win Friends and Influence People* or *How to Stop Worrying and Start Living*? Or maybe you know Stephen R. Covey's *The 7 Habits of Highly Effective People*? The psychologist that influenced these writers was none other than Alfred Adler.

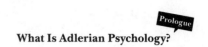

What Is Adlerian Psychology?

In Western psychology, Freud, Adler, and Jung are often referred to as the three great minds of psychology. Adlerian psychology was initially created by Adler and further developed by his successors. The main components of his psychology are outlined below.

1) **Self-Determination:** You are the protagonist of your own life. People are not just the victims of their environment or upbringing; everyone has the power to shape their destiny.
2) **Teleology:** Every human action has a purpose. A unique characteristic of human action is that humans are motivated not by the past but by some future purpose they have in mind.
3) **Holism:** A person's body and mind are a single unit. People are not organisms with contradictions and conflict in their hearts, but rather each person is an irreplaceable and indivisible unit.
4) **Cognitive Theory:** No one else can see life through your eyes. Every individual views things through their own subjective lens.
5) **Interpersonal Relationships:** All human actions are linked to a corresponding partner. Everything that we do is related to the people in our lives.

Adlerian psychology teaches you to overcome the difficulties you face in life and in interpersonal relationships through encouragement. The concept of encouragement will be described in further detail later, but for now, it is enough knowing that it can help us conquer the problems that

23

arise between ourselves and others. When I use the term *encouragement* in Adlerian psychology, I am not simply referring to praise or what the average reader may think of as encouragement. It is not simply a method for making happy people even more happy and energetic; it also has the power to pull people out of their slumps, invigorate them, and give them the strength to change their lives.

Adlerian psychology aims to build a strong **sense of community** through education and counseling. A sense of community is a sort of barometer for the health of our relationships with our families, neighbors, co-workers, and community members. It is a general term for our sense of belonging, our capacity for empathy, our willingness to make contributions to the community, and our ability to trust. A sense of community can be a difficult concept to wrap your head around, so I like to explain it as the feeling of connection and the bonds we have between ourselves and others. Once you can truly understand the sense of bonding and connection and use it to encourage yourself and others, then you can say you have truly mastered Adlerian psychology.

Overview of Adlerian Psychology

Encouragement: Finding the strength to overcome life's difficulties

↓

Components of Adlerian Psychology

> **Self-Determination:** People are not just the victims of their environment or upbringing; everyone has the power to shape their destiny.

> **Teleology:** Every human action has a purpose. A unique characteristic of human action is that humans are motivated not by the past but by some future purpose they have in mind.

> **Holism:** People are not organisms with contradictions and conflict in their hearts, but rather each person is an irreplaceable and indivisible unit.

> **Cognitive Theory:** Every individual views things through their own subjective lens.

> **Interpersonal Relationships:** All human actions are linked to a corresponding partner.

↓

Sense of Community: A barometer for our mental health—the actions that we take to foster our sense of belonging, our capacity for empathy, our willingness to make contributions to the community, and our ability to trust.

⇒ Expansion and Breakthrough from the Field of Education into Personal and Organizational Development

Adler started out as a surgeon and moved into psychology later on. After the First World War, he focused his efforts in the field of education and opened the world's first child guidance center in Vienna, Austria. He contributed to the development of some experimental schools that taught the psychological theories he developed in Austria. In contrast to Freud, who concentrated on healing those with mental illnesses, Adler focused on those who were already mentally healthy but wanted to progress and develop themselves further. When he passed away while still in the prime of his life at the age of 67, his disciples, chiefly in North America, inherited his theories and methods and continued to expand upon them.

Adlerian psychology does not only cover Adler's specialties of psychology and psychiatry; it also encompasses social education in various areas, such as school and home life. I will present a few examples.

First, in the field of psychology, Adler took a different approach than some of his peers who focused on psychoanalysis or behavioral psychology. He did not try to probe deep into the subconscious for unknown damage to the psyche or focus on controlling the behavior of animals with

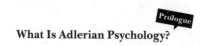
punishment and reward-style experiments (the carrot-and-stick approach). Instead, he used humanistic psychology, focusing on humans as sentient beings with free will, to try and draw out their limitless potential. Abraham Maslow, a prominent figure in New York, visited Adler in Vienna and inherited this approach. Maslow developed his famous theory of the hierarchy of needs and brought humanistic psychology to fruition.

Even in Japan, the effectiveness of Adlerian psychology has been demonstrated in various facets of school and home life, although there are high expectations for its future application in the business world. We can see the application of Adlerian psychology to education in schools with the development of open spaces for student discussions and other techniques for organizing a classroom or school environment. Its influence on education surrounding home life is also evident with the promotion of seminars supporting parent-child interactions.

"SMILE: A Seminar on Parent-Child Interaction with Love and Encouragement" is promoted by the Human Guild, of which I am the managing director. It has garnered much interest and instructed over 50,000 students using the parent-child relationship as a model for interpersonal relationships. This was all achieved due to the undeniable encouragement the students have gained from learning, applying, or even just being influenced by Adlerian psychology.

The Main Components of Adlerian Psychology

2

Now I'd like to present a rough explanation of the five components of Adlerian psychology that were mentioned before.

⇨ Self-Determination: Psychology That Makes You the Protagonist

The first component of Adlerian psychology is **self-determination**, which was discussed on page 23: People are not just the victims of their environment or upbringing; everyone has the power to shape their destiny. The opposite of this would be to assume that problems in your environment and early childhood exert a controlling influence over your whole life—that events in your life have caused you to become a victim.

Adlerian psychology recognizes that environmental circumstances and one's upbringing have an effect on personality development, but how you interpret their effects

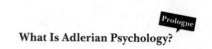
and the attitude that you choose to have are up to you. So-called personality formation is influenced by genes and other physical factors as well as childhood environment, but the final deciding factor is the individual themself.

Adler said that you are the one who made you and you are also the one who can change you. He also said that people are the protagonists in their own destiny—people are the authors, screenwriters, directors, and stars of their own personal life dramas. No one can substitute for you.

Well then, when you self-determine, which direction are you going to point yourself in? For these directions, Adler used the words *useful* and *useless*, but I prefer to use the terms *constructive* and *unconstructive*. That is to say, when you self-determine, you are making a choice to go down either a constructive or an unconstructive (and possibly even destructive) path for yourself and others.

Whenever we deal with difficulties in our lives, we have a tendency to attempt to break everything down into good and bad or right and wrong based on our own principles. But in Adlerian psychology, there is another criterion for judgment: namely, asking the question "Is this constructive

or unconstructive for myself and others?" Answering this
question will prevent you from viewing others as the villain.

Adler believed that people with unconstructive responses can
be guided to make constructive choices through education.

⇨ Teleology: Every Human Action Has a Purpose

The second component of Adlerian psychology is **teleology**—
the view that everyone's actions have their own unique
purpose. Adlerian psychology is a future-focused teleological
psychology—the polar opposite of past-focused etiological
psychology, which was the mainstream for a while. This is a
unique aspect of Adlerian psychology.

Whenever people are motivated to do something, there is
always a future purpose for their actions. Intentions act as a
bridge between the present and the future. They compel us
to move from the negative to the positive, closer to our goals.
The future is something that you can proactively create by
your will. Rather than obsessing over an unchangeable past,
you can focus on the future, which you have control over, by
enlisting the aid of others.

In *The Psychology of the Meaning of Life*, Adler stated, "The
pursuit of supremacy is what motivates all human beings; it is
the source of every contribution we have made to our society."
Further, he said, "Every facet of people's lives should follow this

path, moving from looking down to looking up, from negative to positive, from defeat to victory. . . . [W]hen truly facing life's tasks head on, the only people that can overcome them are those who, in pursuit of that supremacy, have shown a tendency to enrich the lives of everyone else and proceed in a way that benefits others as well."

⇨ Holism: A Person's Body and Mind Are a Single Unit

We frequently say, "I know I should, but I can't quit. I can't break free." Consciously and rationally, we might know that we have a problem, but our subconscious and emotions may hinder our efforts to change. Anyone can relate to thinking things like "I know they make me fat, but I just can't give up sweets" or "I know it is bad for me, but I always end up drinking too much." This shows a contradiction between our conscious and subconscious, between our reason and our emotions.

Adler believed, however, that people are not organisms that can hold contradictions and conflict in their hearts. The third component of his psychology, consequently, is **holism**, which views each person as an irreplaceable and indivisible unit. "I just can't stop" or "I can't come to grips with it" is blaming an uncontrollable environment, habit, or lack of ability. You say, "I can't," but it is not actually the case that you are not able to.

There are other people struggling in the same environment as you are. You are the one that built your habits, and until you try, you cannot know the limits of your abilities. When you look at it like this, "I won't" becomes a more appropriate expression than "I can't," and you can no longer shirk your responsibility. That is to say, reason and emotion, conscious and subconscious, and body and mind all look contradictory at first glance, but they have a complementary relationship. So, in that way, there is a unity contained in our personalities.

⇨ Cognitivism: Every Individual Views Things through Their Own Subjective Lens

The fourth component of Adlerian psychology takes the stance that everyone understands events by assigning their own subjective meaning to them and that it is impossible for people to see things objectively or as they truly are. It is said that there are as many opinions as there are people, but even if the same event is experienced by multiple people, each person will have their own way of interpreting it.

Take, for example, a couple in marriage counseling talking about their honeymoon. The husband says that they never want to go there again because of the food or the smell, that what they remember is the outstanding view and they would love to go there again. Even though the couple had the exact same experience, they each have their own differing opinion

about that experience. As we can see in this example, people cannot objectively grasp external events but rather react based on the subjective meaning that they have attached to these events according to their own experiences and preferences.

With that in mind, when trying to understand someone through Adlerian psychology, it is more important to grasp how they subjectively interpret events than to objectively know what is going on inside of them.

⇨ Interpersonal Relationships: All Human Actions Require a Partner

The fifth component of Adlerian psychology is interpersonal relationships. According to Adler, every human action is interpersonal and requires a partner. So, if you want to understand someone, according to the cognitive theory we've already learned about, observing their interpersonal relationships is a good shortcut. We often try to understand others based on what they are thinking, but their interpersonal relationships (actions) are easier to accurately observe than their ideas (thoughts).

Incidentally, I specifically used the unusual word *partner*. To use a play as an analogy, when you imagine a partner in a certain action, you can think of them as an audience member or a co-star.

The partner role can either be played by others or by yourself. The partner is what we call the person being influenced, made to experience a certain feeling, or having any other reaction. Adlerian psychology holds that without this partner role, human action is really unthinkable.

People are influenced by the actions of their partner, and based on that, they feel certain things and respond with further actions. Then, on that basis, their partner takes further actions and so on. In this way, interpersonal relationships continue to exist in a mutually influencing way.

As I just mentioned, the partner role is not only for others, but includes oneself as well. There is another you that is always having conversations with the real you. When facing some challenge, these two versions of you discuss things with each other before eventually reaching a conclusion.

⇨ Encouragement and Social Interest

And finally, to end this Prologue, I would like to touch on encouragement and social interest. Adlerian psychology is the psychology of encouragement. I realize I am repeating myself here, but it is very important to make the distinction between encouragement and praise. Encouragement is giving the strength to overcome difficulties. It requires mutual respect and trust based on empathy.

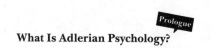
Praise, on the other hand, takes the stance of judging a person to be good or bad. Even if the process is the same, when you praise someone, you are basing this off of the other person achieving some (positive) outcome that you expected. You withhold praise or disparage the person if they fail to live up to those same expectations.

Finally, the education, counseling, and other forms of support provided by Adlerian psychology have a goal: to nurture our capacity for empathy, our willingness to make contributions to the community, and our ability to trust. Collectively, this is known as a *sense of community*. Adlerian psychology aspires to change your interpersonal relationships from revolving around competing with others and seeing them as rivals to one of cooperation. Someone with a good sense of community is psychologically healthy.

Alfred Adler, the Man

Adler was born in 1870 to a Jewish family in a suburb of Vienna. He was prone to illness as a child and suffered from rickets. He was a small man, only 5 feet tall. As the second of seven children, Adler was heavily influenced by his older brother Sigmund, who was only a year and a half older. Adler was not particularly good at school, even flunking out of elementary school. However, he managed to overcome his disabilities, and with the encouragement of his father, his studies improved and he eventually entered Vienna University's medical school. He received his medical degree at 25, starting out as an ophthalmologist and eventually working as a physician and psychiatrist.

In 1902 when Adler was 32, he became a founding member of the Wednesday Psychology Society (now known as The Vienna Psychoanalytic Society), which was presided over by Freud, and remained a member for nine years. His theories conflicted with Freud's, eventually leading him to leave and branch out into his own field of psychology.

After parting with Freud, he named his field *individual psychology*. It's quite clear that he influenced many psychologists, including Victor Frankl, famous for his book *Man's Search for Meaning*; Abraham Maslow, famous for Maslow's hierarchy of needs; Eric Berne, famous for creating the theory of transactional analysis; and Carl Rogers, famous for creating person-centered therapy. The list is not limited to psychologists, however, and also includes social educator Dale Carnegie, famous for opening the road to self-improvement with his books *How to Win Friends and Influence People* and *How to Stop Worrying and Start Living*, as well as some people of Freud's school, including Karen Horney and Erich Fromm, among others.

With this level of influence, there are people who consider him the apostle of courage and hope and a psychologist 100 years ahead of his time.

Part 1

If You Change Your Perspective, Your Life Will Be Easier

BASIC
...
... MISTAKE.
YEAH.
TWITCH
SO I THINK I'LL JUST QUIT MY JOB.
!

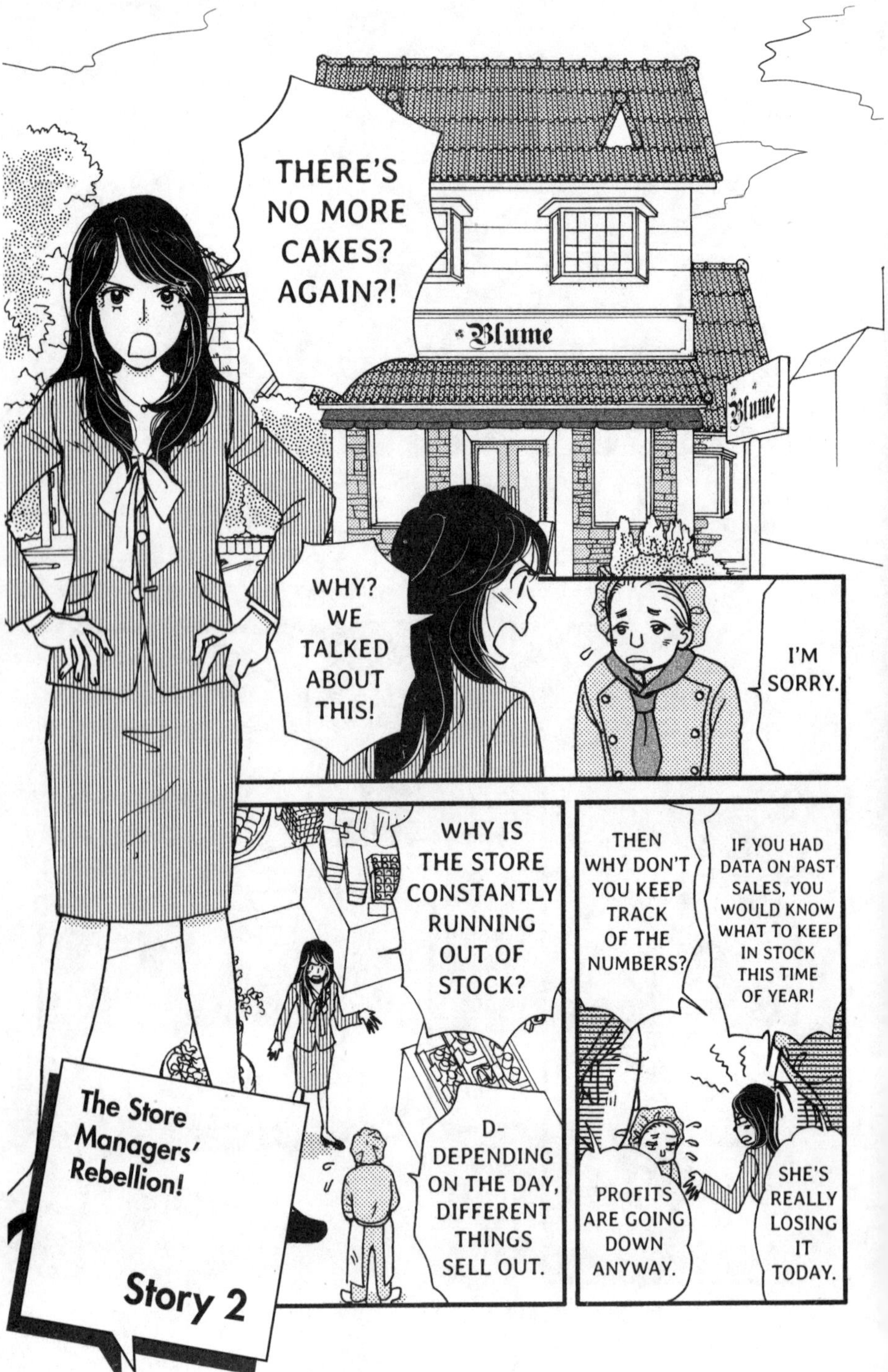
THERE'S NO MORE CAKES? AGAIN?!
WHY? WE TALKED ABOUT THIS!
I'M SORRY.
WHY IS THE STORE CONSTANTLY RUNNING OUT OF STOCK?
D- DEPENDING ON THE DAY, DIFFERENT THINGS SELL OUT.
THEN WHY DON'T YOU KEEP TRACK OF THE NUMBERS?
IF YOU HAD DATA ON PAST SALES, YOU WOULD KNOW WHAT TO KEEP IN STOCK THIS TIME OF YEAR!
PROFITS ARE GOING DOWN ANYWAY.
SHE'S REALLY LOSING IT TODAY.
The Store Managers' Rebellion!
Story 2

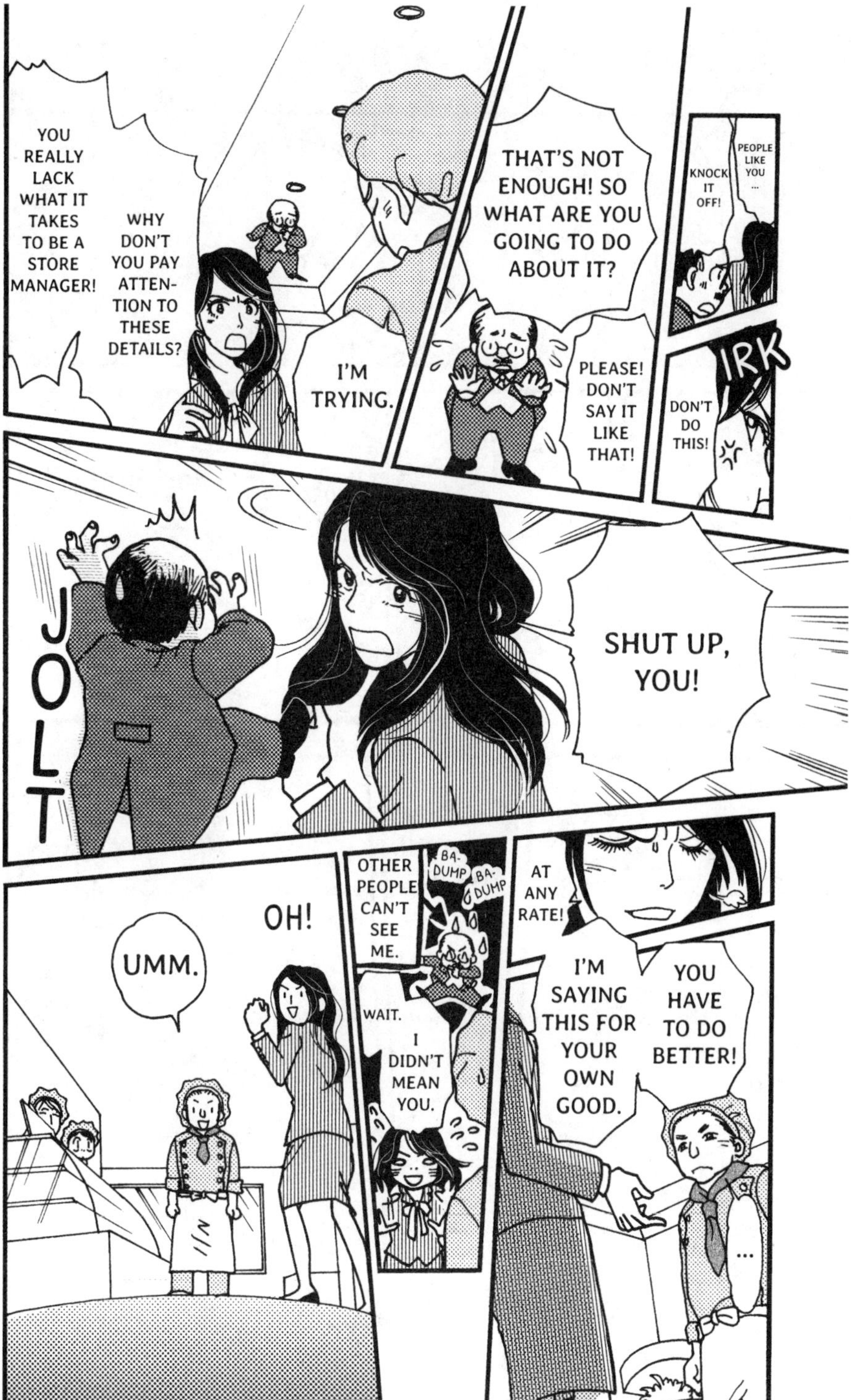
YOU REALLY LACK WHAT IT TAKES TO BE A STORE MANAGER!
WHY DON'T YOU PAY ATTEN- TION TO THESE DETAILS?
I'M TRYING.
THAT'S NOT ENOUGH! SO WHAT ARE YOU GOING TO DO ABOUT IT?
PLEASE! DON'T SAY IT LIKE THAT!
KNOCK IT OFF!
PEOPLE LIKE YOU ...
IRK
DON'T DO THIS!
JOLT
SHUT UP, YOU!
UMM.
OH!
OTHER PEOPLE CAN'T SEE ME.
BA-DUMP BA-DUMP
WAIT.
I DIDN'T MEAN YOU.
AT ANY RATE!
I'M SAYING THIS FOR YOUR OWN GOOD.
YOU HAVE TO DO BETTER!
...

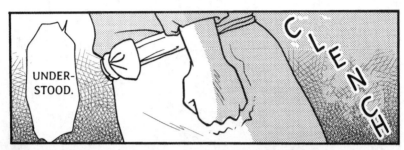

UNDER-STOOD.

CLENCH

PLEASE DON'T TALK TO ME ANYMORE.

I'M WORKING

BUT—

I'M RESPONSIBLE FOR THE STORE MANAGERS, SO IT'S MY JOB TO PROACTIVELY FIND AND FIX THEIR WEAK-NESSES.

POKE

POKE

THAT'S HOW I HAVE TO TALK TO GET THROUGH TO THEM.

C-CUT IT OUT.

THAT'S STILL NO EXCUSE FOR TALKING TO THEM LIKE THAT.

THAT'S HOW PEOPLE TALK IN THE MODERN AGE.

THIS IS NOT ABOUT THAT.

YOU UNDER-STAND MY PROBLEM, RIGHT?

SALES ARE DROPPING AND I'M IN TROUBLE.

MAEJIMA! WHAT DID YOU DO?!

HUH?

SLAM

ALL OF YOUR STORE MANAGERS ARE DOWNSTAIRS DEMANDING A MEETING!

WHAT ?!

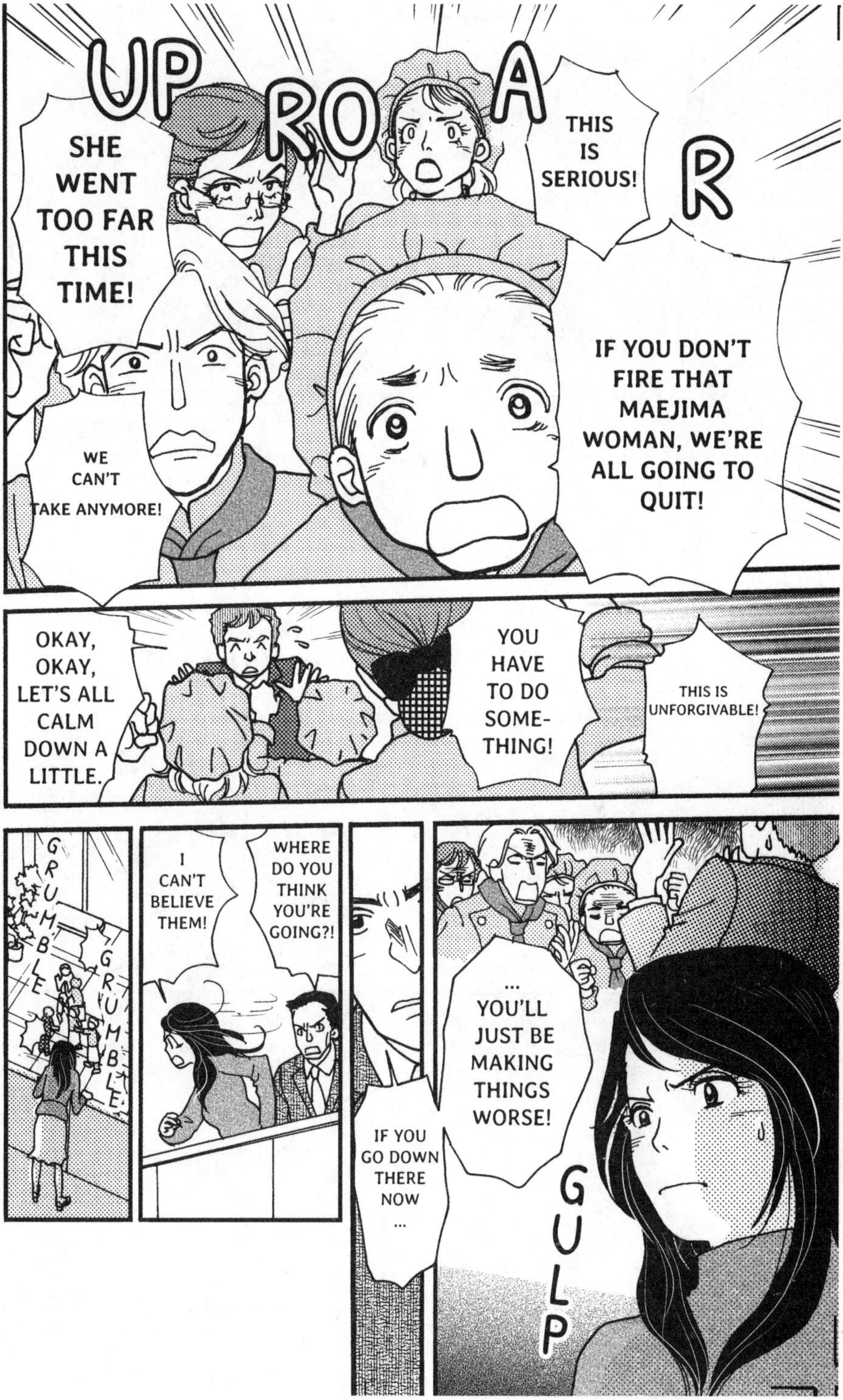
UPROAR
THIS IS SERIOUS!
SHE WENT TOO FAR THIS TIME!
IF YOU DON'T FIRE THAT MAEJIMA WOMAN, WE'RE ALL GOING TO QUIT!
WE CAN'T TAKE ANYMORE!
THIS IS UNFORGIVABLE!
YOU HAVE TO DO SOME-THING!
OKAY, OKAY, LET'S ALL CALM DOWN A LITTLE.
IF YOU GO DOWN THERE NOW ...
... YOU'LL JUST BE MAKING THINGS WORSE!
GULP
WHERE DO YOU THINK YOU'RE GOING?!
I CAN'T BELIEVE THEM!
GRUMBLE
GRUMBLE

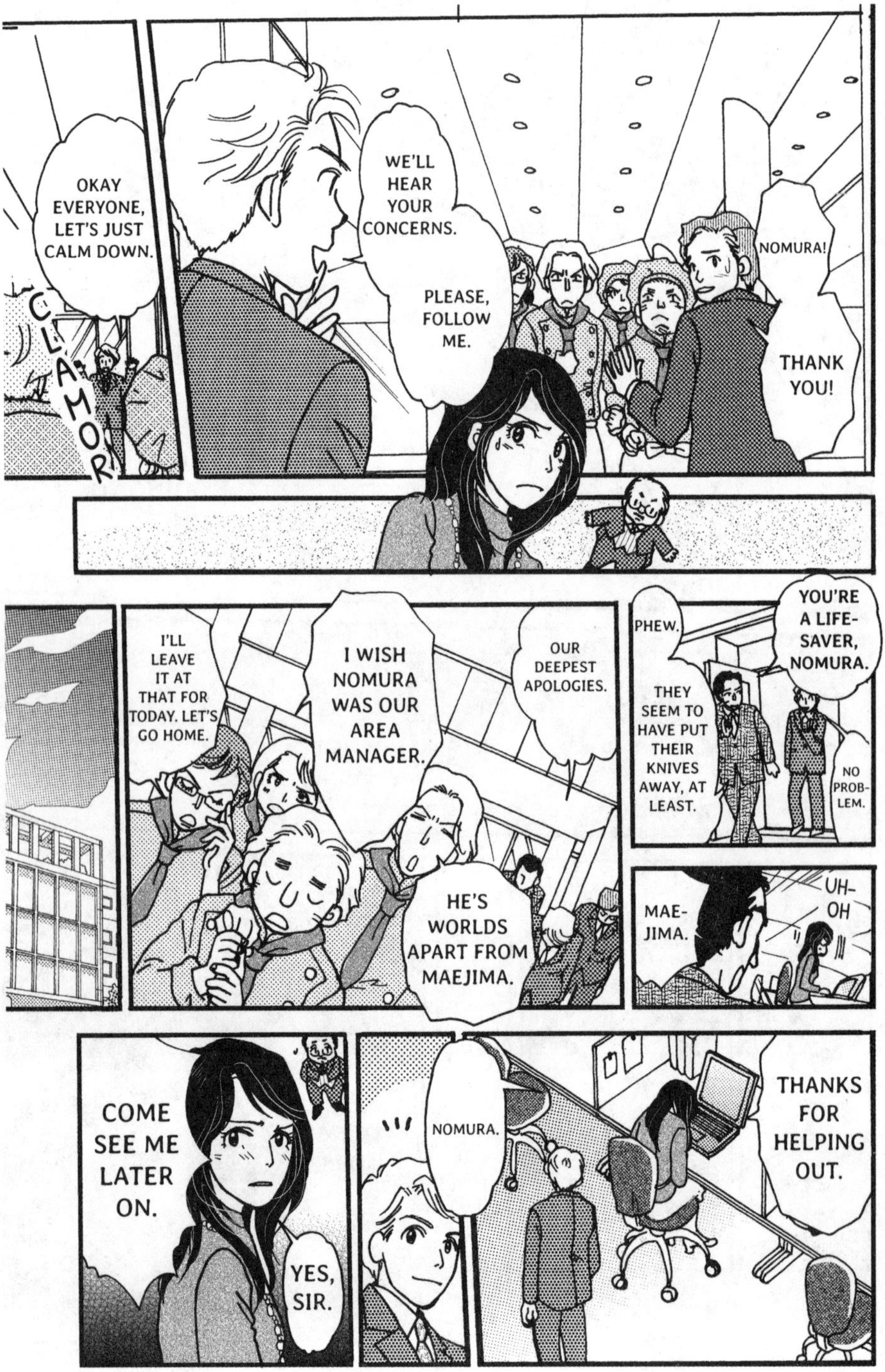
OKAY EVERYONE, LET'S JUST CALM DOWN.
CLAMOR
WE'LL HEAR YOUR CONCERNS.
PLEASE, FOLLOW ME.
NOMURA!
THANK YOU!
I'LL LEAVE IT AT THAT FOR TODAY. LET'S GO HOME.
I WISH NOMURA WAS OUR AREA MANAGER.
OUR DEEPEST APOLOGIES.
HE'S WORLDS APART FROM MAEJIMA.
PHEW.
YOU'RE A LIFE-SAVER, NOMURA.
THEY SEEM TO HAVE PUT THEIR KNIVES AWAY, AT LEAST.
NO PROB-LEM.
MAE-JIMA.
UH-OH
COME SEE ME LATER ON.
YES, SIR.
NOMURA.
THANKS FOR HELPING OUT.

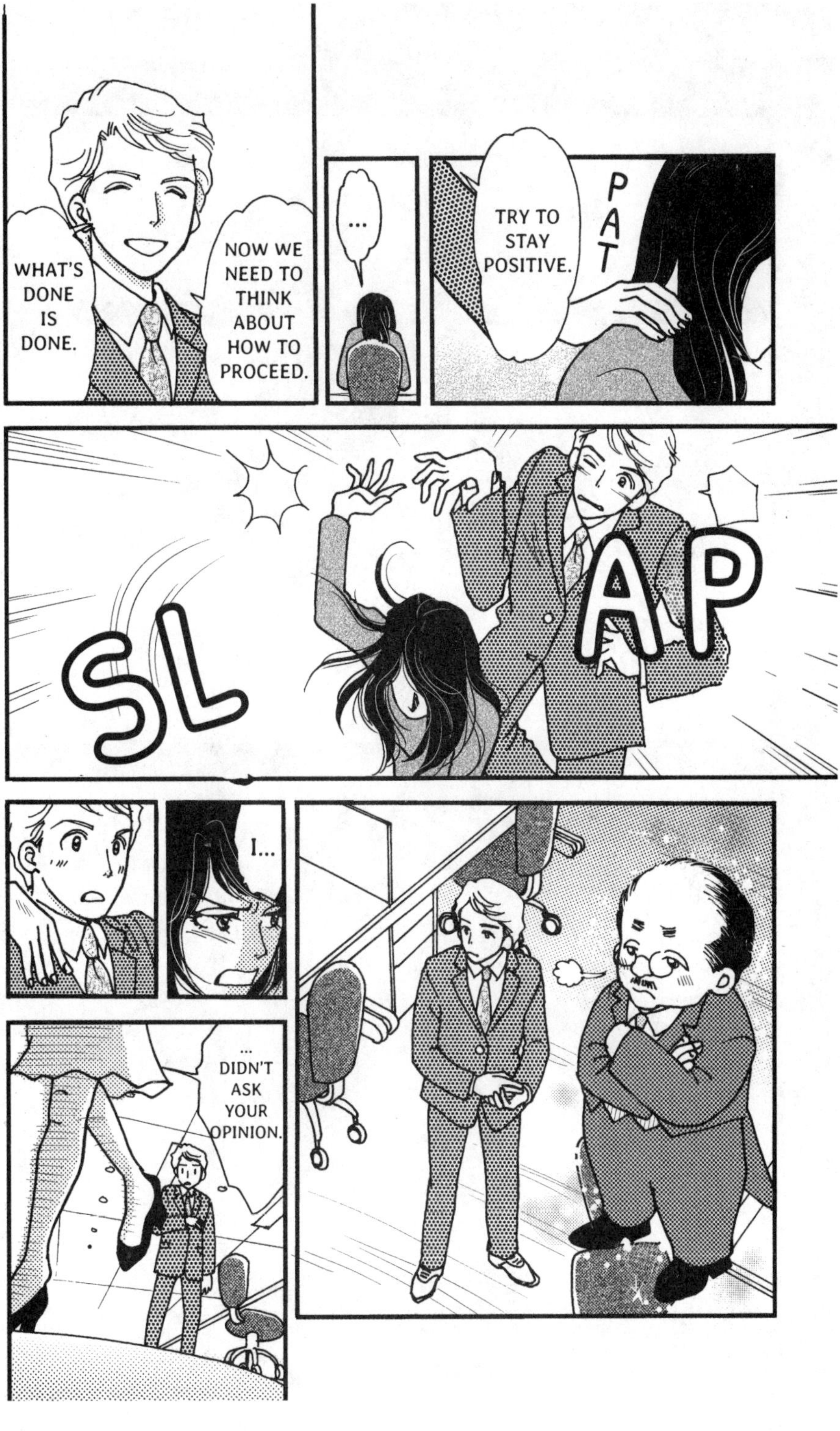
WHAT'S DONE IS DONE.
NOW WE NEED TO THINK ABOUT HOW TO PROCEED.
...
TRY TO STAY POSITIVE.
PAT
SLAP
I...
... DIDN'T ASK YOUR OPINION.

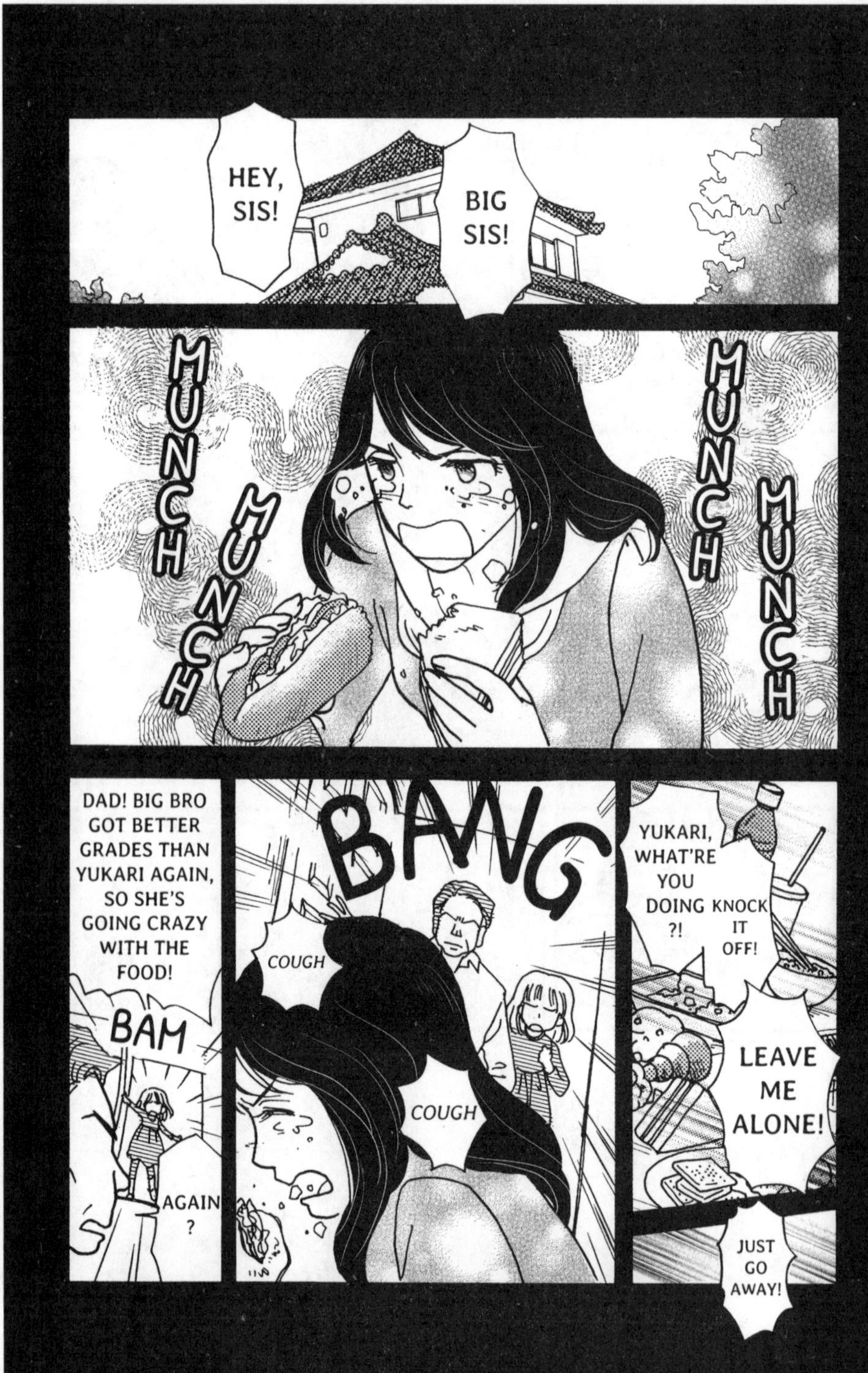

BIG SIS!
HEY, SIS!
MUNCH MUNCH
MUNCH MUNCH
YUKARI, WHAT'RE YOU DOING ?!
KNOCK IT OFF!
LEAVE ME ALONE!
JUST GO AWAY!
BANG
COUGH
COUGH
DAD! BIG BRO GOT BETTER GRADES THAN YUKARI AGAIN, SO SHE'S GOING CRAZY WITH THE FOOD!
BAM
AGAIN ?

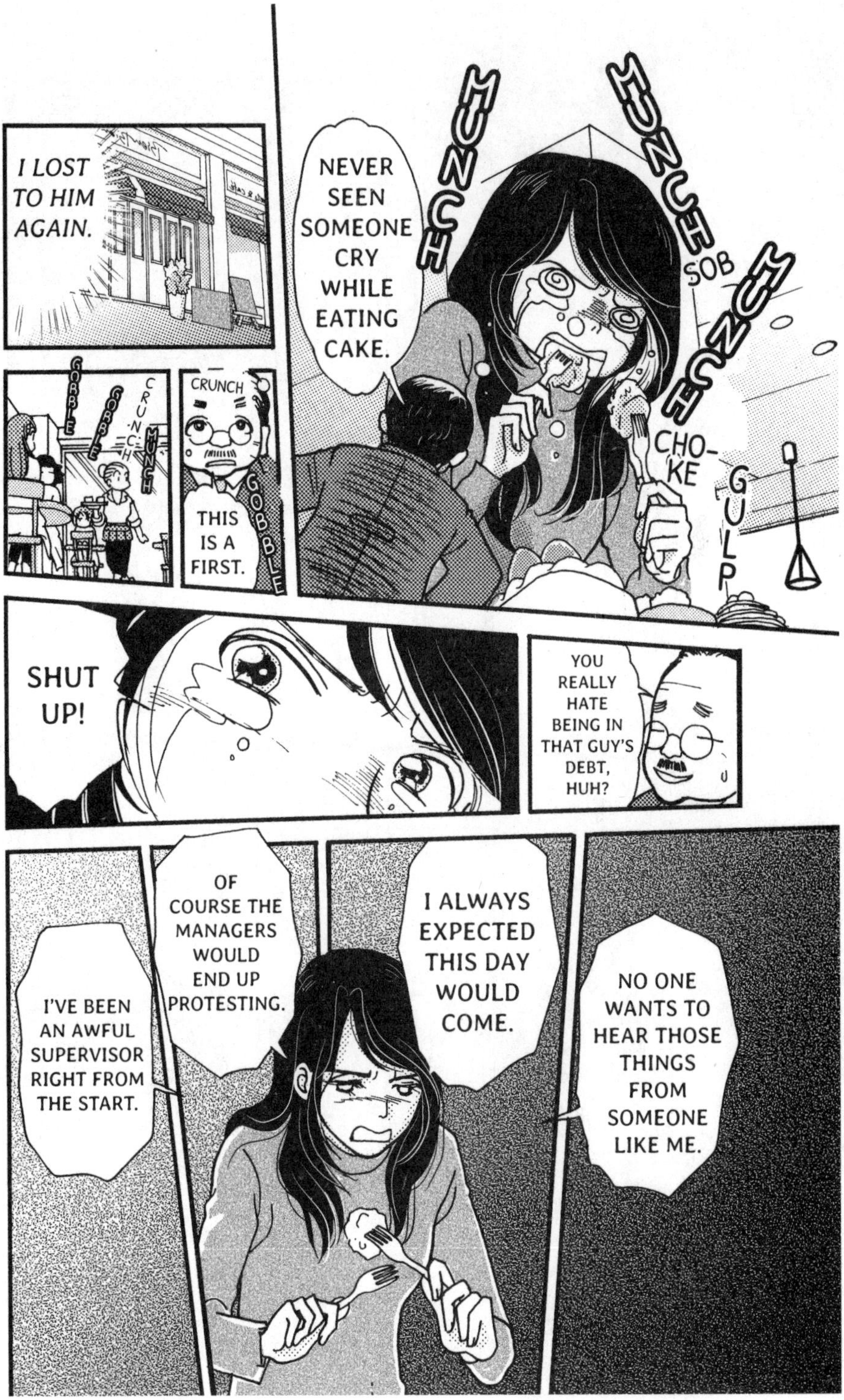
MUNCH
MUNCH
NEVER SEEN SOMEONE CRY WHILE EATING CAKE.
SOB
MUNCH
CHO-KE
GULP
I LOST TO HIM AGAIN.
CRUNCH
THIS IS A FIRST.
GOBBLE
GOBBLE
GOBBLE
CRUNCH
MUNCH
YOU REALLY HATE BEING IN THAT GUY'S DEBT, HUH?
SHUT UP!
NO ONE WANTS TO HEAR THOSE THINGS FROM SOMEONE LIKE ME.
I ALWAYS EXPECTED THIS DAY WOULD COME.
OF COURSE THE MANAGERS WOULD END UP PROTESTING.
I'VE BEEN AN AWFUL SUPERVISOR RIGHT FROM THE START.

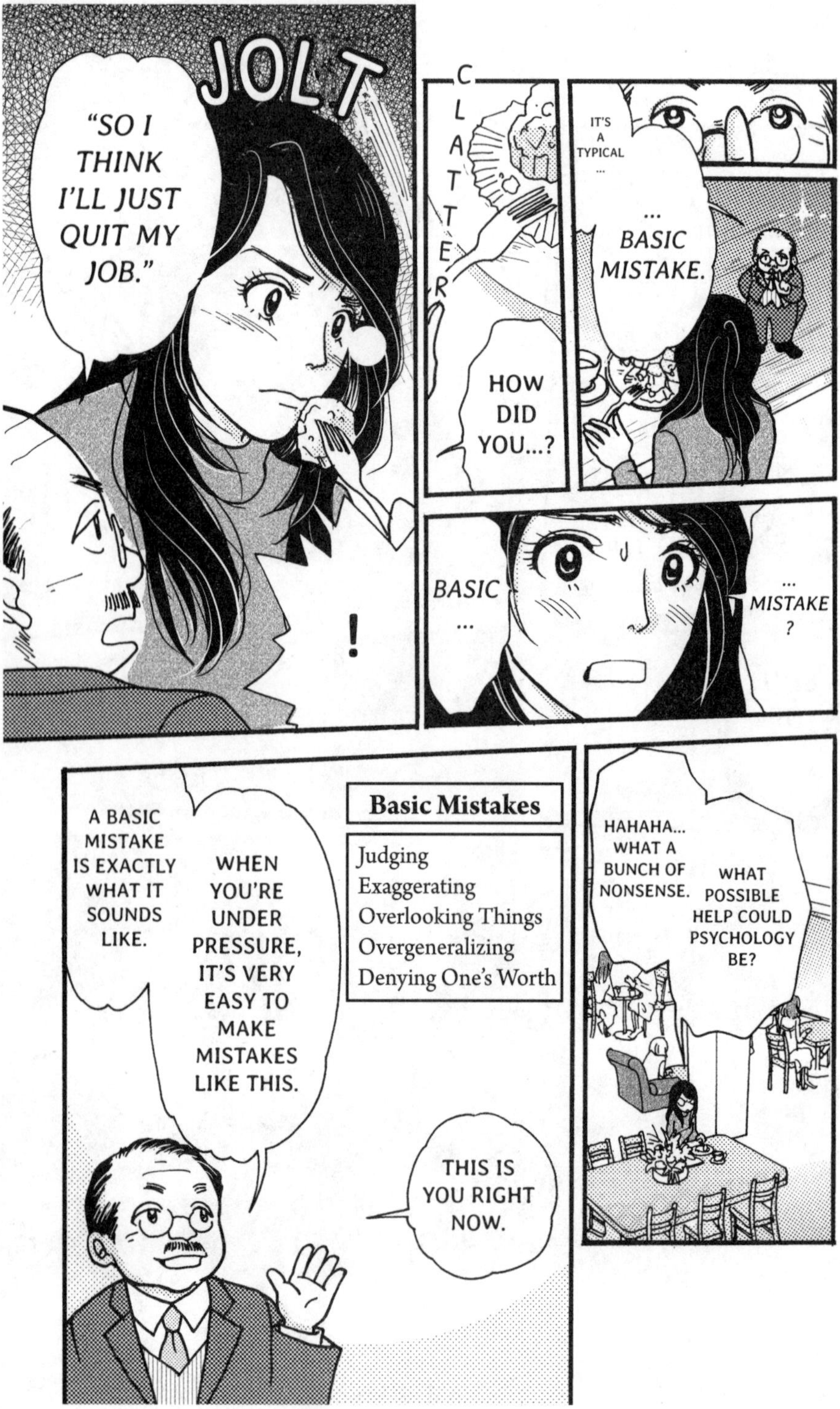
JOLT
"SO I THINK I'LL JUST QUIT MY JOB."
!
CLATTER
HOW DID YOU...?
IT'S A TYPICAL ...
... BASIC MISTAKE.
BASIC ...
... MISTAKE ?
HAHAHA... WHAT A BUNCH OF NONSENSE.
WHAT POSSIBLE HELP COULD PSYCHOLOGY BE?
A BASIC MISTAKE IS EXACTLY WHAT IT SOUNDS LIKE.
WHEN YOU'RE UNDER PRESSURE, IT'S VERY EASY TO MAKE MISTAKES LIKE THIS.
Basic Mistakes
Judging
Exaggerating
Overlooking Things
Overgeneralizing
Denying One's Worth
THIS IS YOU RIGHT NOW.

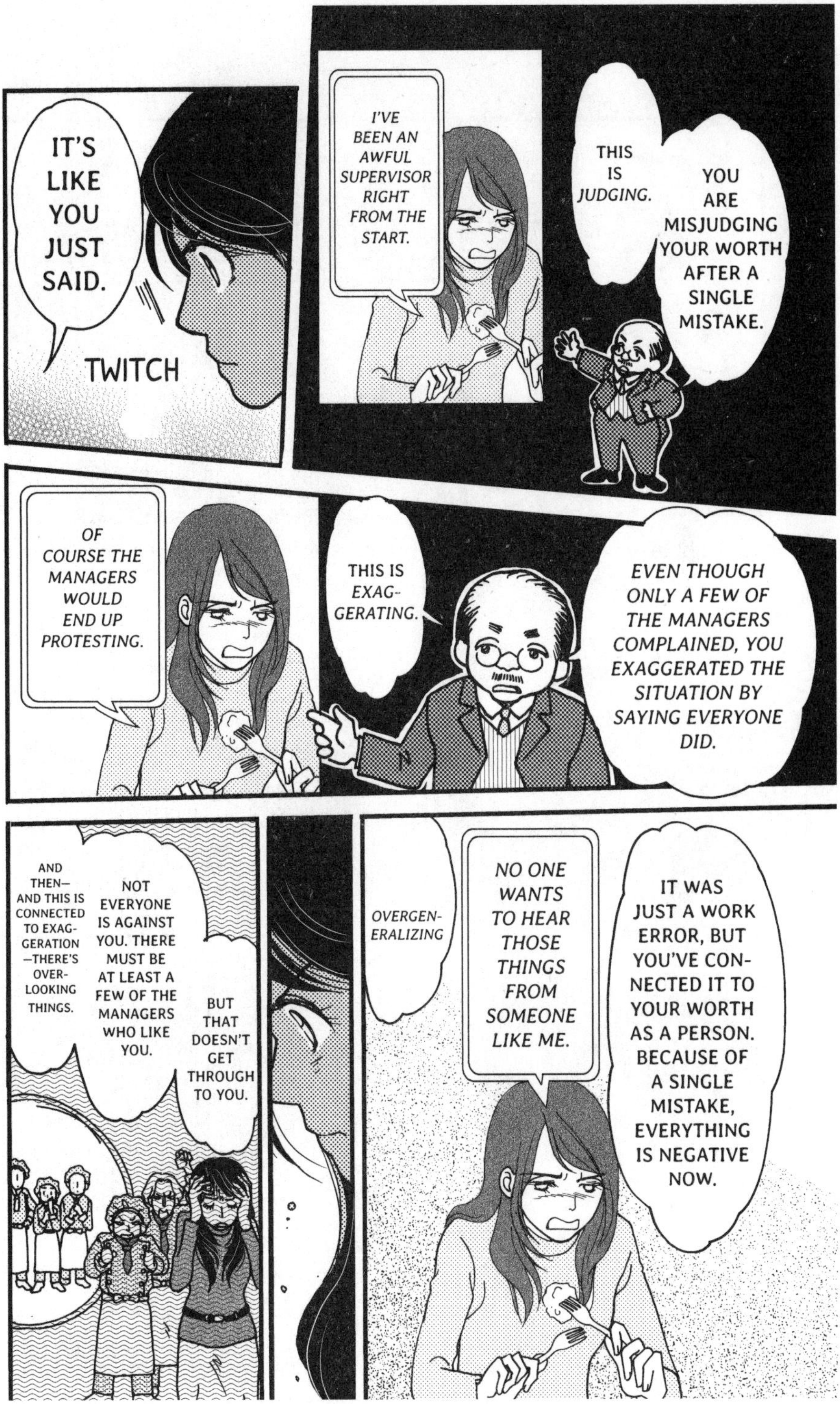
IT'S LIKE YOU JUST SAID.
TWITCH
I'VE BEEN AN AWFUL SUPERVISOR RIGHT FROM THE START.
THIS IS JUDGING.
YOU ARE MISJUDGING YOUR WORTH AFTER A SINGLE MISTAKE.
OF COURSE THE MANAGERS WOULD END UP PROTESTING.
THIS IS EXAG-GERATING.
EVEN THOUGH ONLY A FEW OF THE MANAGERS COMPLAINED, YOU EXAGGERATED THE SITUATION BY SAYING EVERYONE DID.
NO ONE WANTS TO HEAR THOSE THINGS FROM SOMEONE LIKE ME.
OVERGEN-ERALIZING
IT WAS JUST A WORK ERROR, BUT YOU'VE CON-NECTED IT TO YOUR WORTH AS A PERSON. BECAUSE OF A SINGLE MISTAKE, EVERYTHING IS NEGATIVE NOW.
AND THEN—AND THIS IS CONNECTED TO EXAG-GERATION—THERE'S OVER-LOOKING THINGS.
NOT EVERYONE IS AGAINST YOU. THERE MUST BE AT LEAST A FEW OF THE MANAGERS WHO LIKE YOU.
BUT THAT DOESN'T GET THROUGH TO YOU.

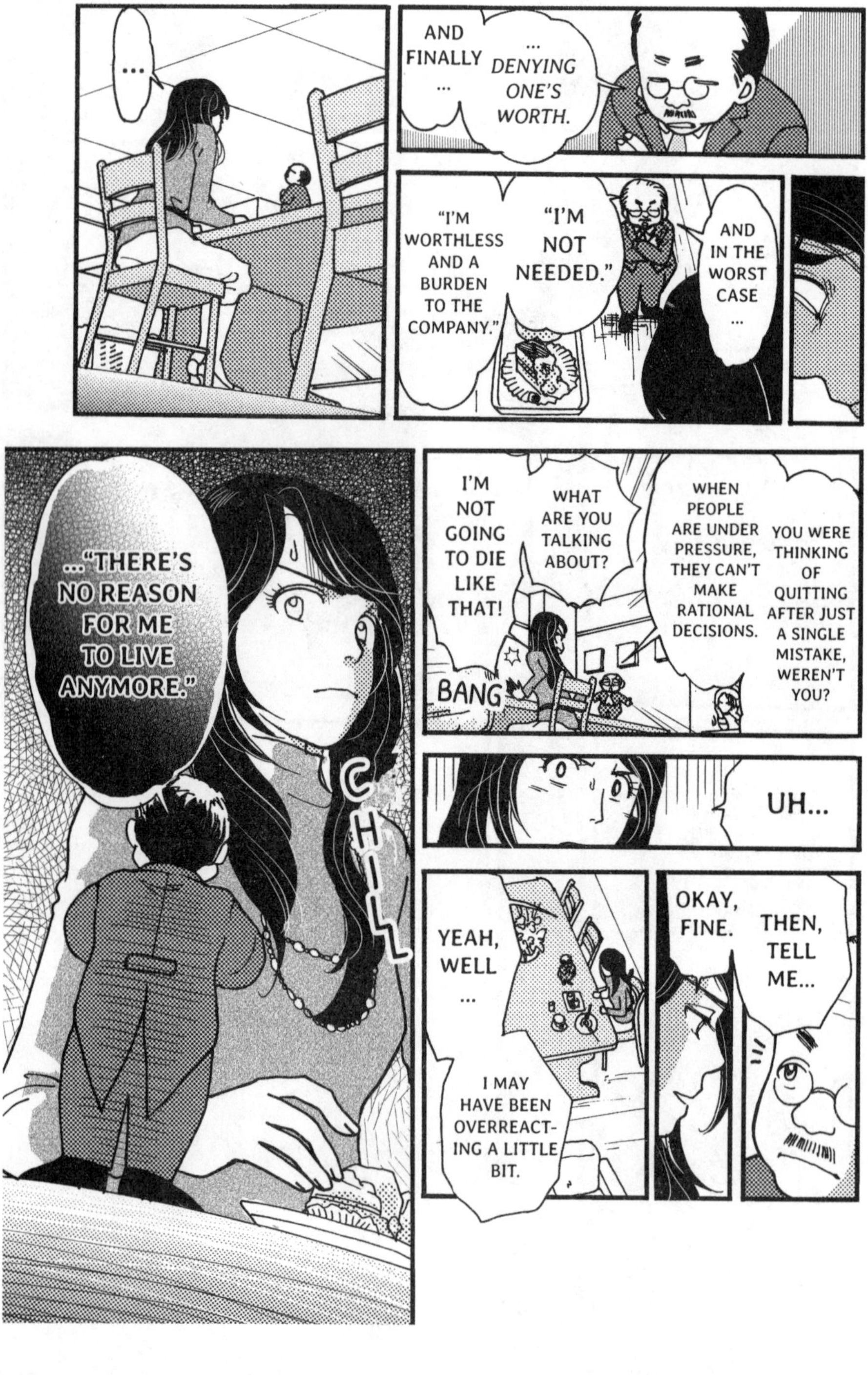

...
AND FINALLY ...
... DENYING ONE'S WORTH.
"I'M WORTHLESS AND A BURDEN TO THE COMPANY."
"I'M NOT NEEDED."
AND IN THE WORST CASE ...
..."THERE'S NO REASON FOR ME TO LIVE ANYMORE."
CHILL
I'M NOT GOING TO DIE LIKE THAT!
BANG
WHAT ARE YOU TALKING ABOUT?
WHEN PEOPLE ARE UNDER PRESSURE, THEY CAN'T MAKE RATIONAL DECISIONS.
YOU WERE THINKING OF QUITTING AFTER JUST A SINGLE MISTAKE, WEREN'T YOU?
UH...
YEAH, WELL ...
I MAY HAVE BEEN OVERREACTING A LITTLE BIT.
OKAY, FINE.
THEN, TELL ME...

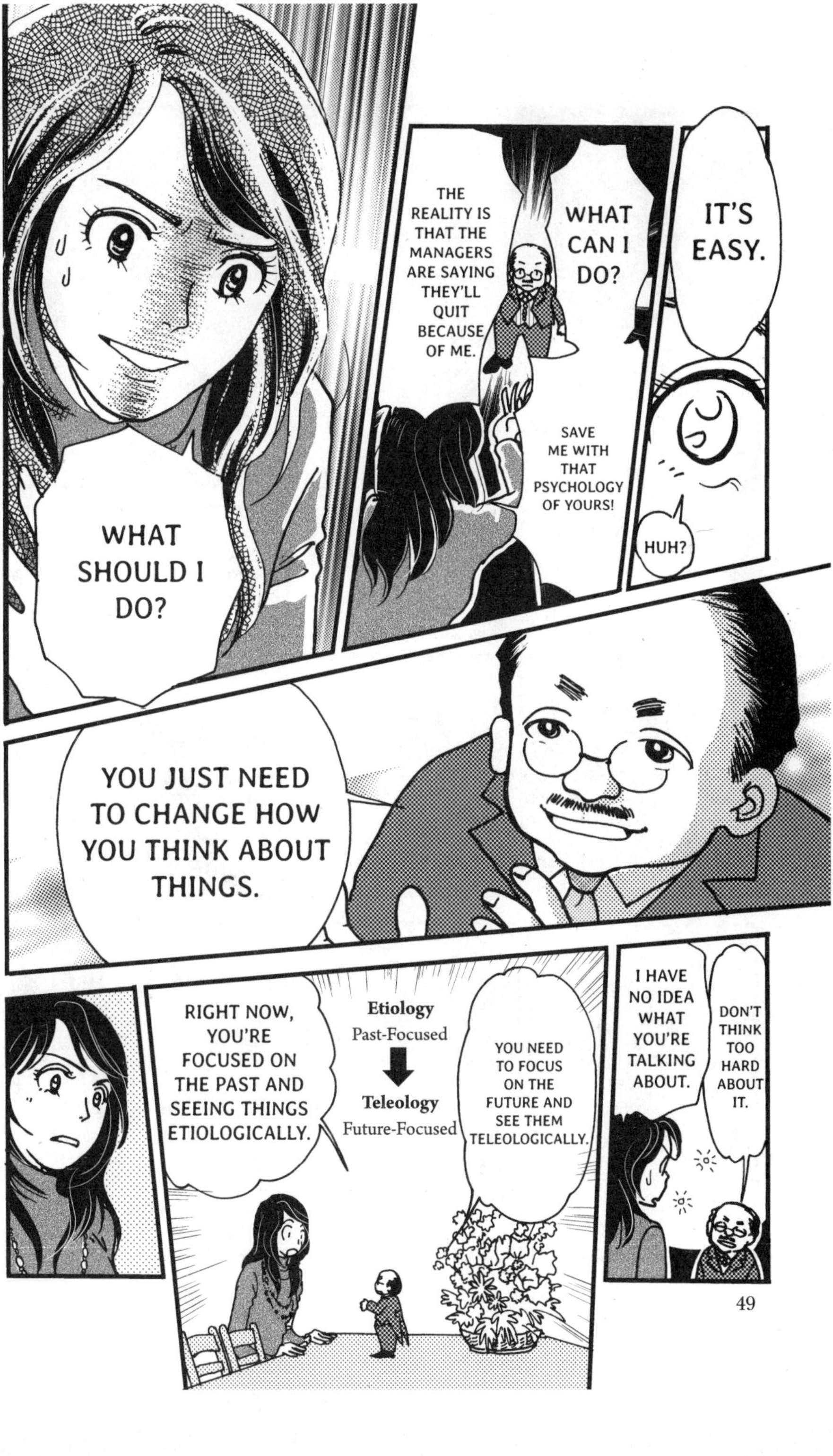
WHAT SHOULD I DO?
THE REALITY IS THAT THE MANAGERS ARE SAYING THEY'LL QUIT BECAUSE OF ME.
WHAT CAN I DO?
SAVE ME WITH THAT PSYCHOLOGY OF YOURS!
IT'S EASY.
HUH?
YOU JUST NEED TO CHANGE HOW YOU THINK ABOUT THINGS.
RIGHT NOW, YOU'RE FOCUSED ON THE PAST AND SEEING THINGS ETIOLOGICALLY.
Etiology
Past-Focused
Teleology
Future-Focused
YOU NEED TO FOCUS ON THE FUTURE AND SEE THEM TELEOLOGICALLY.
I HAVE NO IDEA WHAT YOU'RE TALKING ABOUT.
DON'T THINK TOO HARD ABOUT IT.

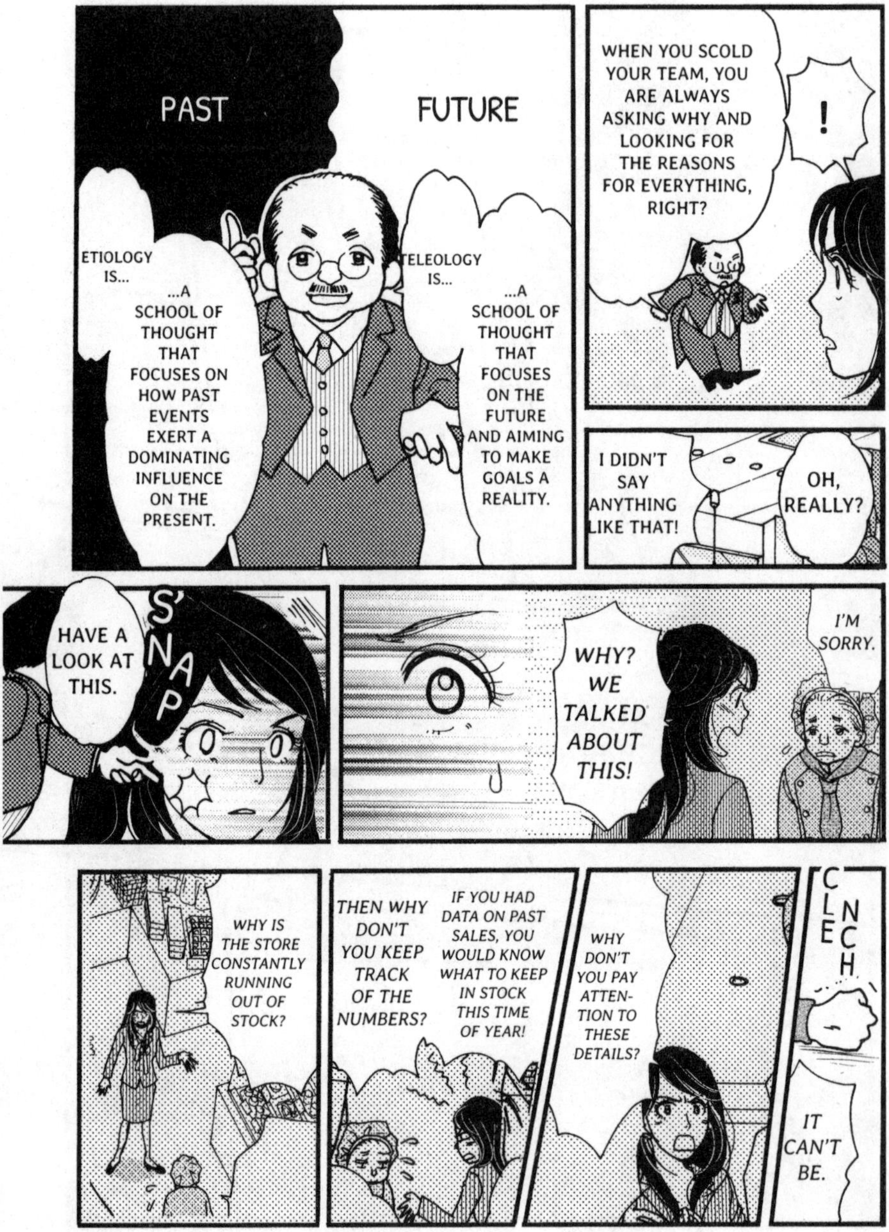
PAST
FUTURE
ETIOLOGY IS...
...A SCHOOL OF THOUGHT THAT FOCUSES ON HOW PAST EVENTS EXERT A DOMINATING INFLUENCE ON THE PRESENT.
TELEOLOGY IS...
...A SCHOOL OF THOUGHT THAT FOCUSES ON THE FUTURE AND AIMING TO MAKE GOALS A REALITY.
WHEN YOU SCOLD YOUR TEAM, YOU ARE ALWAYS ASKING WHY AND LOOKING FOR THE REASONS FOR EVERYTHING, RIGHT?
!
I DIDN'T SAY ANYTHING LIKE THAT!
OH, REALLY?
HAVE A LOOK AT THIS.
SNAP
WHY? WE TALKED ABOUT THIS!
I'M SORRY.
WHY IS THE STORE CONSTANTLY RUNNING OUT OF STOCK?
THEN WHY DON'T YOU KEEP TRACK OF THE NUMBERS?
IF YOU HAD DATA ON PAST SALES, YOU WOULD KNOW WHAT TO KEEP IN STOCK THIS TIME OF YEAR!
WHY DON'T YOU PAY ATTEN-TION TO THESE DETAILS?
CLENCH
IT CAN'T BE.

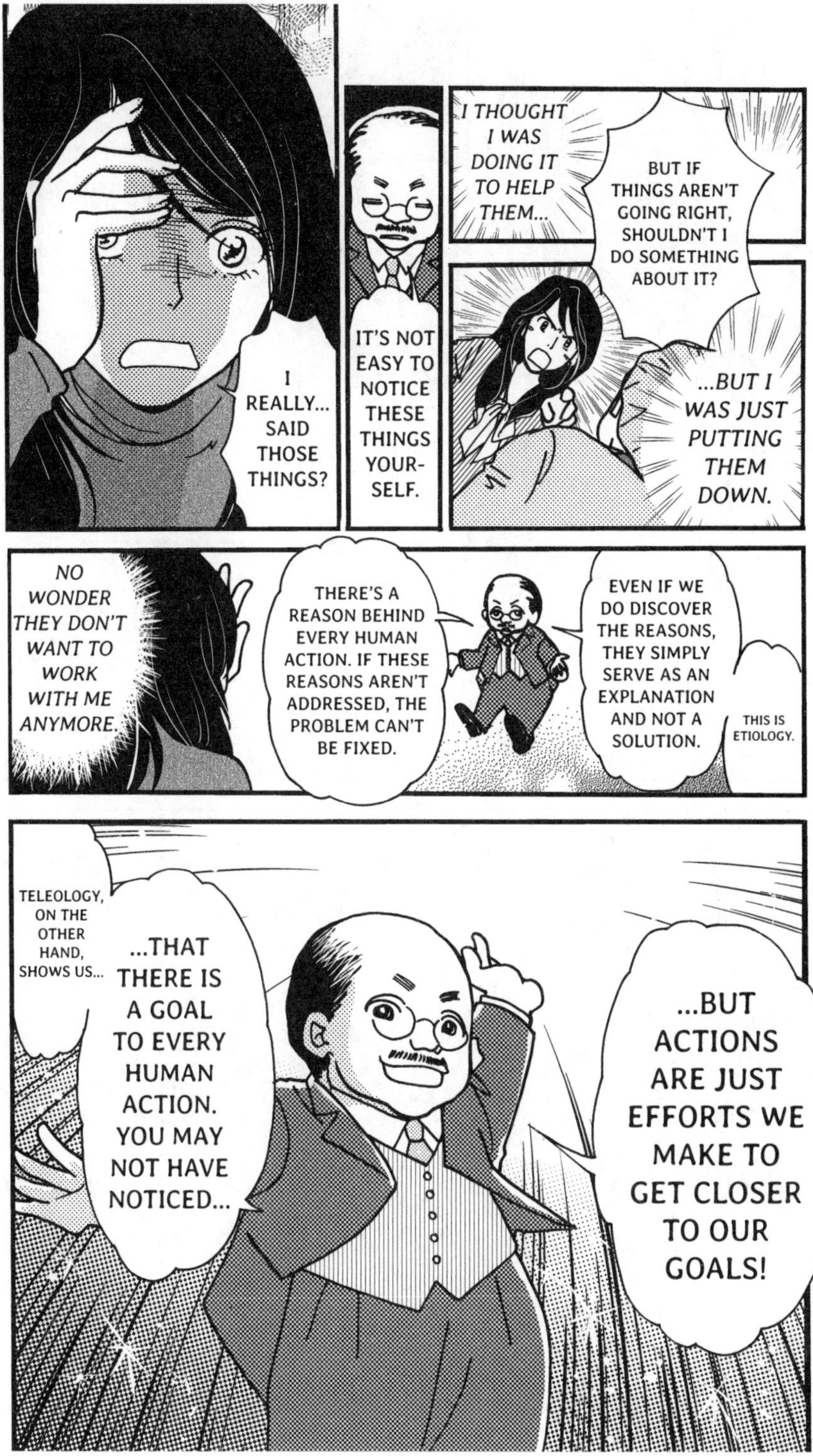
I REALLY... SAID THOSE THINGS?
IT'S NOT EASY TO NOTICE THESE THINGS YOURSELF.
I THOUGHT I WAS DOING IT TO HELP THEM...
BUT IF THINGS AREN'T GOING RIGHT, SHOULDN'T I DO SOMETHING ABOUT IT?
...BUT I WAS JUST PUTTING THEM DOWN.
NO WONDER THEY DON'T WANT TO WORK WITH ME ANYMORE.
THERE'S A REASON BEHIND EVERY HUMAN ACTION. IF THESE REASONS AREN'T ADDRESSED, THE PROBLEM CAN'T BE FIXED.
EVEN IF WE DO DISCOVER THE REASONS, THEY SIMPLY SERVE AS AN EXPLANATION AND NOT A SOLUTION.
THIS IS ETIOLOGY.
TELEOLOGY, ON THE OTHER HAND, SHOWS US...
...THAT THERE IS A GOAL TO EVERY HUMAN ACTION. YOU MAY NOT HAVE NOTICED...
...BUT ACTIONS ARE JUST EFFORTS WE MAKE TO GET CLOSER TO OUR GOALS!

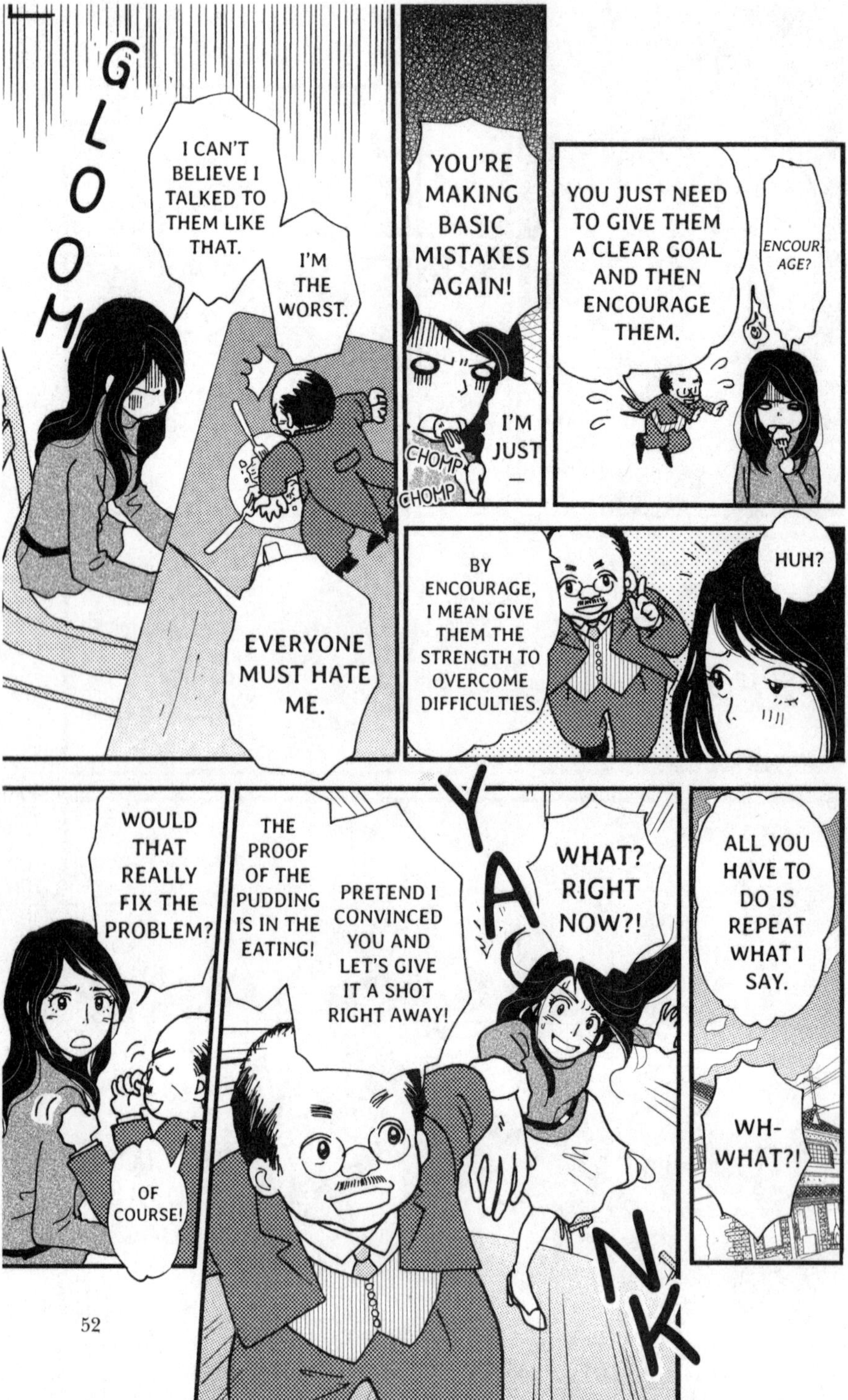
GLOOM
I CAN'T BELIEVE I TALKED TO THEM LIKE THAT.
I'M THE WORST.
EVERYONE MUST HATE ME.
YOU'RE MAKING BASIC MISTAKES AGAIN!
I'M JUST—
CHOMP CHOMP
YOU JUST NEED TO GIVE THEM A CLEAR GOAL AND THEN ENCOURAGE THEM.
ENCOURAGE?
BY ENCOURAGE, I MEAN GIVE THEM THE STRENGTH TO OVERCOME DIFFICULTIES.
HUH?
WOULD THAT REALLY FIX THE PROBLEM?
OF COURSE!
THE PROOF OF THE PUDDING IS IN THE EATING!
PRETEND I CONVINCED YOU AND LET'S GIVE IT A SHOT RIGHT AWAY!
YANK
WHAT? RIGHT NOW?!
ALL YOU HAVE TO DO IS REPEAT WHAT I SAY.
WH-WHAT?!

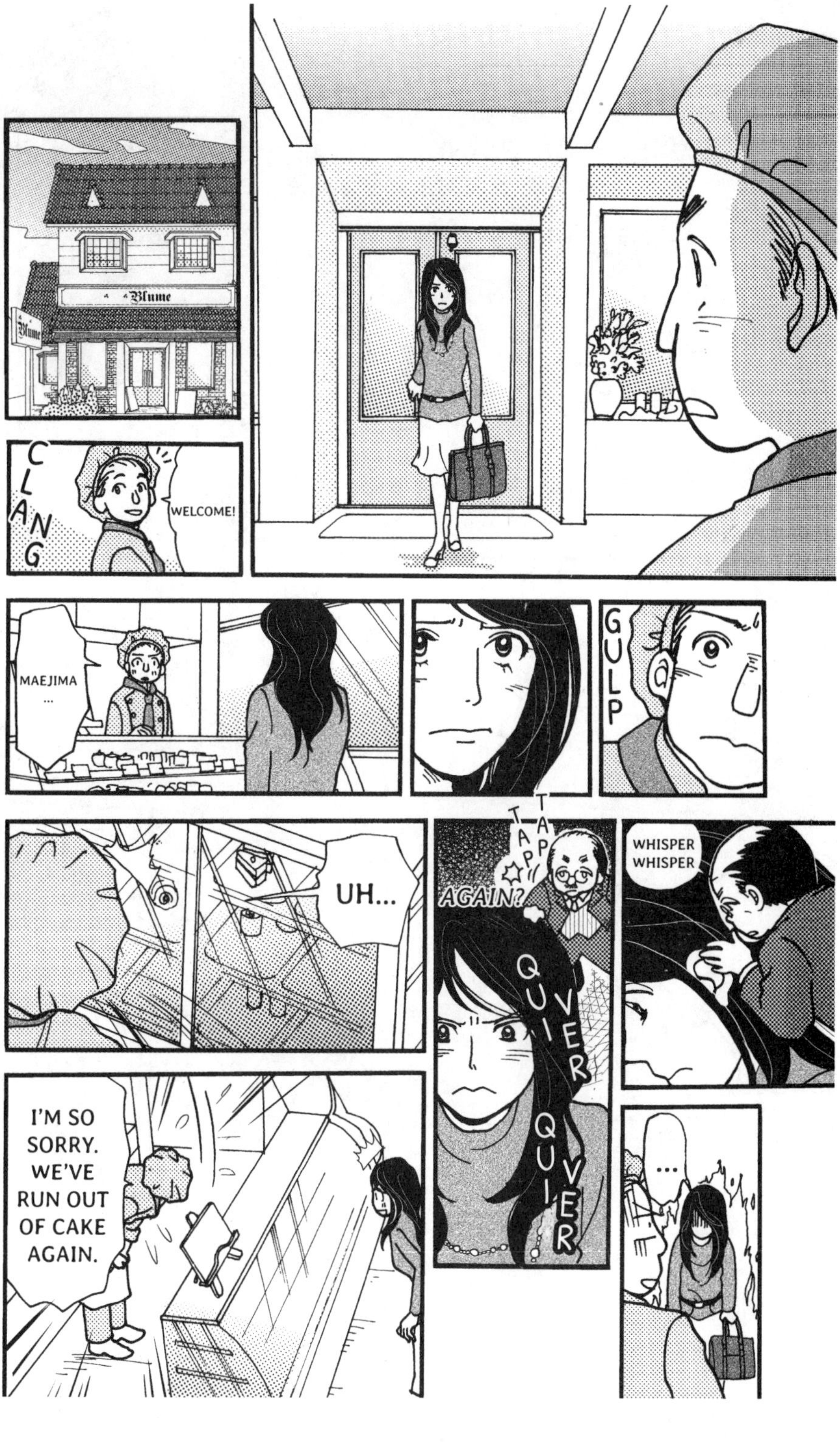
CLANG
WELCOME!
MAEJIMA ...
GULP
UH...
TAP TAP
AGAIN?
QUIVER QUIVER
WHISPER WHISPER
I'M SO SORRY. WE'VE RUN OUT OF CAKE AGAIN.
...

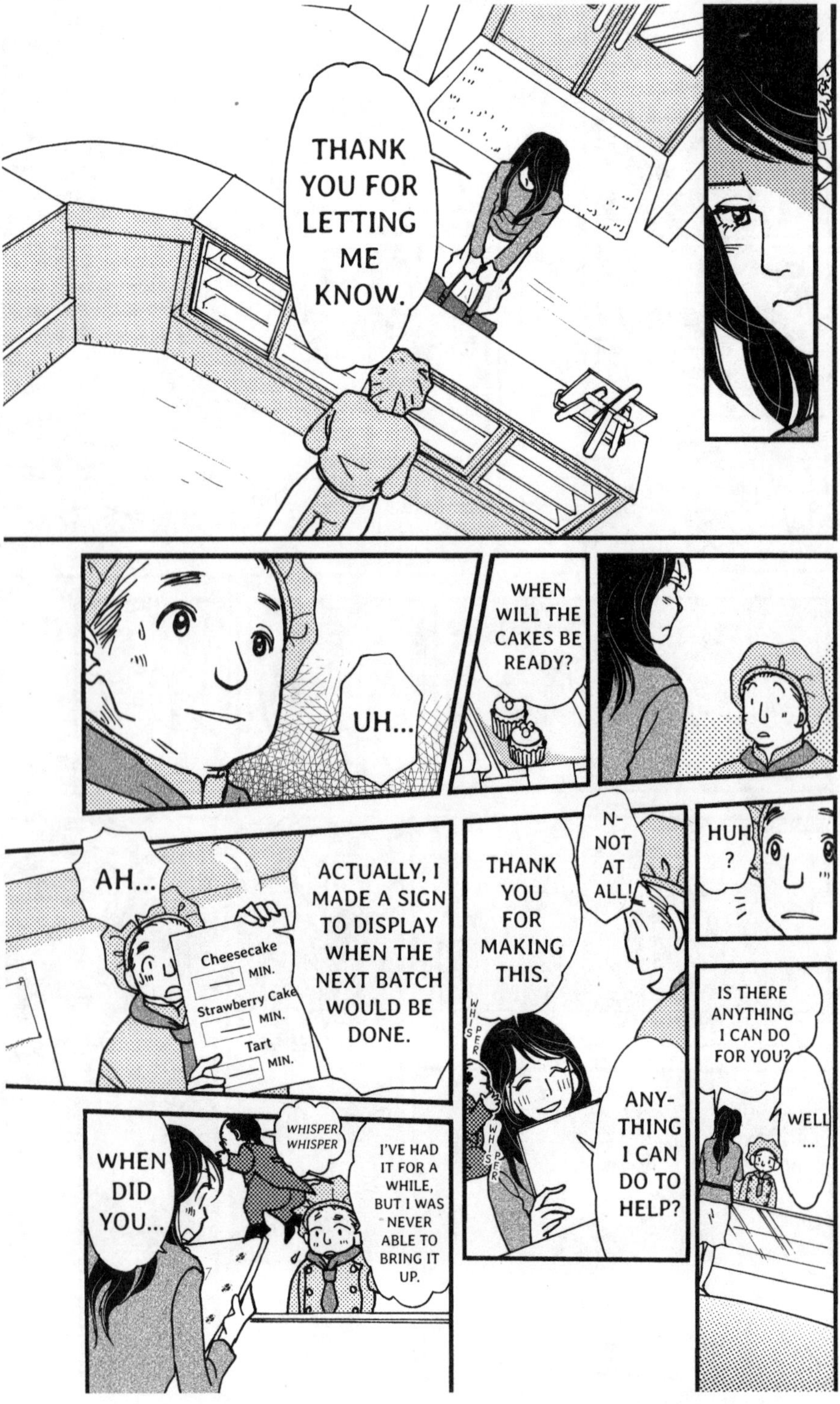
THANK YOU FOR LETTING ME KNOW.
WHEN WILL THE CAKES BE READY?
UH...
HUH?
IS THERE ANYTHING I CAN DO FOR YOU?
WELL...
ANYTHING I CAN DO TO HELP?
AH...
ACTUALLY, I MADE A SIGN TO DISPLAY WHEN THE NEXT BATCH WOULD BE DONE.
Cheesecake
MIN.
Strawberry Cake
MIN.
Tart
MIN.
THANK YOU FOR MAKING THIS.
N-NOT AT ALL!
WHISPER
WHISPER
WHEN DID YOU...
WHISPER WHISPER
I'VE HAD IT FOR A WHILE, BUT I WAS NEVER ABLE TO BRING IT UP.

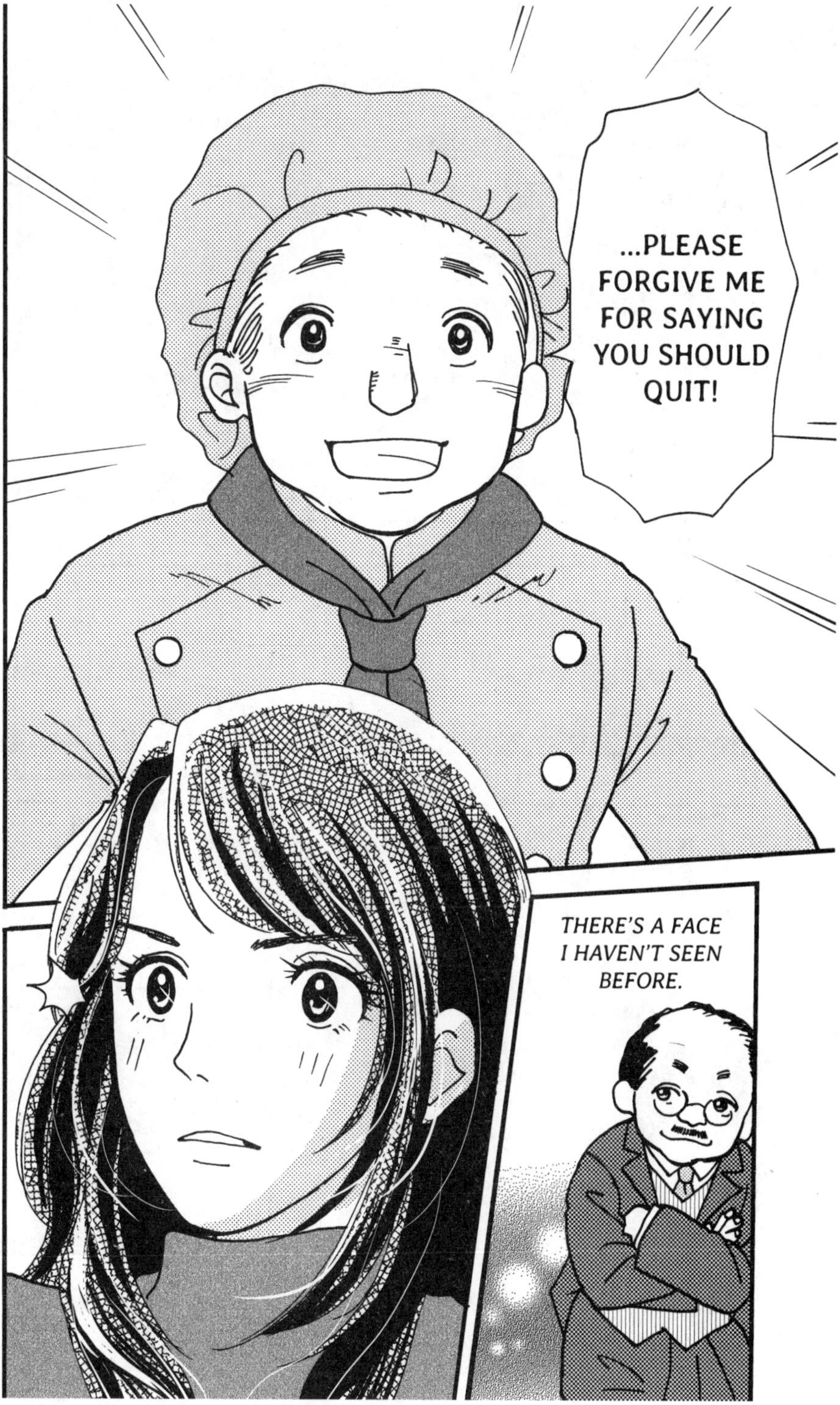
...PLEASE FORGIVE ME FOR SAYING YOU SHOULD QUIT!
THERE'S A FACE I HAVEN'T SEEN BEFORE.

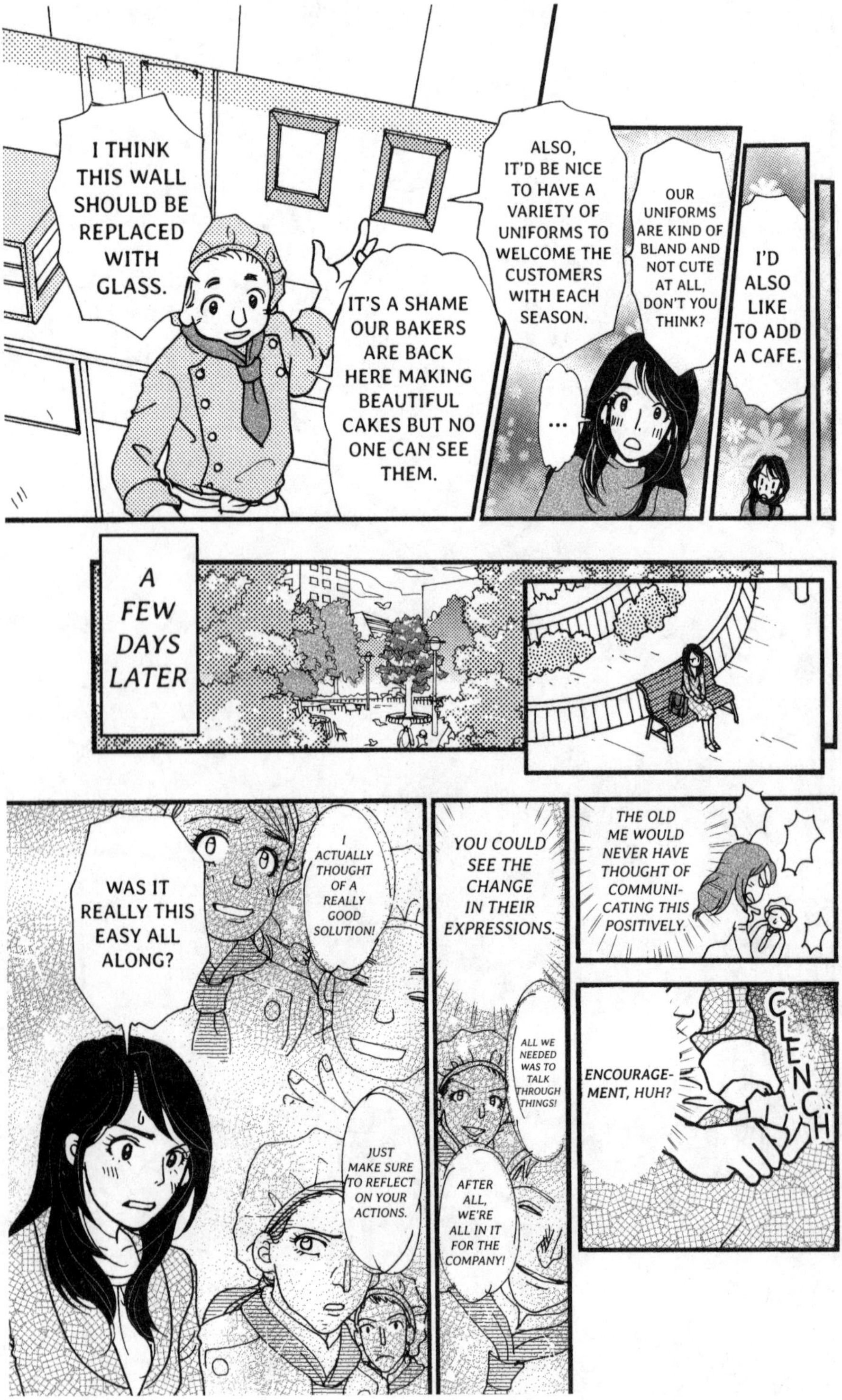
I THINK THIS WALL SHOULD BE REPLACED WITH GLASS.
IT'S A SHAME OUR BAKERS ARE BACK HERE MAKING BEAUTIFUL CAKES BUT NO ONE CAN SEE THEM.
ALSO, IT'D BE NICE TO HAVE A VARIETY OF UNIFORMS TO WELCOME THE CUSTOMERS WITH EACH SEASON.
...
OUR UNIFORMS ARE KIND OF BLAND AND NOT CUTE AT ALL, DON'T YOU THINK?
I'D ALSO LIKE TO ADD A CAFE.
A FEW DAYS LATER
WAS IT REALLY THIS EASY ALL ALONG?
I ACTUALLY THOUGHT OF A REALLY GOOD SOLUTION!
JUST MAKE SURE TO REFLECT ON YOUR ACTIONS.
YOU COULD SEE THE CHANGE IN THEIR EXPRESSIONS.
ALL WE NEEDED WAS TO TALK THROUGH THINGS!
AFTER ALL, WE'RE ALL IN IT FOR THE COMPANY!
THE OLD ME WOULD NEVER HAVE THOUGHT OF COMMUNI-CATING THIS POSITIVELY.
ENCOURAGE-MENT, HUH?
CLENCH

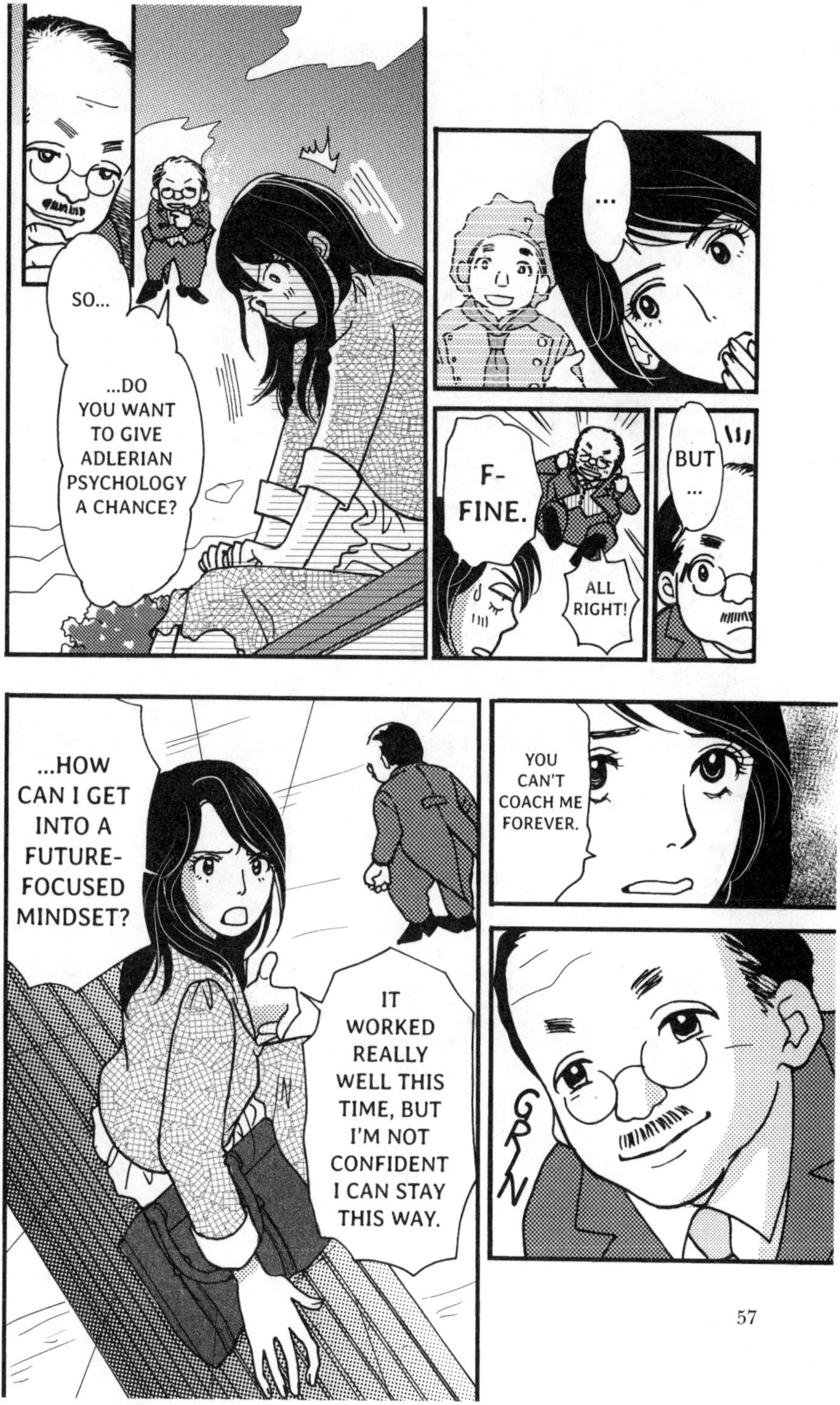
SO...
...DO YOU WANT TO GIVE ADLERIAN PSYCHOLOGY A CHANCE?
...
F-FINE.
ALL RIGHT!
BUT ...
...HOW CAN I GET INTO A FUTURE-FOCUSED MINDSET?
IT WORKED REALLY WELL THIS TIME, BUT I'M NOT CONFIDENT I CAN STAY THIS WAY.
YOU CAN'T COACH ME FOREVER.
GRIN

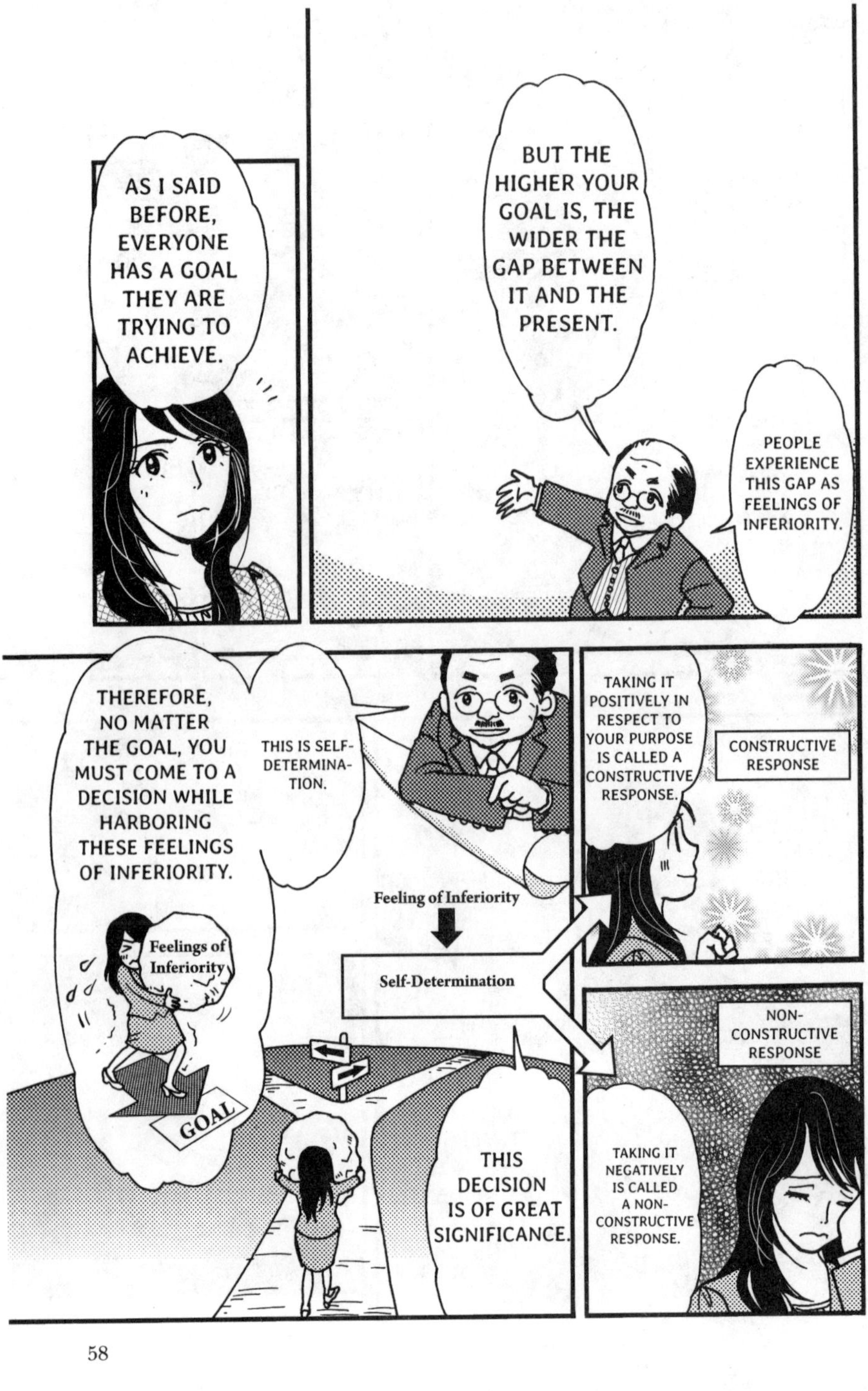

AS I SAID BEFORE, EVERYONE HAS A GOAL THEY ARE TRYING TO ACHIEVE.
BUT THE HIGHER YOUR GOAL IS, THE WIDER THE GAP BETWEEN IT AND THE PRESENT.
PEOPLE EXPERIENCE THIS GAP AS FEELINGS OF INFERIORITY.
THEREFORE, NO MATTER THE GOAL, YOU MUST COME TO A DECISION WHILE HARBORING THESE FEELINGS OF INFERIORITY.
Feelings of Inferiority
GOAL
THIS IS SELF-DETERMINATION.
Feeling of Inferiority
Self-Determination
THIS DECISION IS OF GREAT SIGNIFICANCE.
TAKING IT POSITIVELY IN RESPECT TO YOUR PURPOSE IS CALLED A CONSTRUCTIVE RESPONSE.
CONSTRUCTIVE RESPONSE
NON-CONSTRUCTIVE RESPONSE
TAKING IT NEGATIVELY IS CALLED A NON-CONSTRUCTIVE RESPONSE.

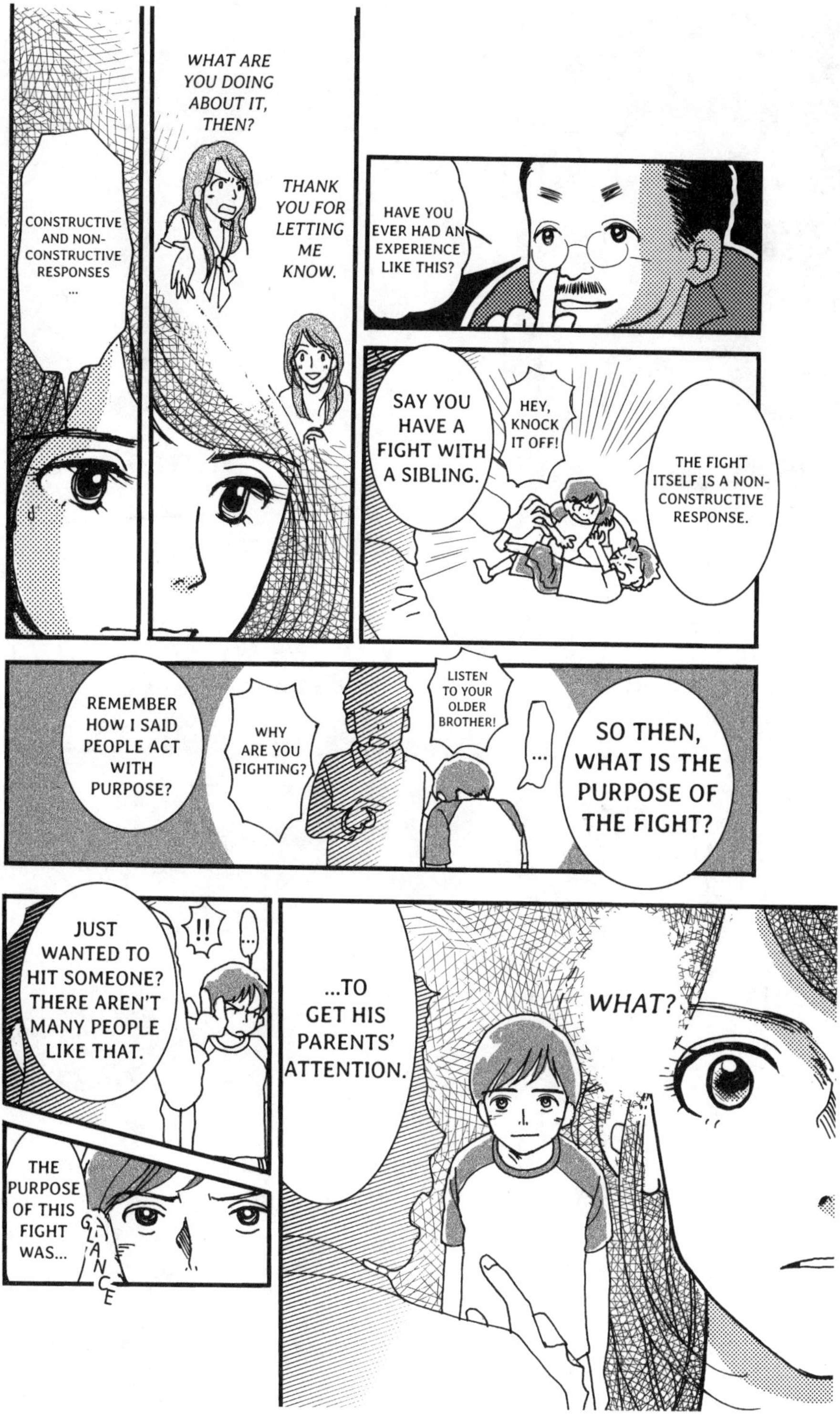
WHAT ARE YOU DOING ABOUT IT, THEN?
THANK YOU FOR LETTING ME KNOW.
CONSTRUCTIVE AND NON-CONSTRUCTIVE RESPONSES ...
HAVE YOU EVER HAD AN EXPERIENCE LIKE THIS?
SAY YOU HAVE A FIGHT WITH A SIBLING.
HEY, KNOCK IT OFF!
THE FIGHT ITSELF IS A NON-CONSTRUCTIVE RESPONSE.
REMEMBER HOW I SAID PEOPLE ACT WITH PURPOSE?
WHY ARE YOU FIGHTING?
LISTEN TO YOUR OLDER BROTHER!
...
SO THEN, WHAT IS THE PURPOSE OF THE FIGHT?
JUST WANTED TO HIT SOMEONE? THERE AREN'T MANY PEOPLE LIKE THAT.
!!
...
THE PURPOSE OF THIS FIGHT WAS...
GLANCE
...TO GET HIS PARENTS' ATTENTION.
WHAT?

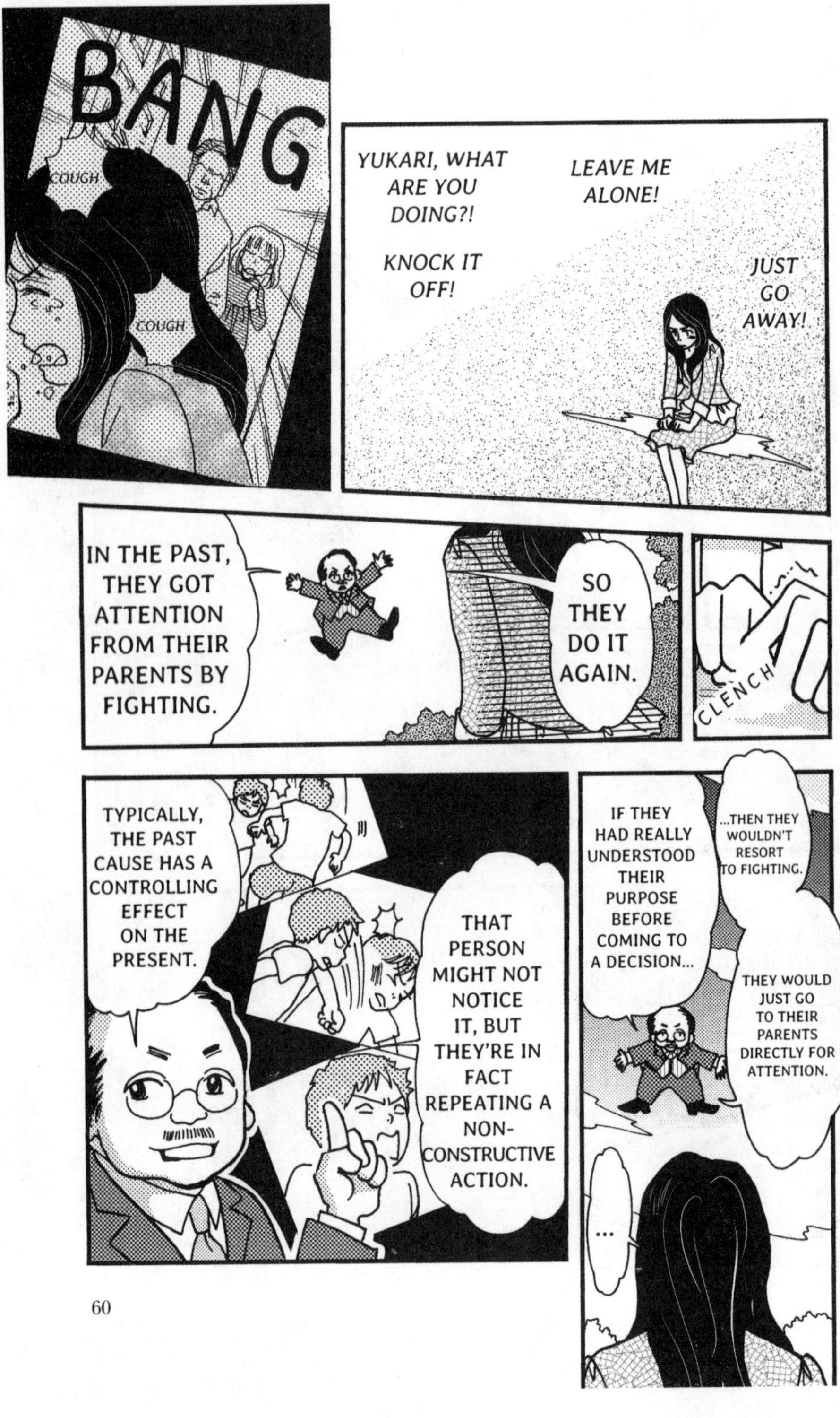
BANG
COUGH
COUGH
YUKARI, WHAT ARE YOU DOING?!
KNOCK IT OFF!
LEAVE ME ALONE!
JUST GO AWAY!
IN THE PAST, THEY GOT ATTENTION FROM THEIR PARENTS BY FIGHTING.
SO THEY DO IT AGAIN.
CLENCH
TYPICALLY, THE PAST CAUSE HAS A CONTROLLING EFFECT ON THE PRESENT.
THAT PERSON MIGHT NOT NOTICE IT, BUT THEY'RE IN FACT REPEATING A NON-CONSTRUCTIVE ACTION.
IF THEY HAD REALLY UNDERSTOOD THEIR PURPOSE BEFORE COMING TO A DECISION...
...THEN THEY WOULDN'T RESORT TO FIGHTING.
THEY WOULD JUST GO TO THEIR PARENTS DIRECTLY FOR ATTENTION.
...

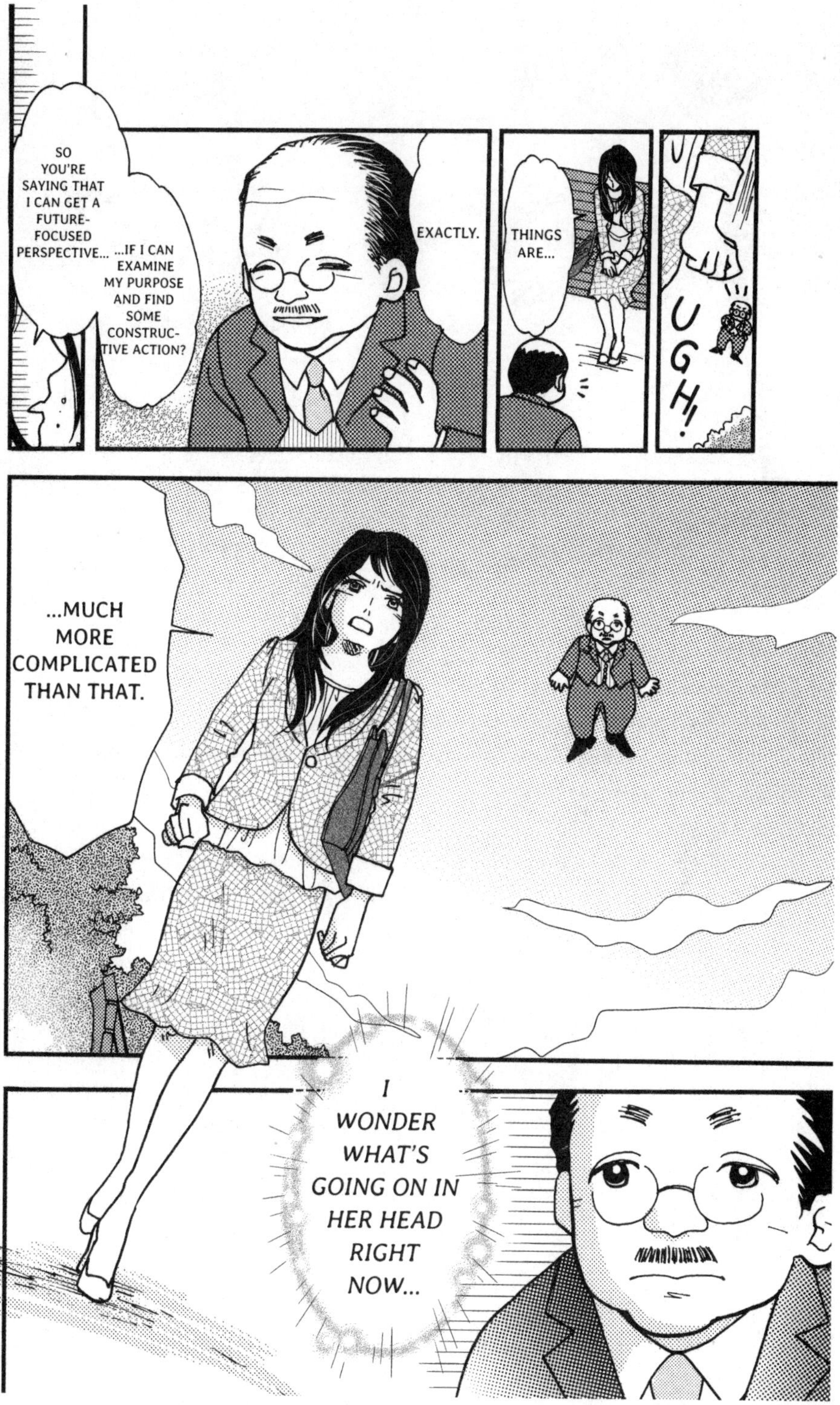
SO YOU'RE SAYING THAT I CAN GET A FUTURE-FOCUSED PERSPECTIVE...
...IF I CAN EXAMINE MY PURPOSE AND FIND SOME CONSTRUCTIVE ACTION?
EXACTLY.
THINGS ARE...
UGH!
...MUCH MORE COMPLICATED THAN THAT.
I WONDER WHAT'S GOING ON IN HER HEAD RIGHT NOW...

Lifestyle and Life Tasks

1

⇨ What Is Lifestyle?

Although lifestyle wasn't touched on in the Prologue, it is an integral concept in Adlerian psychology. When you hear the word *lifestyle*, you may associate it with the societal trends surrounding how you live your life. But in Adlerian psychology, lifestyle is more closely associated with how each individual lives their life—how they exist. So why does Adler specifically use the term *lifestyle* in this way rather than *character* or *personality*?

Each person's unique way of thinking, feeling, expressing emotions, and taking actions based on their considerations, feelings, and conduct is called their *character*. Adler believed the word *character* had a sense of weight and immutability to it. So, in order to convey a broader meaning than character, including the belief in one's self and the world around them, he used the word *lifestyle*.

It seems that Adler believed from the beginning that even one's character could be changed. Sydney M. Roth, one of Adler's disciples, once asked him around what age it was too late to change one's character. Adler's reply was "Probably one or two days before death." Adler, who didn't place much emphasis on definitions, called the pursuit of one's goals the *law of motion*. Adler also called this *lifestyle*. After Adler's passing, this was accepted as a basic definition in the continually developing Adlerian psychology:

> Lifestyle is a system of beliefs about the present and the ideal states of the self and the world.

Your present self is how you see your situation and could also be called your *self-image*. It's your subjective view of your body, personality, abilities, and so on. Next is your ideal self. It's things like wanting to be excellent, wanting to be perfect, wanting attention, and wanting to be loved by those around you. It's the answer to the questions "How do I want to be?" and "How should I be?"

The world is your surrounding environment. It encompasses everything from large concepts like the world, life, fate, and people, down to small concepts such as men, women, your surrounding environment, family, friends, superiors, and subordinates. How you see them is the present world. How you would like them to be in regards to yourself is the ideal world.

⇛ The Elements and Effects of Lifestyle

In modern Adlerian psychology, lifestyle is made up of three parts:

1) **Concept of Self:** Your beliefs about your present self
   "I am _____."

2) **World Image:** Your beliefs about the world
   "The world (life, people, men/women, friends, etc.) is __."

3) **Personal Ideals:** Your beliefs about your ideal self and ideal world
   "I should be _____."
   "I want life (the people around you, etc.) to be ___."

In order to explain the concept of self easier, let's use the king of invention, Thomas Edison, as an example. Edison, who is famously quoted as saying "Genius is 1% inspiration and 99% perspiration," didn't seem to have the kind of concept of self where he thought he was frequently failing. On the contrary, if he had had such a concept of himself, he would have given up trying after a few failures and never would have become known as the king of inventors. Another famous quote of his, "I am not discouraged because every wrong attempt discarded is another step forward," supports this contention.

Next, let's use Yukari's lifestyle to deepen our understanding of the concept of self, world image, and personal ideal.

Her concept of herself is that she is a bad person. So it doesn't matter how much the people around her affirm her abilities; she still doesn't see herself as adequate and ends up despising herself. Her world image is "I cannot rely on my subordinates." So she ends up unable to depend on them and does everything herself. This makes it very difficult for her to achieve anything with other people in her organization. Her personal ideal is "I have to surpass my rivals." So her focus is always on competition, and it becomes difficult for her to build any other type of relationship with the people she works with. You can see on the next page how we can analyze Yukari's lifestyle based on what we have learned so far.

Lifestyle Classification

	Self	World
Present	**Concept of Self:** Your beliefs about your current self "I am ____." *Yukari's Example:* "I'm a terrible person."  	**World Image:** Your beliefs about the world "The world (life, people, men/women, friends, etc.) is ____." *Yukari's Example:* "I cannot rely on my subordinates." 
Ideal	**Personal Ideal:** Your beliefs about your ideal self and world "I should be ____." "The world (the people around you, etc.) should be ____." *Yukari's Example:* "I have to surpass my rivals." 	

The reality is that there are still many aspects of Yukari's lifestyle that she needs to take control of. Luckily, according to Adlerian psychology, she can change her lifestyle, and we can enjoy watching Yukari's transformation.

Lifestyles are often written deeply in our hearts, as Yukari's lifestyle is for her, even if she is not aware of this. When she faces a difficult life task, her thoughts and ways of responding will be based on her lifestyle.

⇨ What Are Life Tasks?

Life tasks are those tasks that we have to meet head on in life. They are the things that we deal with every day from morning to night. If you work in an office, it's getting on the train and getting to work on time, it's greeting your coworkers at the office, it's following orders from superiors, it's dealing with customer complaints, and perhaps at the end of the day, it's helping your child with homework or finding quiet time with your spouse.

Adler divided life tasks into three categories: work, friendship, and love. They all make up the essence of interpersonal relationships and can be defined as follows:

1) Work tasks: roles, obligations, and responsibilities that constitute your daily output
2) Friendship tasks: relationships with those around you
3) Love tasks: relationships between couples and parents/children

In Yukari's case, since being promoted from store manager to area manager, her work tasks include leading the stores that she is in charge of. Her friendship tasks don't include any close friends and she is facing alienation from some of her store managers. Her love tasks are issues with her family—particularly her father and her brother—that she has yet to resolve. It also doesn't seem like she has a close relationship with her younger sister.

Life Tasks

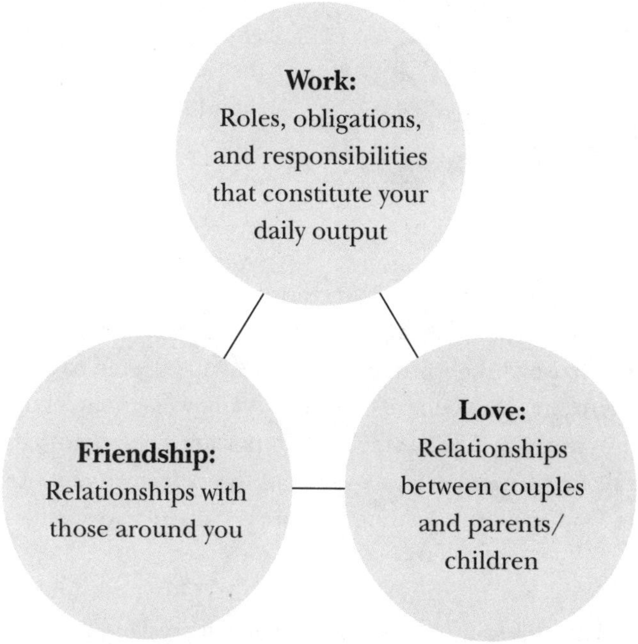
Work:
Roles, obligations, and responsibilities that constitute your daily output
Friendship:
Relationships with those around you
Love:
Relationships between couples and parents/ children

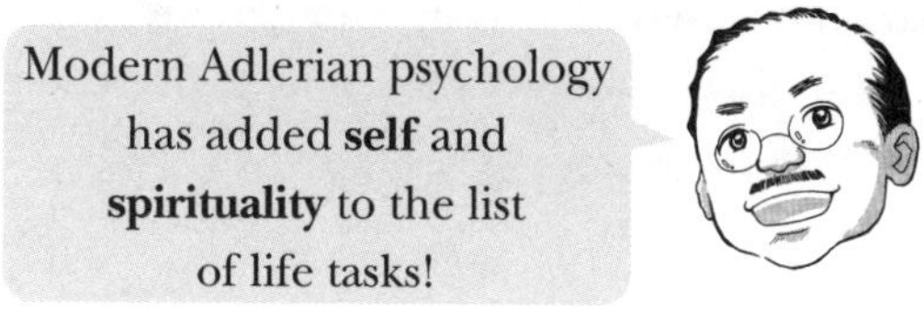
Modern Adlerian psychology has added **self** and **spirituality** to the list of life tasks!

From an Etiological Approach to a Teleological One

2

⇨ The Three Patterns of Discouragement

There are probably a lot of people around you that have difficulties in their life or friction with their environment similar to Yukari. This type of person has low self-esteem and doesn't trust those around them. One characteristic of this type of person is that they are always seeing problems *etiologically*, looking for the cause of their problems in the unchangeable past. Furthermore, they believe that this somehow has control over their present. So when something important doesn't go right, they make themselves into a victim of their environment or in some kind of martyr, leading to more self-discouragement.

In Yukari's case, it doesn't even end there. Others around her also adopt this same approach—the managers get discouraged and the alienation between them festers and grows. Discouragement, which eliminates the ability to overcome difficulties, comes in three patterns:

1) The setting of unrealistic expectations
2) Focusing on unaccomplished areas
3) Self-deprecation

For the first pattern, setting expectations too low makes success too easy, doesn't lead to growth, and gives no sense of achievement. On the other hand, if expectations are too high, you still fail after many attempts and you lose motivation (1). Then you focus on the areas that weren't successful (2) and begin asking why they weren't successful. When you ask this of others, it makes them uncomfortable and damages your relationships with them. Depending on your subordinates, they may just make up a story to avoid the issue. Some subordinates may even respond by getting angry themselves.

Additionally, if only the situation or their actions are considered, some people may take this as an attack on their character and start to believe that no matter what they do, it won't be enough (3). The next step is to doubt the character of the one accusing them, at which point there is no longer any trust, and any chance of working together as a team disappears.

⇒ Searching for the Cause Does Not Lead to the Solution

As Dr. Adler advised Yukari, "Everyone's actions have their own unique purpose."

If we recognize that searching for the cause of our problems does not lead to solutions, we can have a future-focused perspective. Then, when we are faced with a negative outcome from our interactions with others, we can try and understand what their motivation was and encourage them rather than approaching the problem etiologically and devaluing them. See the chart below for a comparison of the two methods. It's easier to see the differences in etiology and teleology with a concrete example.

There was a period when I was mainly focused on helping truant kids. Once I started searching for the reason for their truancy, usually some problem with their mother, their environment, or their early life would appear.

Etiology and Teleology

Etiology (Causality) Cause and Effect Approach	Teleology Goal and Method Approach
① Past causes exert a controlling influence on the present (past-focused perspective) ② Intention doesn't matter (the individual is weak or has no independence) ③ Individuals paint themselves as a victim of the environment or a martyr (victim or martyr mentality) ④ People are discouraged (discouragement)	① Future goals rule the present (future-focused perspective) ② Intention makes a difference (individual independence) ③ A creative mindset can flourish (individual's mindset) ④ People are encouraged (encouragement)

This was the same mentality found in factories, where quality control was constantly searching for the perpetrator of some kind of error. Once I dropped this kind of etiological approach and searched for the purpose behind the truancy, I found that the cause was usually a longing for their parents' affection or revenge for some corporal punishment from a teacher. At this point, the truancy became much easier to deal with. I experienced this difference in etiology and teleology firsthand myself and came to the following conclusion: *searching for the cause leads you to an explanation but not a resolution.*

The fact that the child is truant because their mother didn't raise them or there wasn't enough physical contact during their childhood may sound like a plausible explanation, but that doesn't change the fact that what's done is done. In truth, it only creates a hostile environment in the parent-child relationship. What's more important is reestablishing a parent-child relationship based on respect and trust. Then the parent and child can work hand-in-hand in order to resolve the issues between them.

If we take Yukari's competitive, perfectionist lifestyle as an example, we can see that it's full of basic mistakes. The way that she interrogates her subordinates ultimately shows that she is demanding the same level of perfectionism in them and is just trying to dominate them into doing things her way. Seeing this, Dr. Adler explained that "There is a goal to every human action" and "Actions are just efforts we make to get closer to our goals," while encouraging her to shift from a causal, blaming, etiological mindset to an encouraging, teleological one.

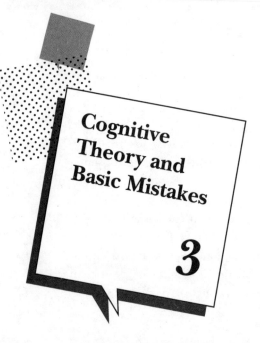

Cognitive Theory and Basic Mistakes

3

⇨ **What Is Private Logic?**

As we said in the Prologue, cognitive theory, the basic underpinning of Adlerian psychology, holds that people interpret events in their own subjective way. That is to say, people cannot view events objectively as they really are.

This subjective interpretation—the individual's unique viewpoint, way of thinking, and valuation of themselves and the world (both humanity as a whole and other individuals)—is called *private logic* in Adlerian psychology. Private logic is, so to speak, like a set of unique glasses that each person wears. Through these glasses, the wearer perceives things that are to a certain extent distorted from what others see. Others may see things more positively or negatively than we do. This private logic can create non-constructive (and occasionally destructive) interpretations, making life more difficult and causing friction with our surroundings. These warped perceptions and self-defeating thoughts are known as *basic mistakes.*

⇒ Basic Mistakes

The five quintessential basic mistakes are *judging, exaggerating, overlooking, overgeneralizing,* and *denying one's worth.* Everyone tends to make these mistakes in stressful situations.

Judging is when you come to a conclusion and label something with certainty when that label is actually only one of the possibilities. For example, Yukari judged that she was a terrible supervisor.

Exaggerating is making a mountain out of a molehill and blowing things out of proportion. For example, Yukari acted like every store manager was rebelling against her when in fact there were some who supported her. *Everyone, always,* and *everything* are words often used when exaggerating.

Overlooking is when you consider only one part of a whole and miss important aspects of the situation. Yukari saw only the store managers rebelling against her, so she didn't consider those who did support her.

Overgeneralizing is viewing everything as a problem when in reality the problem is confined to only a certain area. Yukari took a problem at work, specifically how she handled her subordinates, and overgeneralized that into a problem with her entire personality.

Denying one's worth is having a diminished or destructive opinion of oneself. Yukari said she was worthless and there was no point in her living.

⇨ Three Ways to Guide Yourself Back to Common Sense (Our Shared Sense)

Dr. Adler guided Yukari away from a warped manner of thinking to a healthy and constructive view of herself and others using common sense. Common sense is often thought of as general knowledge or good sense, but philosophers and Adlerian psychology see it as a sense (such as sight or hearing) that all of us possess. We are going to cover common sense in a different form in the next chapter, but here Adlerian psychology is encouraging us to switch to future-focused teleology by honing our common sense. For this, Adler often said it was necessary to see through others' eyes, hear with their ears, and feel with their heart.

In order to grow out of making basic mistakes and into common sense, Adler recommended these three things: *looking for evidence, seizing the moment,* and *using useful (constructive) expressions.* The first strategy that you can use to grow wiser is looking for evidence. In Yukari's example, she said that everyone was rebelling against her. She should have stopped and asked herself if that was true and looked for evidence to support that view. She would have then recognized that she was mistaken.

The second strategy is seizing the moment, knowing that basic mistakes usually come in twos or threes when under stress and recognizing in that moment what is happening. It's stopping yourself a step or two before entering the danger zone.

The third strategy is using useful (constructive) expressions. It is used to sever the rope drawing you in a destructive and self-defeating direction.

Self-Determination

4

⇨ **You Have All of the Judgment Criteria**

I wrote about self-determination in the Prologue when I said that people are not just the victims of their environment and upbringing and that everyone has the power to shape their own destiny. While recognizing the influence of genes and environment on the formation of character, the final deciding factor is the person themself. By this, I mean that it is you that made yourself. It is also you that can change yourself. I want to reiterate that here.

Please take a look at the chart on the next page. Self-determination affects every part of you; it's not just about deciding your own character in spite of your upbringing or feelings of inferiority. Continuing with private logic, you are the one that chooses to remain in a shackled lifestyle with no control over your thoughts, responding to situations in an unconstructive way rather than using the three precepts of common sense (looking for evidence, seizing the moment, and using useful expressions) to approach things in a constructive manner. Constructive response or unconstructive response— you already possess all of the criteria to make that judgment.

Self-Determination
Physical Inferiority
Inferiority Complex
Upbringing Environment
Influencing Factors
Self-Determination
Determinant Factors
Constructive Response Compensation & Inventiveness
Unconstructive Response Inferiority Complex
It is you that built yourself. It is also you that can change yourself.

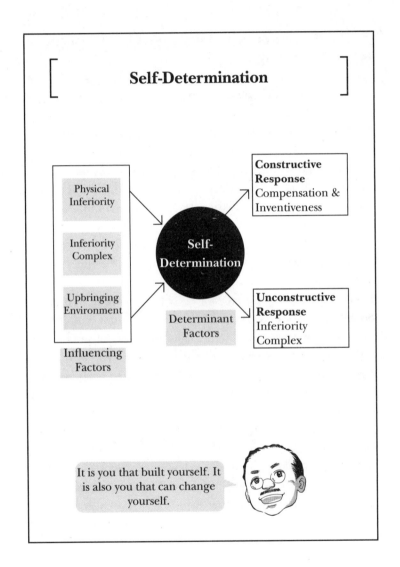

⇒ Physical Inferiority, Feelings of Inferiority, and Inferiority Complex

You can think of the concept of inferiority in three ways:

- **Physical Inferiority:** A part of your body being objectively physically inferior.
- **Feelings of Inferiority:** The subjective feeling that something about yourself is inferior. This negative feeling is based less on a comparison with others and more on a comparison with your ideal self.
- **Inferiority Complex:** Flaunting your inferiority while avoiding the things you need to do in your life (life tasks).

Physical inferiority is when your body (senses, internal organs, bones, etc.) has some form of lessened function, whether it be from birth or an acquired handicap. Adler himself suffered from rickets, and he called this *organ inferiority*. When you hear the words *feelings of inferiority*, it's normal to imagine this involves comparison with others, but in Adlerian psychology, it refers to negative feelings caused by the gap in how we really are compared with our ideal self.

In Part 4, I go into more details regarding feelings of inferiority. The fundamental difference between physical inferiority and feelings of inferiority is that *one is objective and the other is subjective.* The subjective nature of feelings of inferiority means that there are cases where a person is objectively not inferior but perceives themselves that way, as well as the opposite situation where someone is objectively inferior but they do not perceive themselves to be so.

In *The Science of Living,* Adler calls an inferiority complex "none other than excessive feeling of inferiority" and "almost akin to a disease." It's the condition where one's inferiority is used as an excuse for avoiding work-, friendship-, and love-related life tasks. An inferiority complex is when one even actively displays their inferiority and draws attention to it. Likewise, there is also an opposite condition where one draws attention to their superiority. It's called a *superiority complex,* and it has its roots in the same lack of courage as an inferiority complex.

Adler, the Feminist

In December 1897, Adler married Raissa Epstein (born November 1873 in Moscow) after meeting her at a political rally that spring. Raissa was a Jewish Russian and had come to Vienna, the political, cultural, and artistic capital of the world at that time, to study. (Note that women were not allowed to formally enter universities at this time.) Wise and beautiful, Raissa married Adler, who didn't really stand out for his looks. The picture of them together in the manga is quite realistic.

Eventually, they had four children: Valentine (in 1898), Alexandra (in 1901), Kurt (in 1905), and Cornelia (in 1909). Adler is said to have cherished his family. Raissa, despite the strict gender roles of the era, participated in Adler's discussions with his friends, had her own radical ideas, and participated in political and cultural activities.

It may have been his wife Raissa's influence, but Adler proposed the idea of male and female equality earlier than any other psychologist and supported women's rights. Because of this, the Danish sculptor Thyra Boldsen included Adler in a memorial statue she created. The statue depicted 99 famous women and one famous man, Adler.

Heinz Ansbacher and his wife, Rowena, who co-authored *The Individual Psychology of Alfred Adler*, which included various writings by Adler as well as their own commentary, and *Cooperation Between the Sexes,* noted that Adler strongly argued for equality between the sexes.

Part 2

Understanding the Role of Emotion in the Formation of Lifestyle

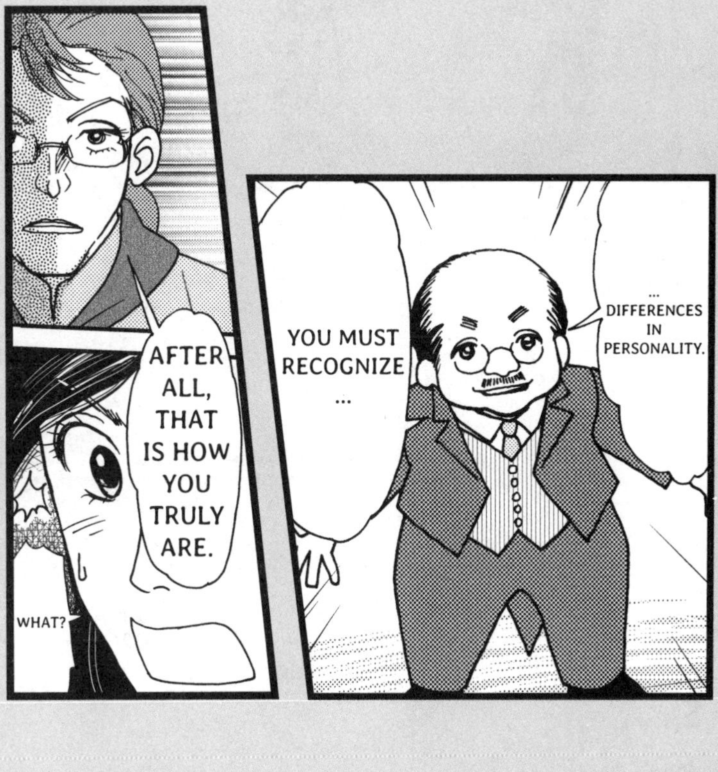
AFTER ALL, THAT IS HOW YOU TRULY ARE.
WHAT?
YOU MUST RECOGNIZE ...
... DIFFERENCES IN PERSONALITY.

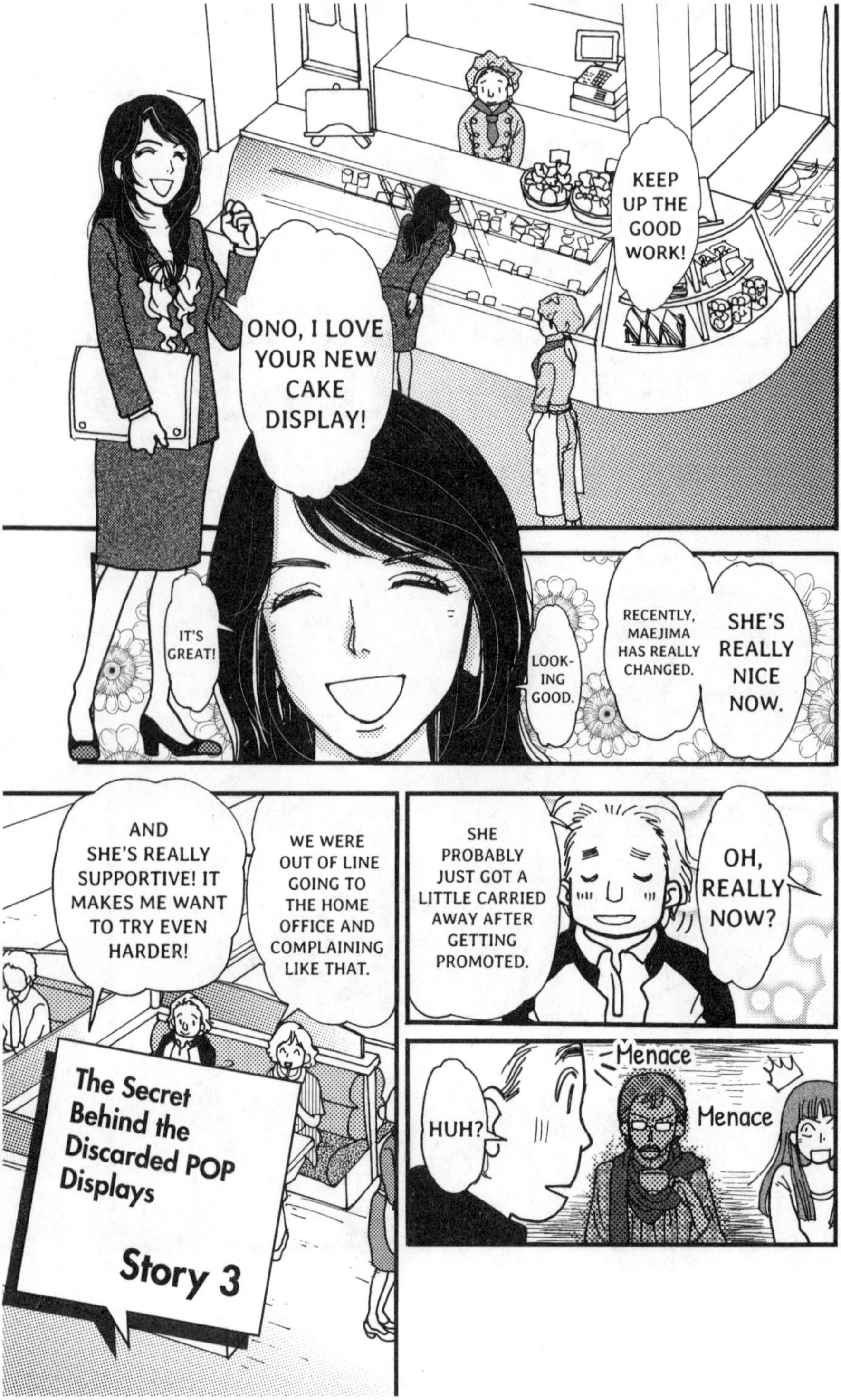
ONO, I LOVE YOUR NEW CAKE DISPLAY!
KEEP UP THE GOOD WORK!
IT'S GREAT!
LOOK-ING GOOD.
RECENTLY, MAEJIMA HAS REALLY CHANGED.
SHE'S REALLY NICE NOW.
AND SHE'S REALLY SUPPORTIVE! IT MAKES ME WANT TO TRY EVEN HARDER!
WE WERE OUT OF LINE GOING TO THE HOME OFFICE AND COMPLAINING LIKE THAT.
The Secret Behind the Discarded POP Displays
Story 3
SHE PROBABLY JUST GOT A LITTLE CARRIED AWAY AFTER GETTING PROMOTED.
OH, REALLY NOW?
HUH?
Menace
Menace

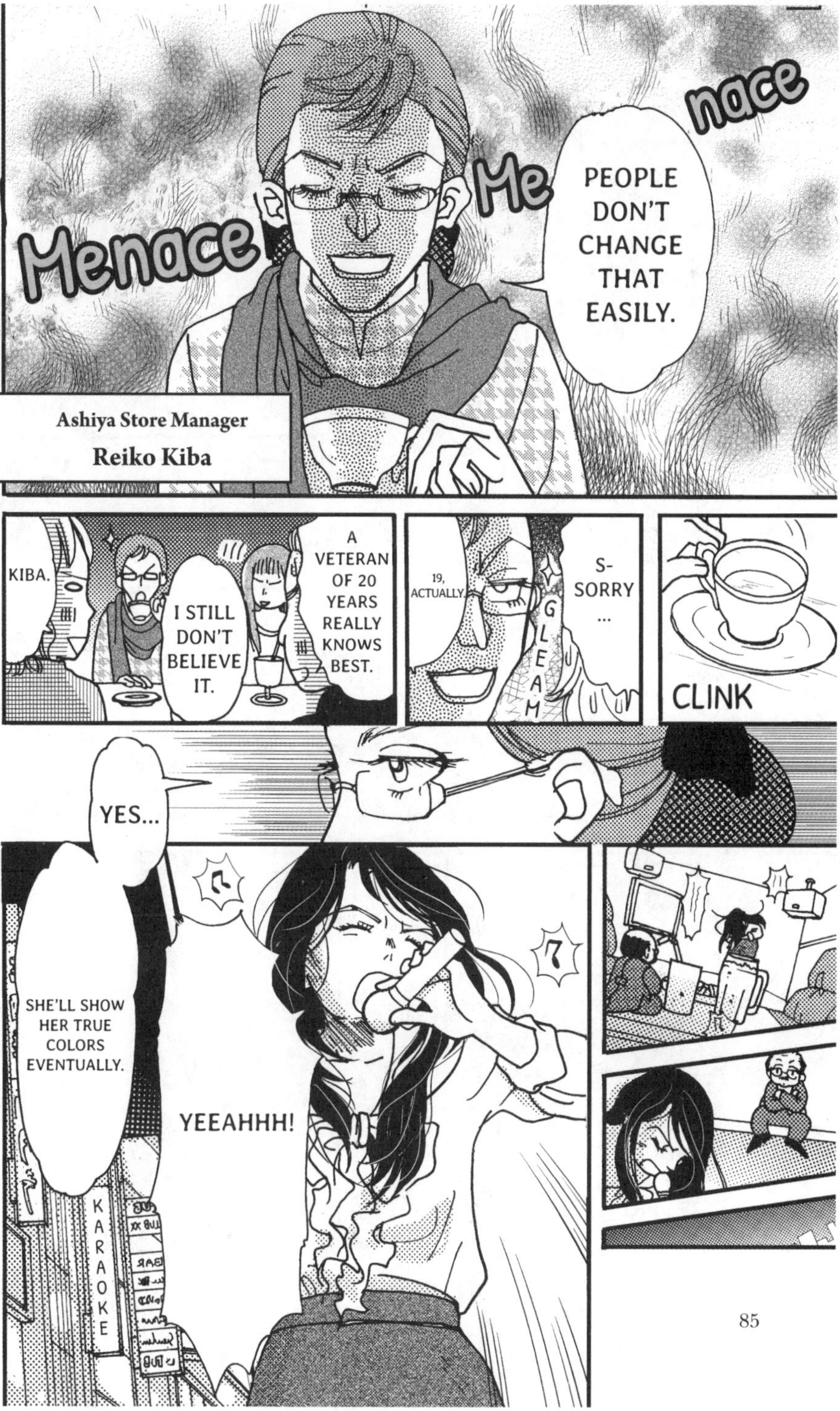
Menace
Me
nace
PEOPLE DON'T CHANGE THAT EASILY.
Ashiya Store Manager
Reiko Kiba
KIBA.
I STILL DON'T BELIEVE IT.
A VETERAN OF 20 YEARS REALLY KNOWS BEST.
19, ACTUALLY.
GLEAM
S-SORRY ...
CLINK
YES...
SHE'LL SHOW HER TRUE COLORS EVENTUALLY.
YEEAHHH!
KARAOKE

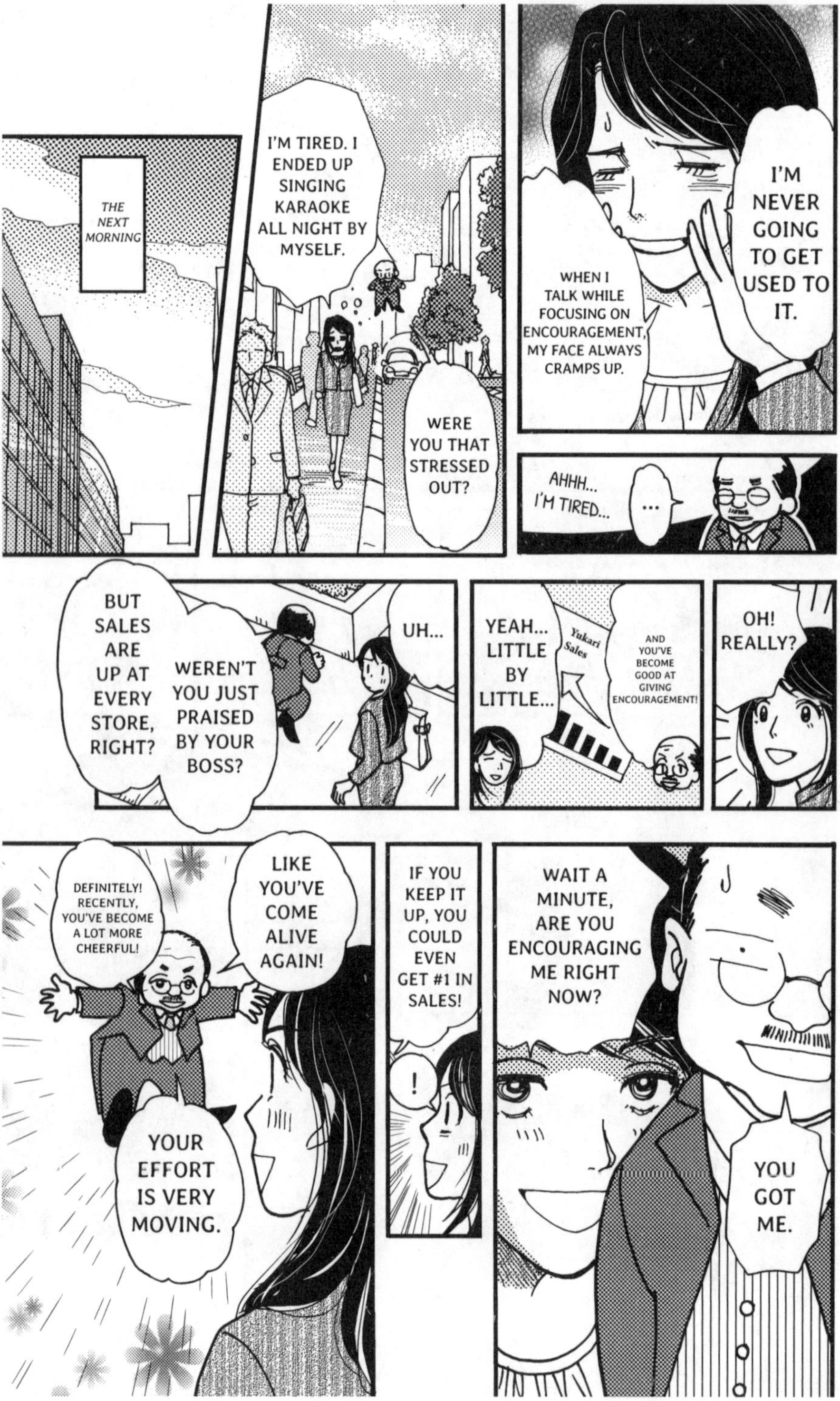
THE NEXT MORNING
I'M TIRED. I ENDED UP SINGING KARAOKE ALL NIGHT BY MYSELF.
WERE YOU THAT STRESSED OUT?
I'M NEVER GOING TO GET USED TO IT.
WHEN I TALK WHILE FOCUSING ON ENCOURAGEMENT, MY FACE ALWAYS CRAMPS UP.
AHHH... I'M TIRED...
...
BUT SALES ARE UP AT EVERY STORE, RIGHT?
WEREN'T YOU JUST PRAISED BY YOUR BOSS?
UH...
YEAH... LITTLE BY LITTLE...
Yukari Sales
AND YOU'VE BECOME GOOD AT GIVING ENCOURAGEMENT!
OH! REALLY?
DEFINITELY! RECENTLY, YOU'VE BECOME A LOT MORE CHEERFUL!
LIKE YOU'VE COME ALIVE AGAIN!
YOUR EFFORT IS VERY MOVING.
IF YOU KEEP IT UP, YOU COULD EVEN GET #1 IN SALES!
!
WAIT A MINUTE, ARE YOU ENCOURAGING ME RIGHT NOW?
YOU GOT ME.

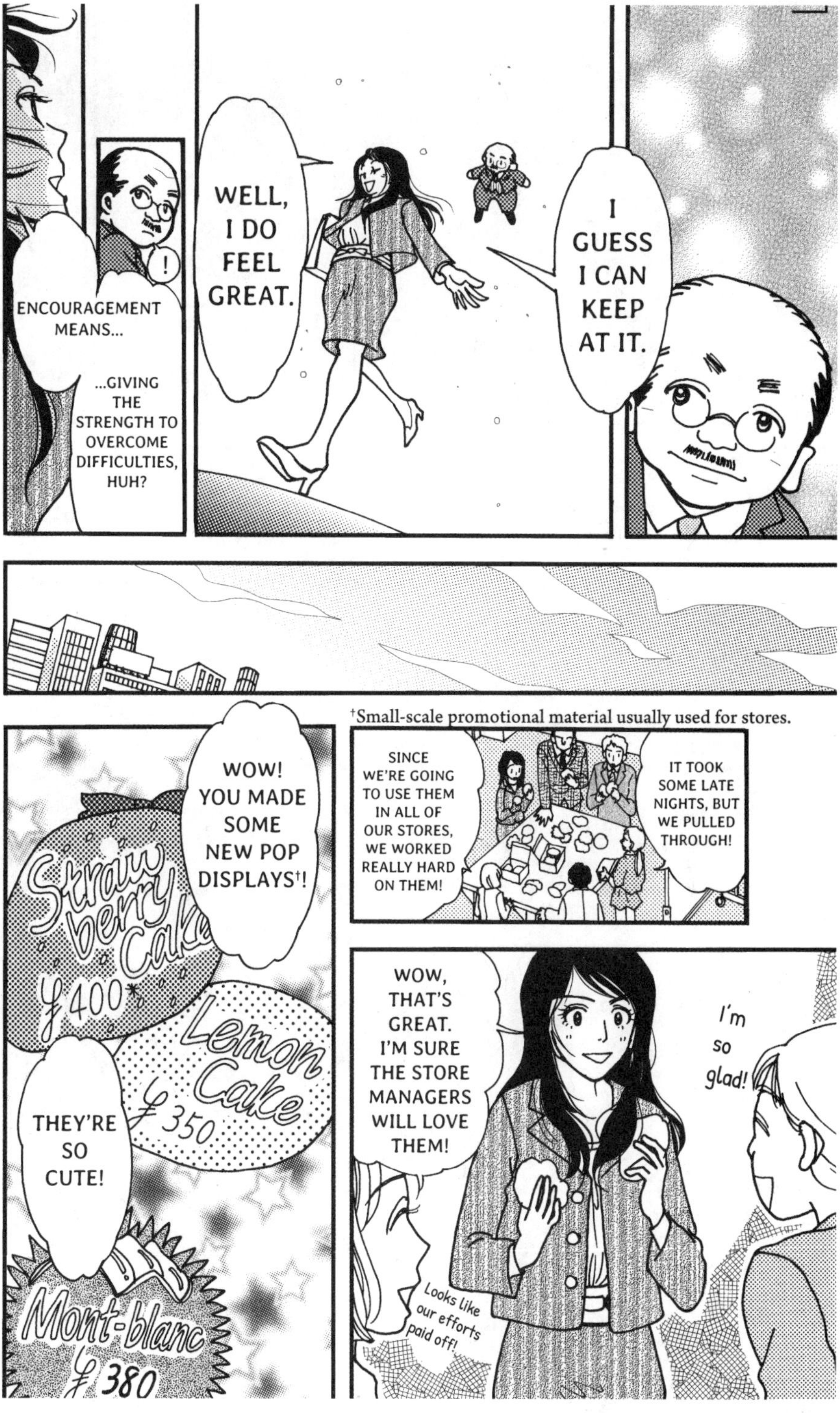
ENCOURAGEMENT MEANS...
...GIVING THE STRENGTH TO OVERCOME DIFFICULTIES, HUH?
!
WELL, I DO FEEL GREAT.
I GUESS I CAN KEEP AT IT.
WOW! YOU MADE SOME NEW POP DISPLAYS†!
Strawberry Cake ¥400*
Lemon Cake ¥350
THEY'RE SO CUTE!
Mont-blanc ¥380
SINCE WE'RE GOING TO USE THEM IN ALL OF OUR STORES, WE WORKED REALLY HARD ON THEM!
IT TOOK SOME LATE NIGHTS, BUT WE PULLED THROUGH!
WOW, THAT'S GREAT. I'M SURE THE STORE MANAGERS WILL LOVE THEM!
I'm so glad!
Looks like our efforts paid off!

†Small-scale promotional material usually used for stores.

*Approximately 100 Japanese yen (¥) = 1 U.S. dollar.

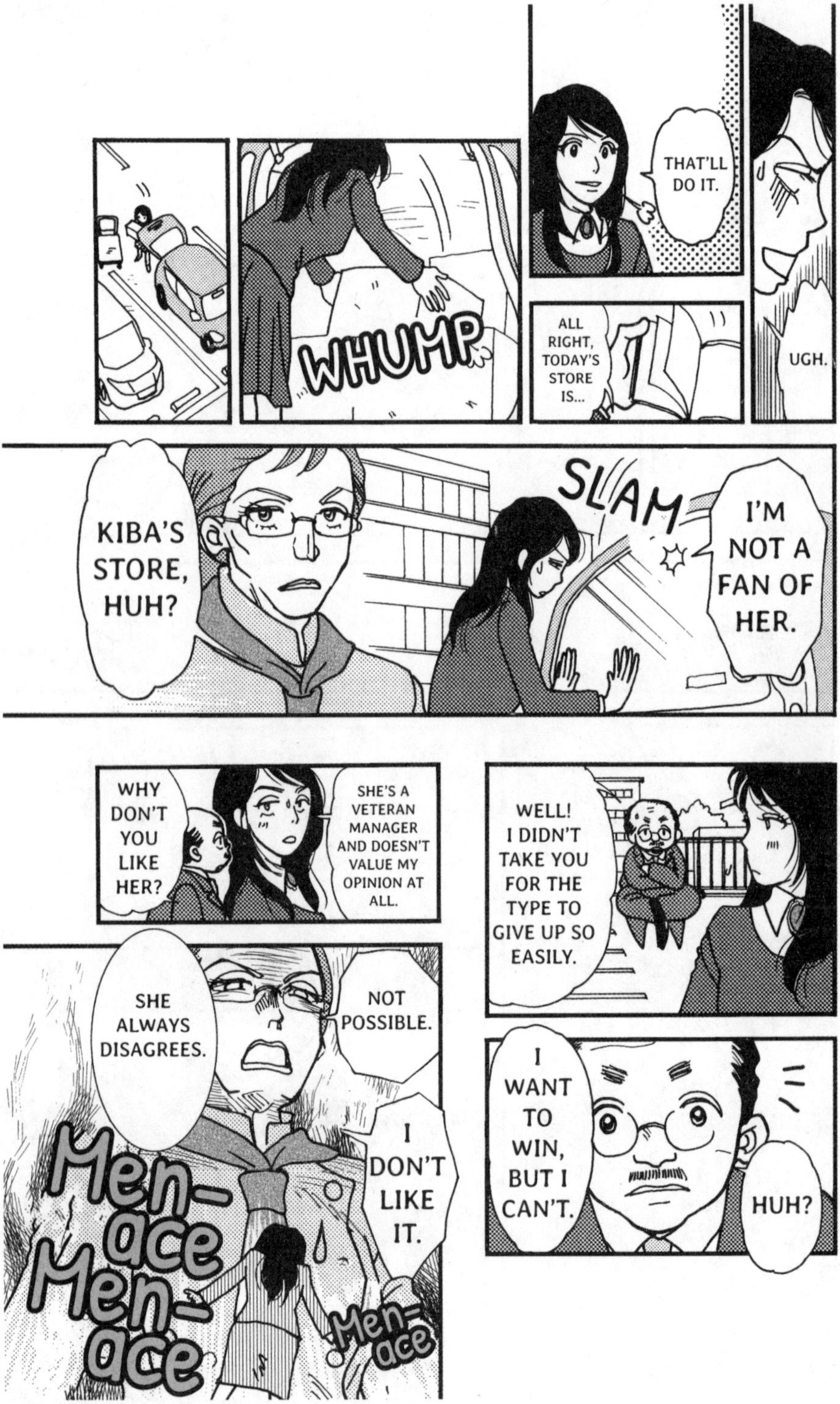

WHUMP
THAT'LL DO IT.
ALL RIGHT, TODAY'S STORE IS...
UGH.
KIBA'S STORE, HUH?
SLAM
I'M NOT A FAN OF HER.
WHY DON'T YOU LIKE HER?
SHE'S A VETERAN MANAGER AND DOESN'T VALUE MY OPINION AT ALL.
SHE ALWAYS DISAGREES.
NOT POSSIBLE.
I DON'T LIKE IT.
Men-ace Men-ace
Men-ace
WELL! I DIDN'T TAKE YOU FOR THE TYPE TO GIVE UP SO EASILY.
I WANT TO WIN, BUT I CAN'T.
HUH?

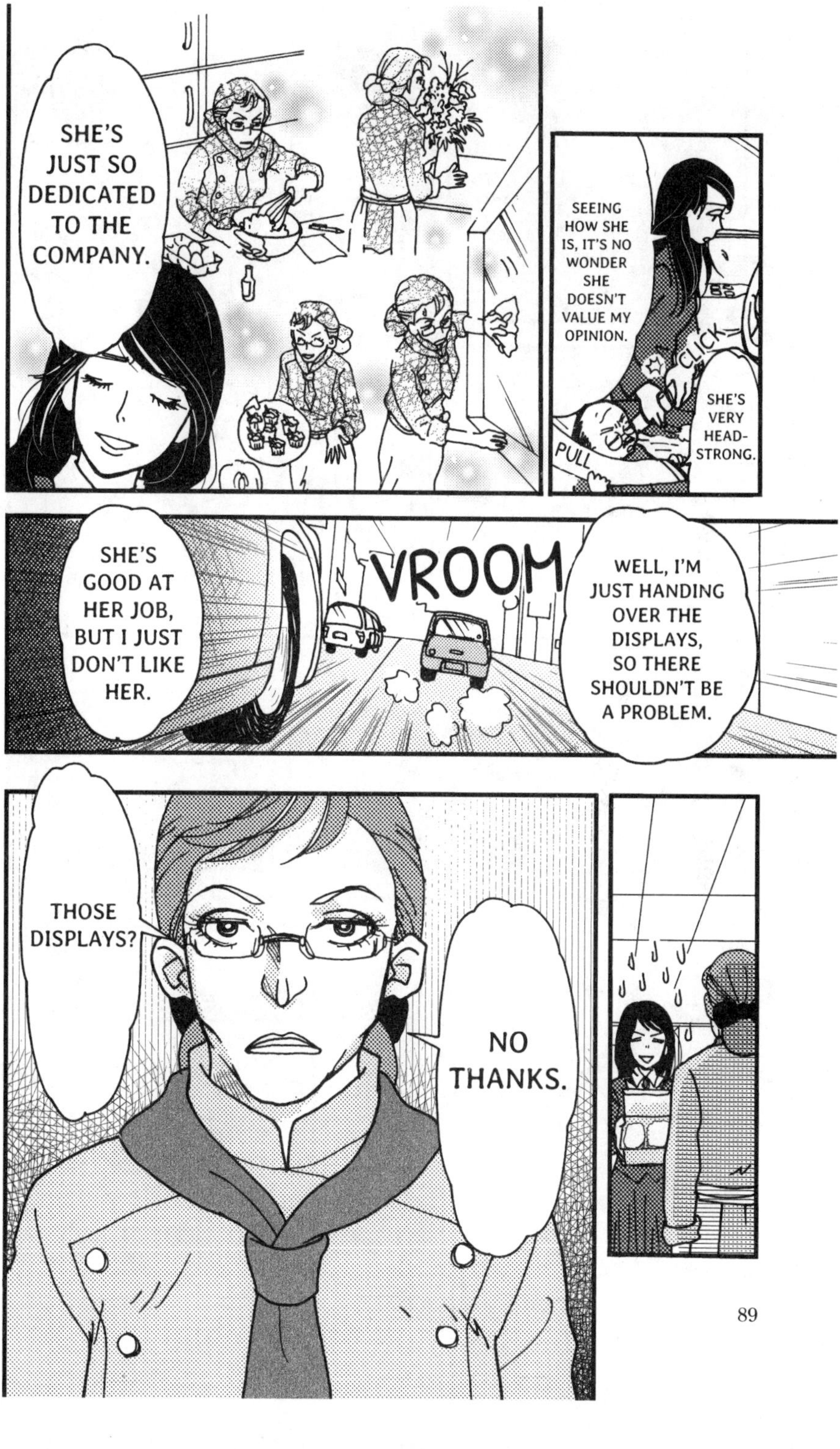
SHE'S JUST SO DEDICATED TO THE COMPANY.
SEEING HOW SHE IS, IT'S NO WONDER SHE DOESN'T VALUE MY OPINION.
CLICK
PULL
SHE'S VERY HEAD-STRONG.
SHE'S GOOD AT HER JOB, BUT I JUST DON'T LIKE HER.
VROOM
WELL, I'M JUST HANDING OVER THE DISPLAYS, SO THERE SHOULDN'T BE A PROBLEM.
THOSE DISPLAYS?
NO THANKS.

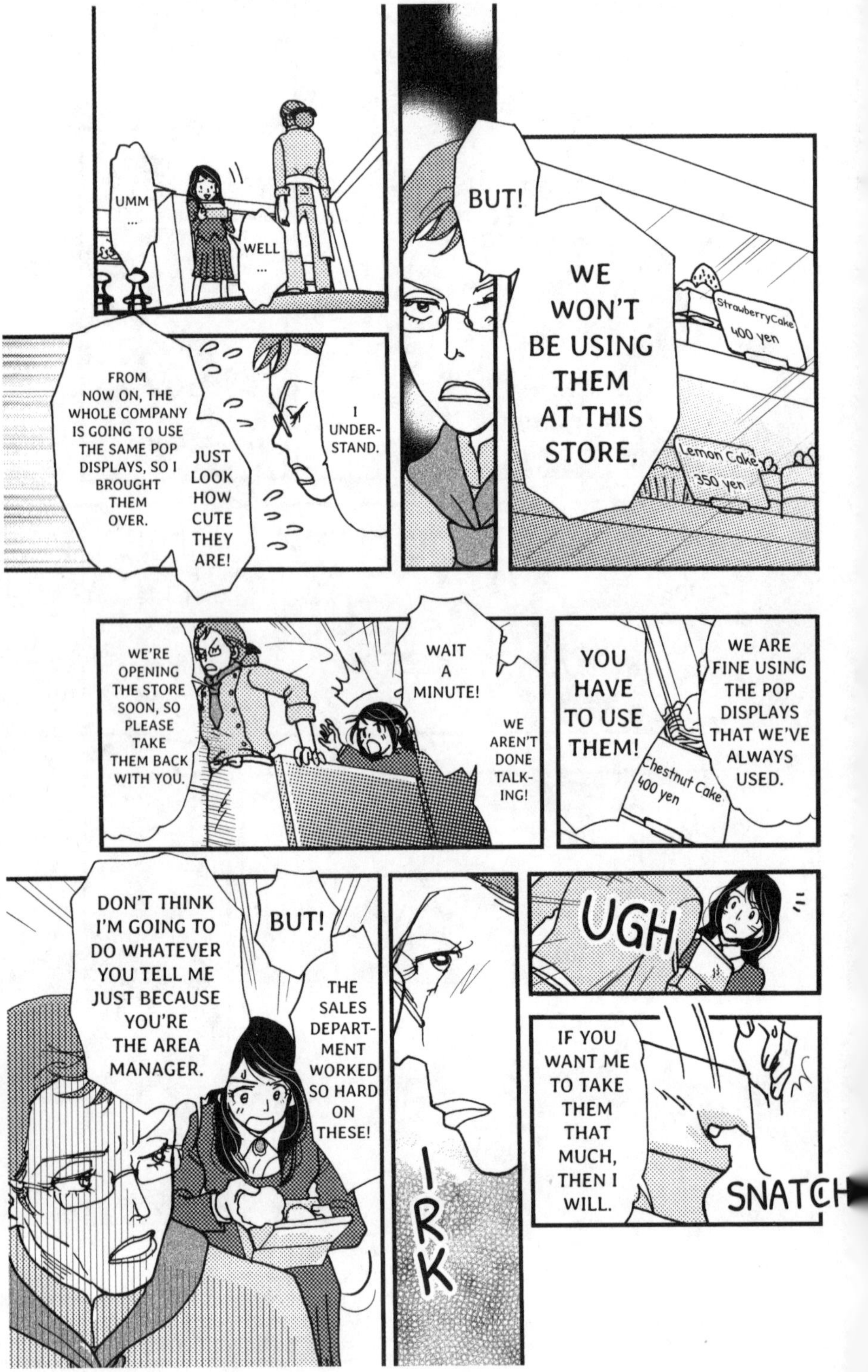

BUT!
WE WON'T BE USING THEM AT THIS STORE.
Strawberry Cake 400 yen
Lemon Cake 350 yen
UMM ...
WELL ...
I UNDERSTAND.
FROM NOW ON, THE WHOLE COMPANY IS GOING TO USE THE SAME POP DISPLAYS, SO I BROUGHT THEM OVER.
JUST LOOK HOW CUTE THEY ARE!
WE ARE FINE USING THE POP DISPLAYS THAT WE'VE ALWAYS USED.
YOU HAVE TO USE THEM!
Chestnut Cake 400 yen
WAIT A MINUTE!
WE AREN'T DONE TALKING!
WE'RE OPENING THE STORE SOON, SO PLEASE TAKE THEM BACK WITH YOU.
UGH
IF YOU WANT ME TO TAKE THEM THAT MUCH, THEN I WILL.
SNATCH
IRK
BUT!
THE SALES DEPARTMENT WORKED SO HARD ON THESE!
DON'T THINK I'M GOING TO DO WHATEVER YOU TELL ME JUST BECAUSE YOU'RE THE AREA MANAGER.

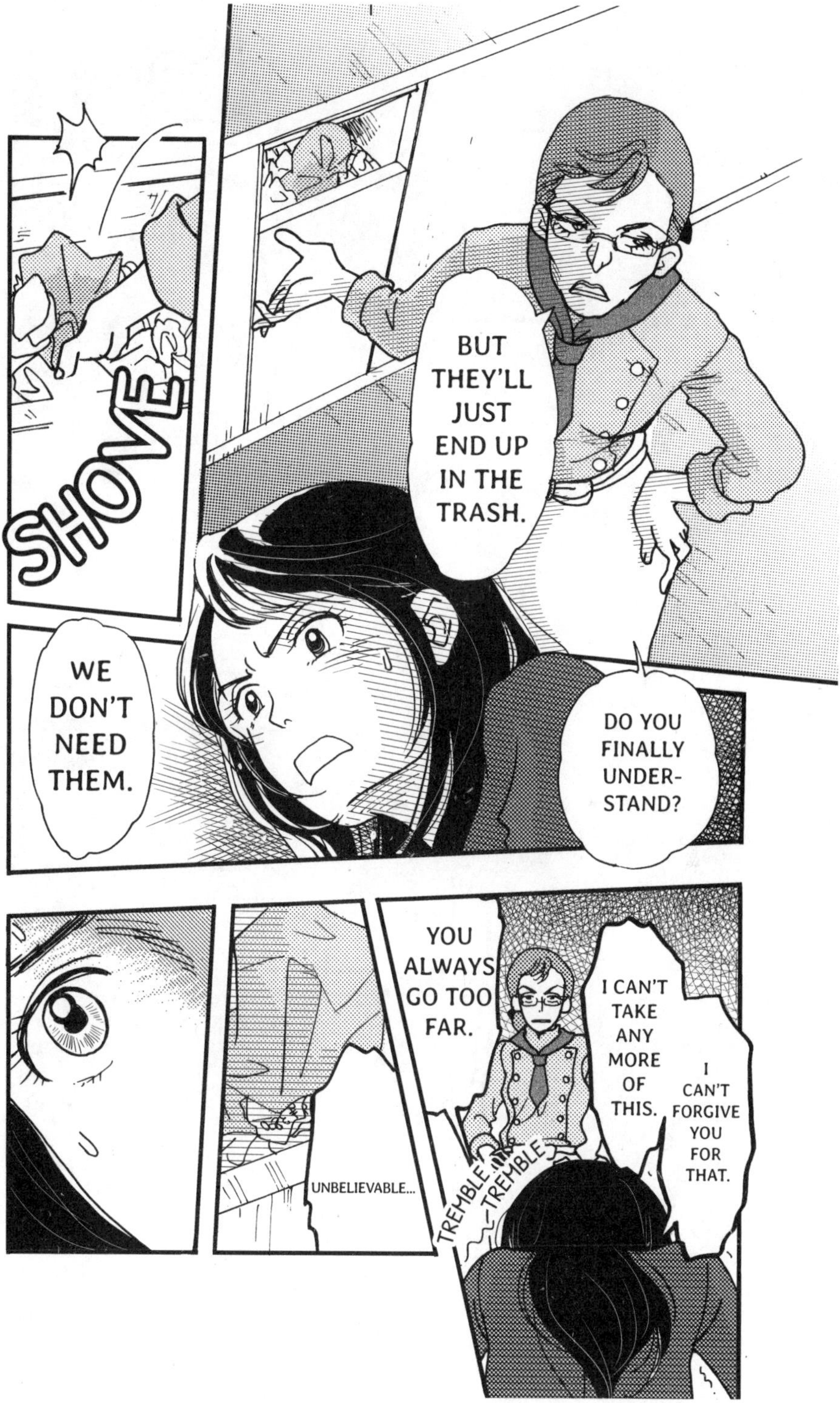
SHOVE
BUT THEY'LL JUST END UP IN THE TRASH.
WE DON'T NEED THEM.
DO YOU FINALLY UNDER-STAND?
YOU ALWAYS GO TOO FAR.
I CAN'T TAKE ANY MORE OF THIS.
I CAN'T FORGIVE YOU FOR THAT.
TREMBLE TREMBLE
UNBELIEVABLE...

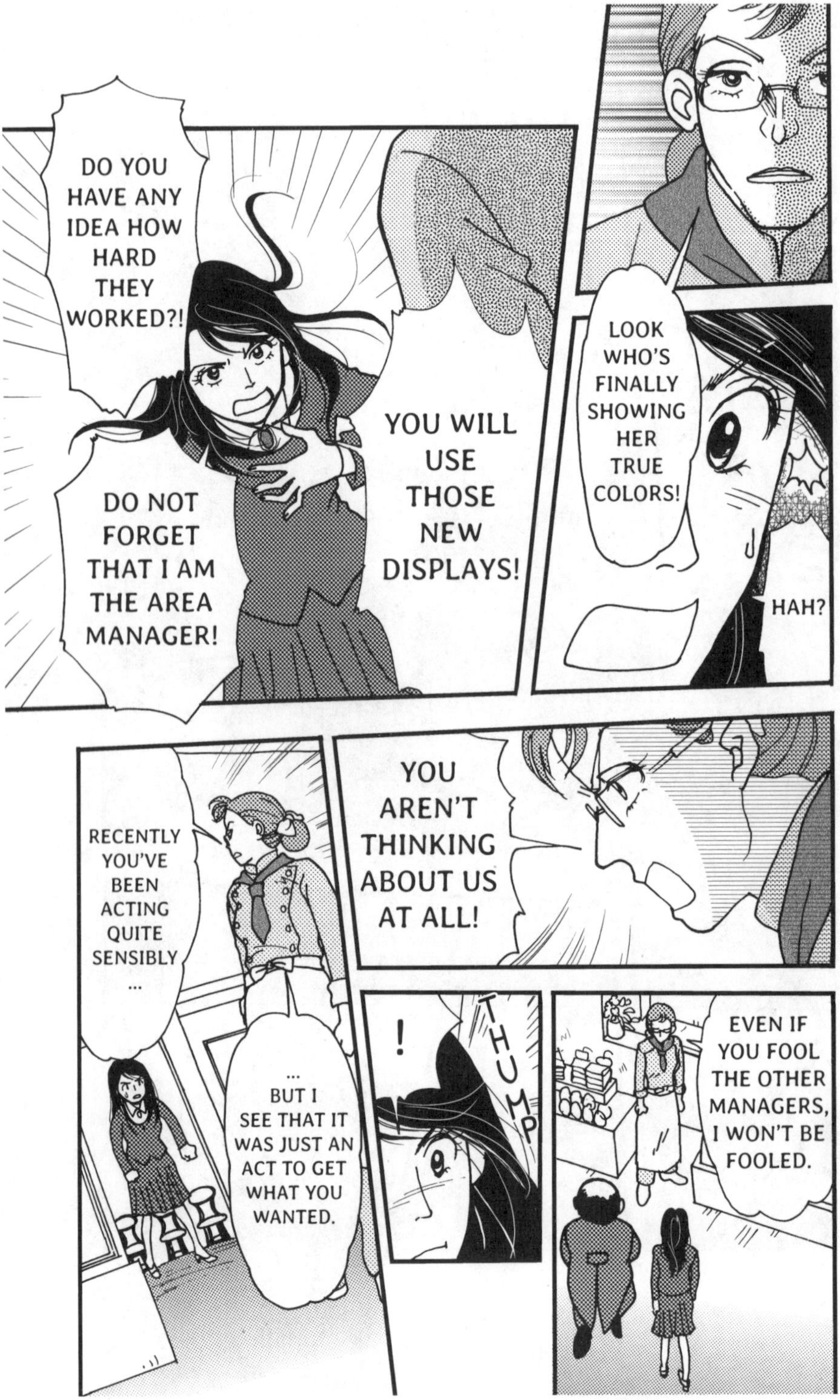
LOOK WHO'S FINALLY SHOWING HER TRUE COLORS!
HAH?
YOU WILL USE THOSE NEW DISPLAYS!
DO YOU HAVE ANY IDEA HOW HARD THEY WORKED?!
DO NOT FORGET THAT I AM THE AREA MANAGER!
YOU AREN'T THINKING ABOUT US AT ALL!
EVEN IF YOU FOOL THE OTHER MANAGERS, I WON'T BE FOOLED.
!
THUMP
RECENTLY YOU'VE BEEN ACTING QUITE SENSIBLY ...
... BUT I SEE THAT IT WAS JUST AN ACT TO GET WHAT YOU WANTED.

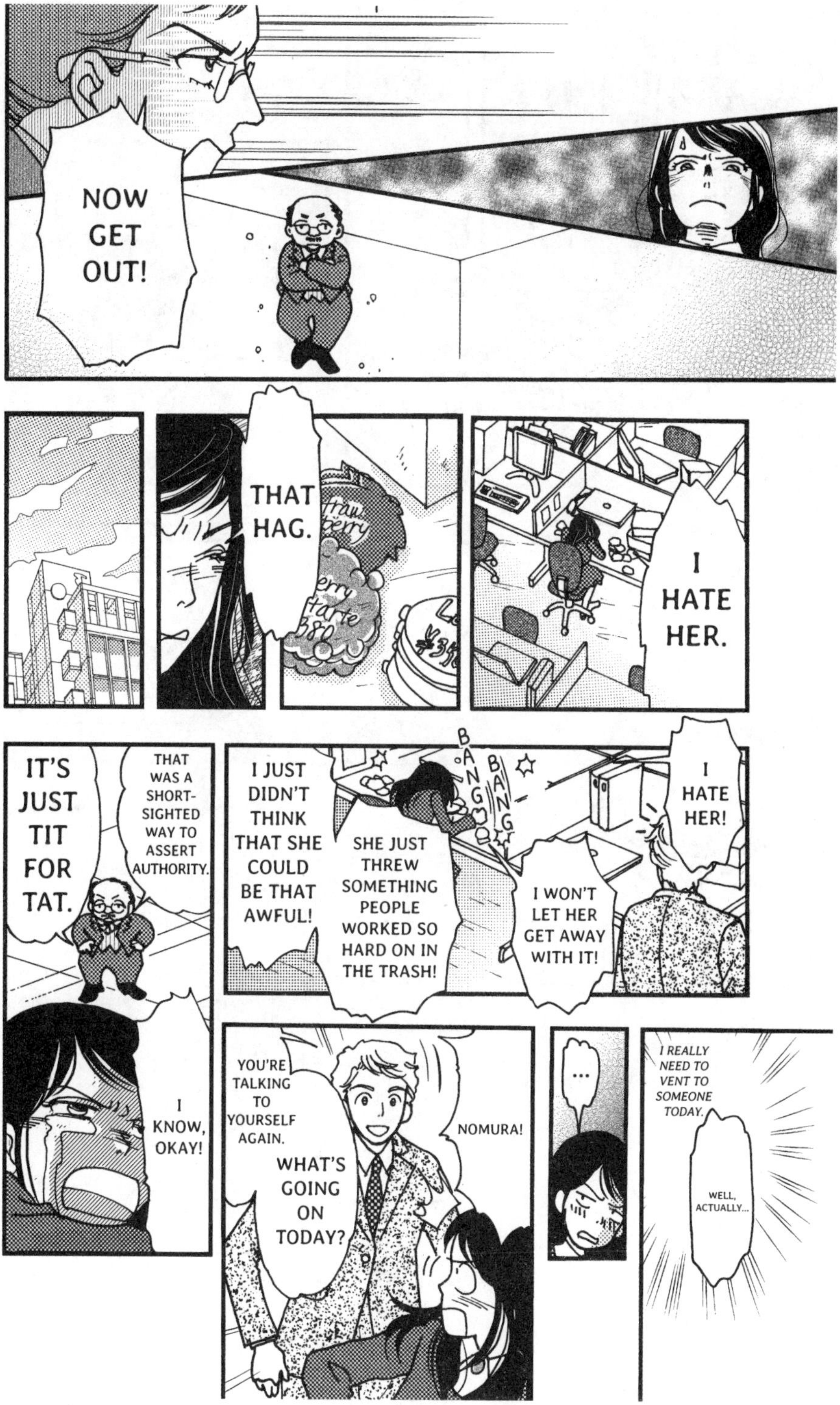
NOW GET OUT!
THAT HAG.
I HATE HER.
THAT WAS A SHORT-SIGHTED WAY TO ASSERT AUTHORITY.
IT'S JUST TIT FOR TAT.
I KNOW, OKAY!
I JUST DIDN'T THINK THAT SHE COULD BE THAT AWFUL!
SHE JUST THREW SOMETHING PEOPLE WORKED SO HARD ON IN THE TRASH!
BANG
BANG
I WON'T LET HER GET AWAY WITH IT!
I HATE HER!
YOU'RE TALKING TO YOURSELF AGAIN.
WHAT'S GOING ON TODAY?
NOMURA!
...
I REALLY NEED TO VENT TO SOMEONE TODAY.
WELL, ACTUALLY...

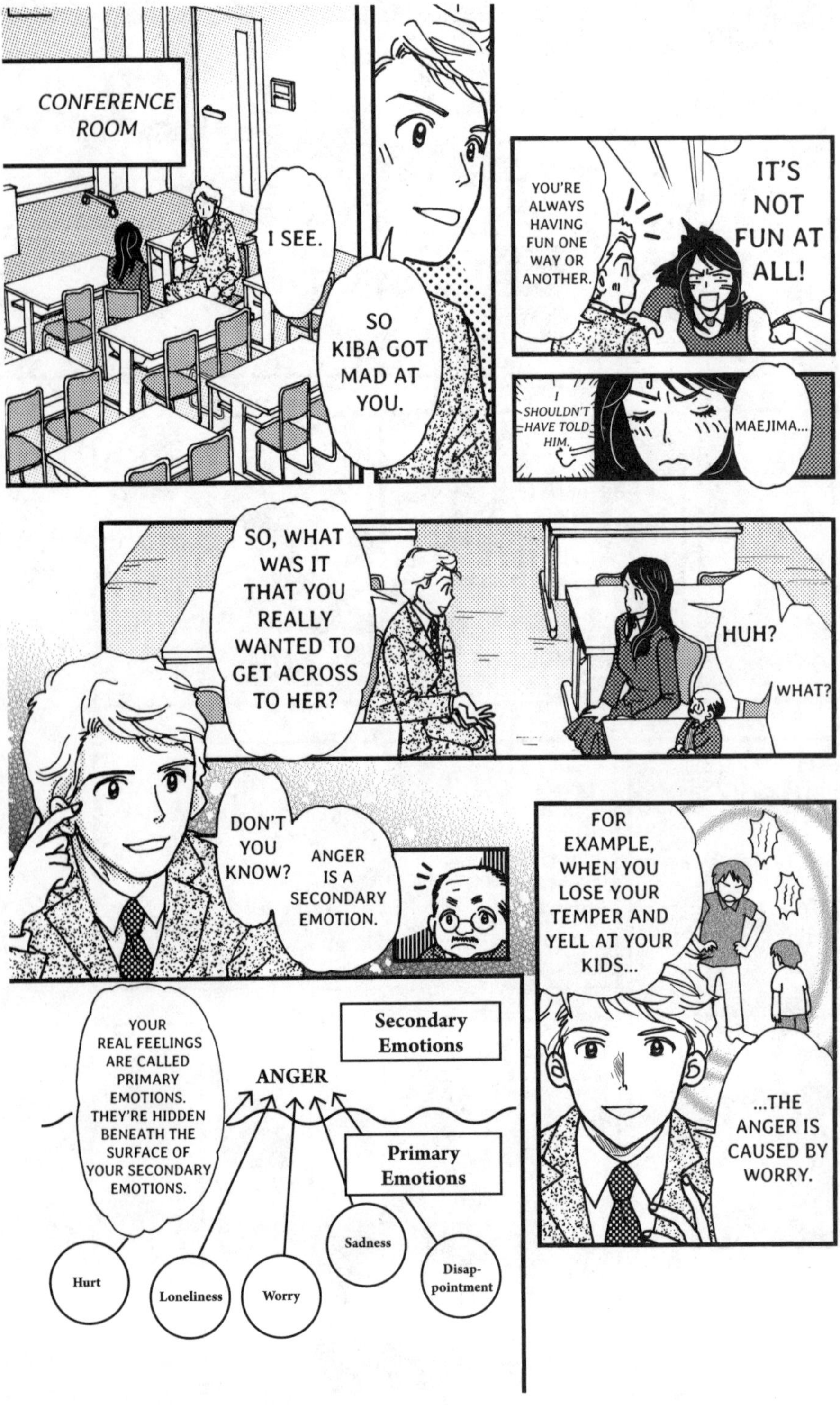
CONFERENCE ROOM
I SEE.
SO KIBA GOT MAD AT YOU.
YOU'RE ALWAYS HAVING FUN ONE WAY OR ANOTHER.
IT'S NOT FUN AT ALL!
I SHOULDN'T HAVE TOLD HIM.
MAEJIMA...
SO, WHAT WAS IT THAT YOU REALLY WANTED TO GET ACROSS TO HER?
HUH?
WHAT?
DON'T YOU KNOW?
ANGER IS A SECONDARY EMOTION.
FOR EXAMPLE, WHEN YOU LOSE YOUR TEMPER AND YELL AT YOUR KIDS...
...THE ANGER IS CAUSED BY WORRY.
YOUR REAL FEELINGS ARE CALLED PRIMARY EMOTIONS. THEY'RE HIDDEN BENEATH THE SURFACE OF YOUR SECONDARY EMOTIONS.
Secondary Emotions
ANGER
Primary Emotions
Hurt
Loneliness
Worry
Sadness
Disap-pointment

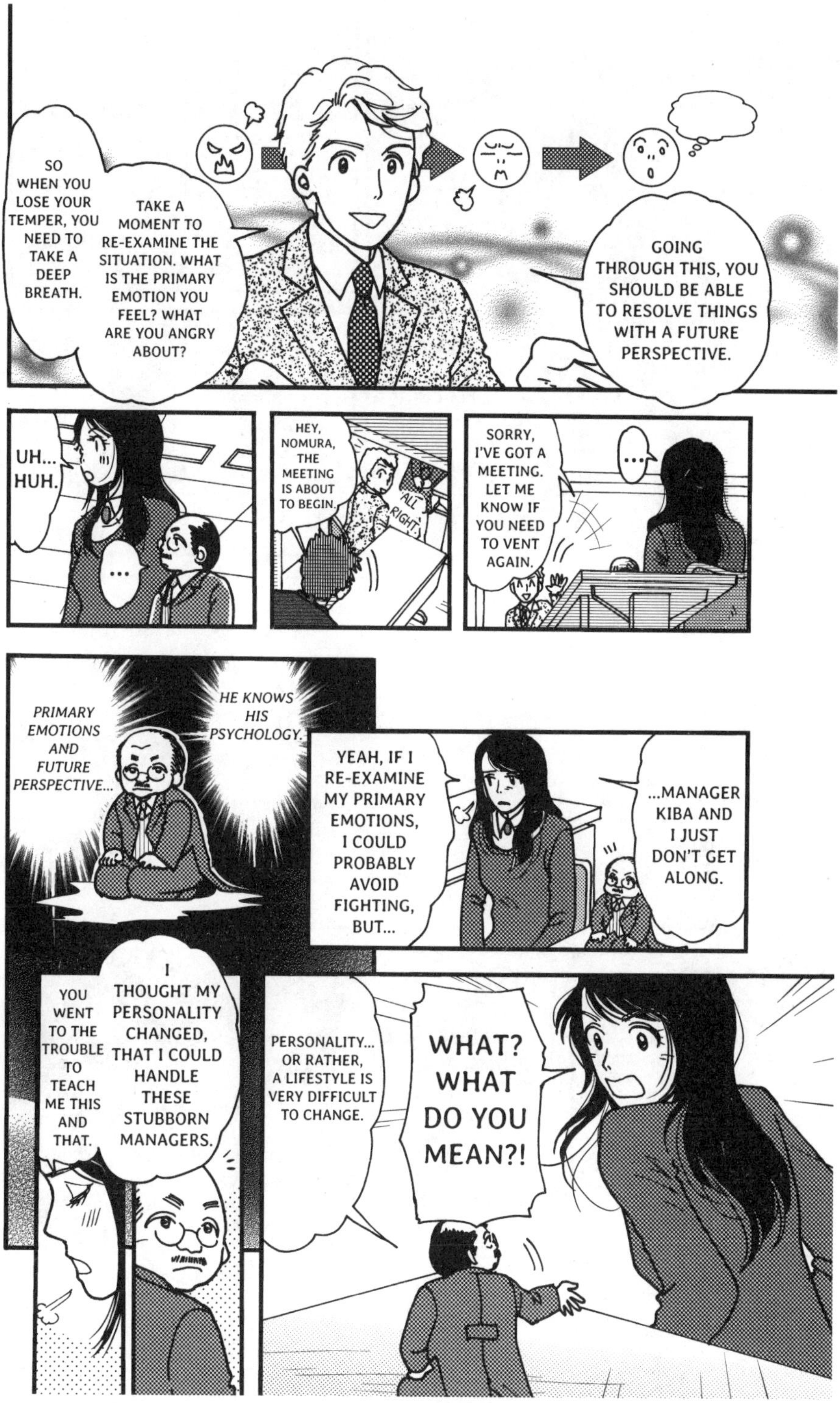
SO WHEN YOU LOSE YOUR TEMPER, YOU NEED TO TAKE A DEEP BREATH.
TAKE A MOMENT TO RE-EXAMINE THE SITUATION. WHAT IS THE PRIMARY EMOTION YOU FEEL? WHAT ARE YOU ANGRY ABOUT?
GOING THROUGH THIS, YOU SHOULD BE ABLE TO RESOLVE THINGS WITH A FUTURE PERSPECTIVE.
UH... HUH.
...
HEY, NOMURA, THE MEETING IS ABOUT TO BEGIN.
ALL RIGHT.
SORRY, I'VE GOT A MEETING. LET ME KNOW IF YOU NEED TO VENT AGAIN.
...
PRIMARY EMOTIONS AND FUTURE PERSPECTIVE...
HE KNOWS HIS PSYCHOLOGY.
YEAH, IF I RE-EXAMINE MY PRIMARY EMOTIONS, I COULD PROBABLY AVOID FIGHTING, BUT...
...MANAGER KIBA AND I JUST DON'T GET ALONG.
YOU WENT TO THE TROUBLE TO TEACH ME THIS AND THAT.
I THOUGHT MY PERSONALITY CHANGED, THAT I COULD HANDLE THESE STUBBORN MANAGERS.
PERSONALITY... OR RATHER, A LIFESTYLE IS VERY DIFFICULT TO CHANGE.
WHAT? WHAT DO YOU MEAN?!

LIKE I EXPLAINED TO YOU BEFORE, YOU DECIDE WHAT ACTIONS YOU TAKE.

BUT WHAT IS REALLY INFLUENCING YOU IS YOUR LIFESTYLE.

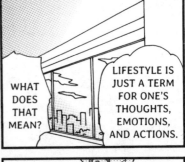

WHAT DOES THAT MEAN?

LIFESTYLE IS JUST A TERM FOR ONE'S THOUGHTS, EMOTIONS, AND ACTIONS.

YOU ARE YOU BECAUSE YOU'VE BEEN SHAPED AND INFLUENCED BY YOUR EXPERIENCES.

WELL... YEAH, OF COURSE.

HOW THAT LIFESTYLE IS SHAPED...

...IS HEAVILY CONNECTED TO YOUR PHYSICAL CONDITION, ENVIRONMENT, AND CULTURE.

Community-Specific Values
• Activities based on those values (culture)

Physical Condition
• Inherited temperament
• Physical ability

Environment
• Birth order
• Family values
• Family atmosphere

YEAH, IT'S NOT EASY TO CHANGE A LIFESTYLE THAT'S BEEN DEVELOPED OVER DECADES.

EXACTLY. IT'S BECAUSE OF THE PROCESS OF FORMATION OF THAT LIFESTYLE THAT THERE ARE BOUND TO BE INCOMPATIBLE PEOPLE.

FOR EXAMPLE, DISLIKING OLDER MEN BECAUSE ONE THAT LIVED NEARBY GOT MAD AT YOU BEFORE.

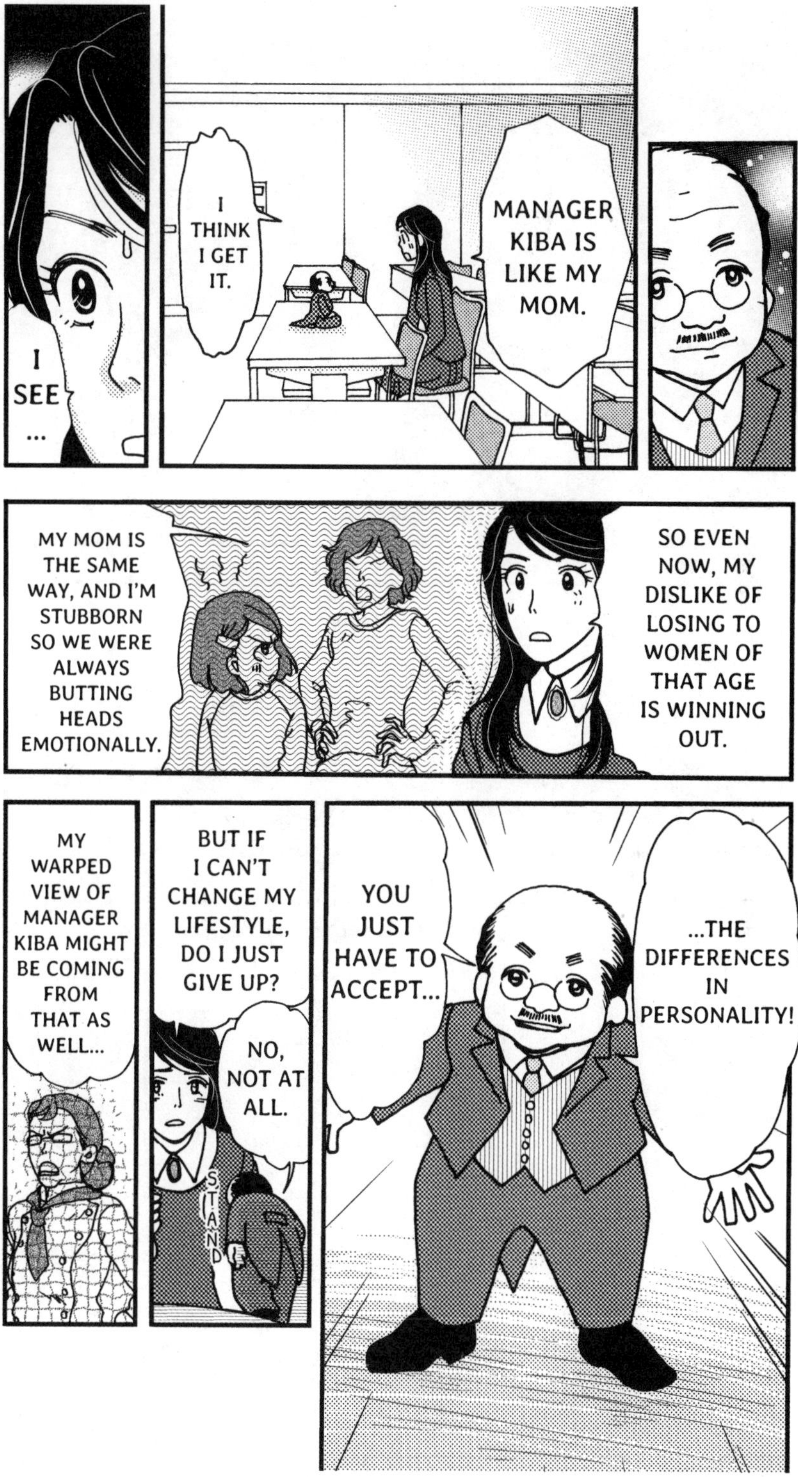
I SEE ...
I THINK I GET IT.
MANAGER KIBA IS LIKE MY MOM.
MY MOM IS THE SAME WAY, AND I'M STUBBORN SO WE WERE ALWAYS BUTTING HEADS EMOTIONALLY.
SO EVEN NOW, MY DISLIKE OF LOSING TO WOMEN OF THAT AGE IS WINNING OUT.
MY WARPED VIEW OF MANAGER KIBA MIGHT BE COMING FROM THAT AS WELL...
BUT IF I CAN'T CHANGE MY LIFESTYLE, DO I JUST GIVE UP?
NO, NOT AT ALL.
STAND
YOU JUST HAVE TO ACCEPT...
...THE DIFFERENCES IN PERSONALITY!

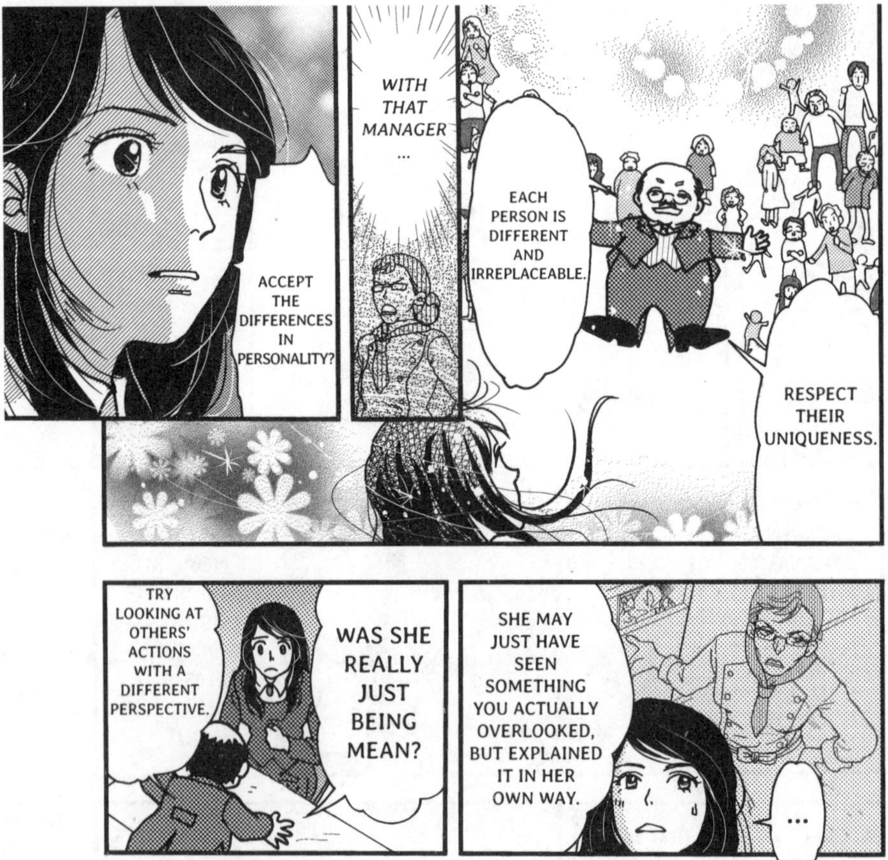
ACCEPT THE DIFFERENCES IN PERSONALITY?
WITH THAT MANAGER ...
EACH PERSON IS DIFFERENT AND IRREPLACEABLE.
RESPECT THEIR UNIQUENESS.
TRY LOOKING AT OTHERS' ACTIONS WITH A DIFFERENT PERSPECTIVE.
WAS SHE REALLY JUST BEING MEAN?
SHE MAY JUST HAVE SEEN SOMETHING YOU ACTUALLY OVERLOOKED, BUT EXPLAINED IT IN HER OWN WAY.
...

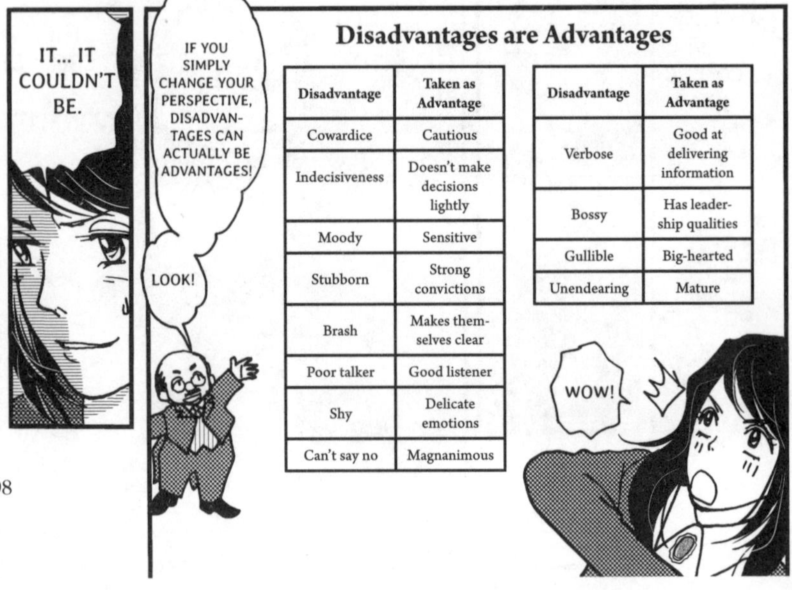
IT... IT COULDN'T BE.
IF YOU SIMPLY CHANGE YOUR PERSPECTIVE, DISADVANTAGES CAN ACTUALLY BE ADVANTAGES!
LOOK!
WOW!

Disadvantages are Advantages

Disadvantage	Taken as Advantage
Cowardice	Cautious
Indecisiveness	Doesn't make decisions lightly
Moody	Sensitive
Stubborn	Strong convictions
Brash	Makes themselves clear
Poor talker	Good listener
Shy	Delicate emotions
Can't say no	Magnanimous

Disadvantage	Taken as Advantage
Verbose	Good at delivering information
Bossy	Has leadership qualities
Gullible	Big-hearted
Unendearing	Mature

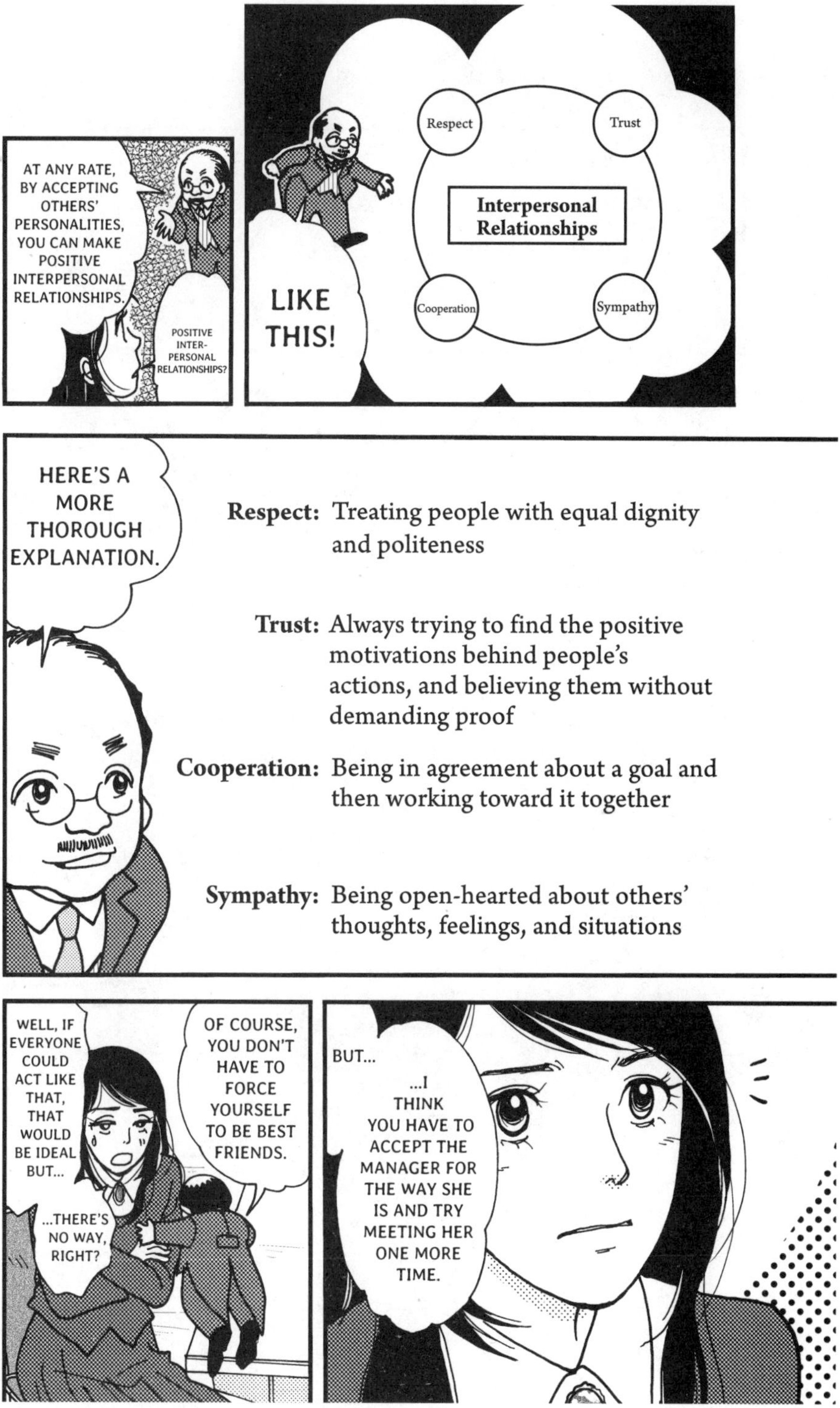
AT ANY RATE, BY ACCEPTING OTHERS' PERSONALITIES, YOU CAN MAKE POSITIVE INTERPERSONAL RELATIONSHIPS.
POSITIVE INTER-PERSONAL RELATIONSHIPS?
LIKE THIS!
Respect
Trust
Interpersonal Relationships
Cooperation
Sympathy
HERE'S A MORE THOROUGH EXPLANATION.
Respect: Treating people with equal dignity and politeness
Trust: Always trying to find the positive motivations behind people's actions, and believing them without demanding proof
Cooperation: Being in agreement about a goal and then working toward it together
Sympathy: Being open-hearted about others' thoughts, feelings, and situations
WELL, IF EVERYONE COULD ACT LIKE THAT, THAT WOULD BE IDEAL BUT...
...THERE'S NO WAY, RIGHT?
OF COURSE, YOU DON'T HAVE TO FORCE YOURSELF TO BE BEST FRIENDS.
BUT...
...I THINK YOU HAVE TO ACCEPT THE MANAGER FOR THE WAY SHE IS AND TRY MEETING HER ONE MORE TIME.

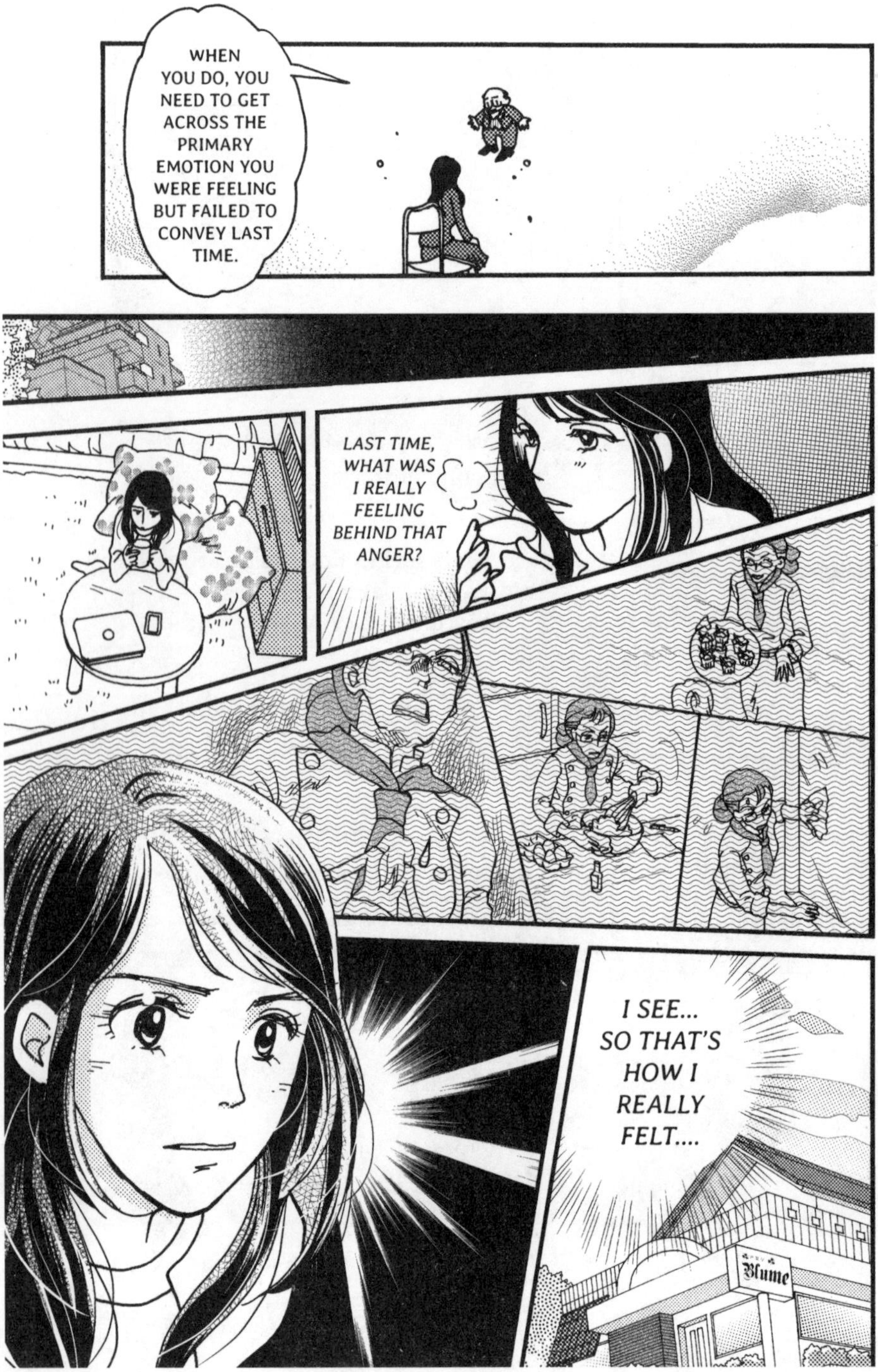
WHEN YOU DO, YOU NEED TO GET ACROSS THE PRIMARY EMOTION YOU WERE FEELING BUT FAILED TO CONVEY LAST TIME.
LAST TIME, WHAT WAS I REALLY FEELING BEHIND THAT ANGER?
I SEE... SO THAT'S HOW I REALLY FELT....
Blume

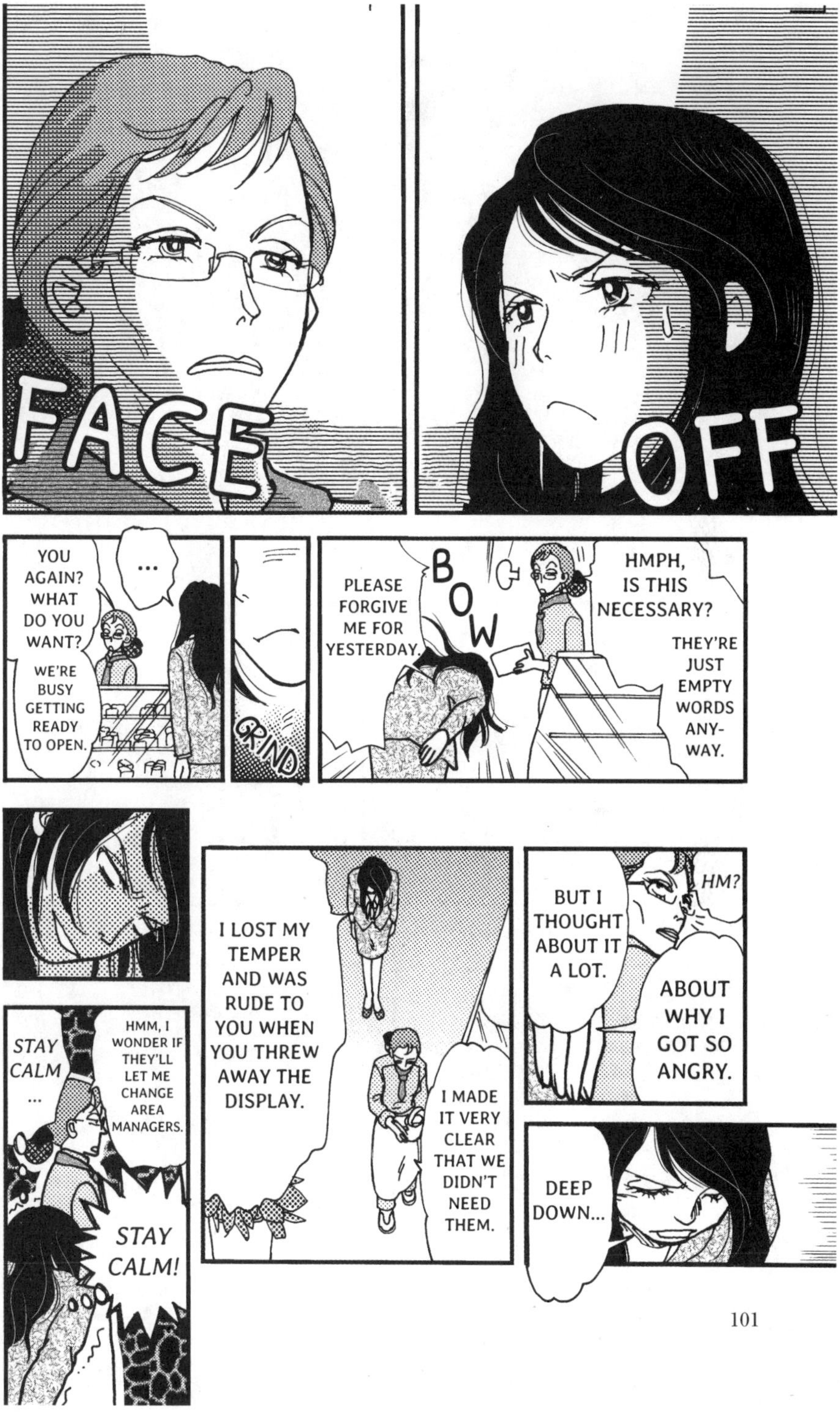
FACE
OFF
YOU AGAIN? WHAT DO YOU WANT?
WE'RE BUSY GETTING READY TO OPEN.
...
GRIND
PLEASE FORGIVE ME FOR YESTERDAY.
BOW
HMPH, IS THIS NECESSARY?
THEY'RE JUST EMPTY WORDS ANY-WAY.
I LOST MY TEMPER AND WAS RUDE TO YOU WHEN YOU THREW AWAY THE DISPLAY.
I MADE IT VERY CLEAR THAT WE DIDN'T NEED THEM.
HM?
BUT I THOUGHT ABOUT IT A LOT.
ABOUT WHY I GOT SO ANGRY.
STAY CALM...
HMM, I WONDER IF THEY'LL LET ME CHANGE AREA MANAGERS.
STAY CALM!
DEEP DOWN...

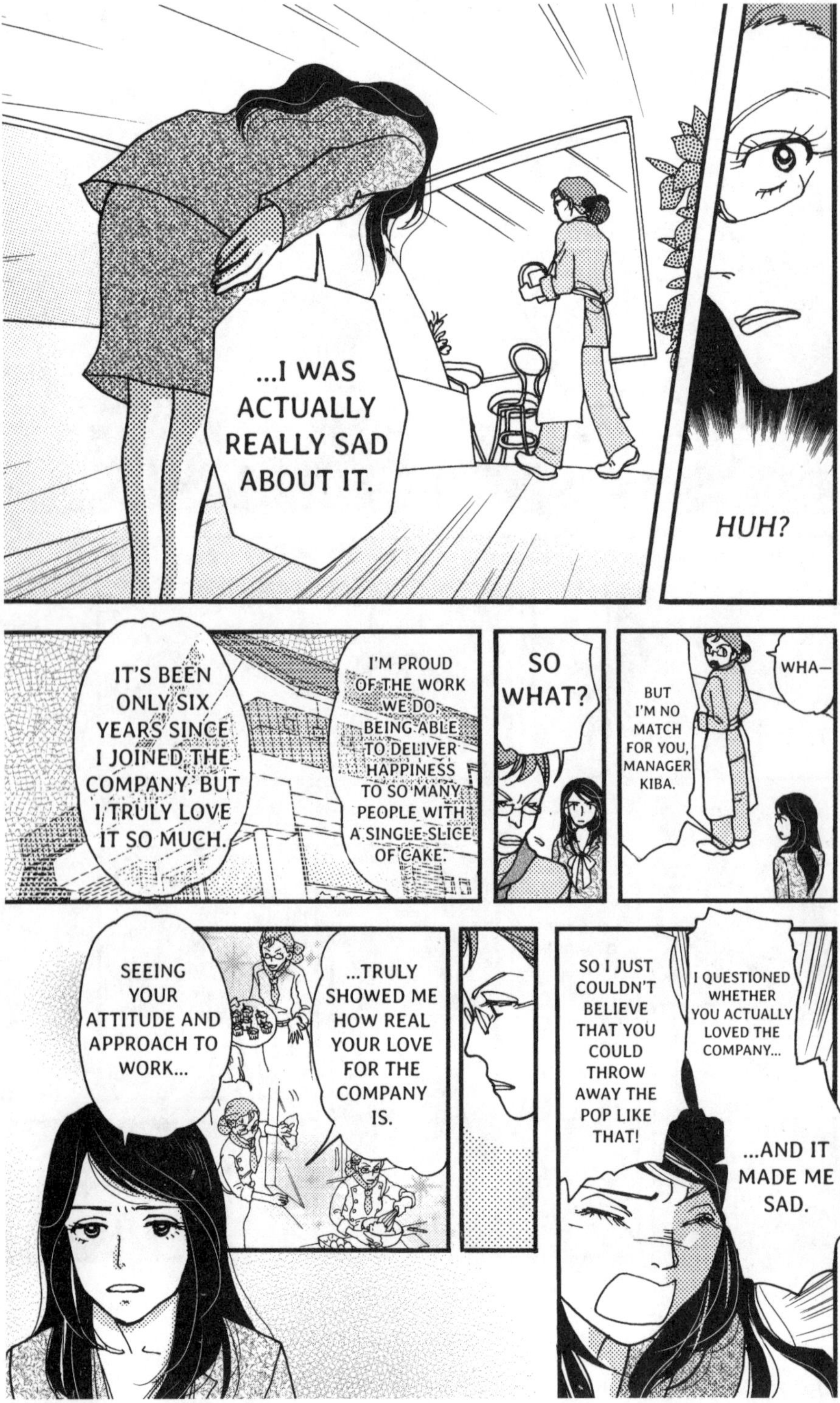
...I WAS ACTUALLY REALLY SAD ABOUT IT.
HUH?
IT'S BEEN ONLY SIX YEARS SINCE I JOINED THE COMPANY, BUT I TRULY LOVE IT SO MUCH.
I'M PROUD OF THE WORK WE DO BEING ABLE TO DELIVER HAPPINESS TO SO MANY PEOPLE WITH A SINGLE SLICE OF CAKE.
SO WHAT?
BUT I'M NO MATCH FOR YOU, MANAGER KIBA.
WHA—
SEEING YOUR ATTITUDE AND APPROACH TO WORK...
...TRULY SHOWED ME HOW REAL YOUR LOVE FOR THE COMPANY IS.
SO I JUST COULDN'T BELIEVE THAT YOU COULD THROW AWAY THE POP LIKE THAT!
I QUESTIONED WHETHER YOU ACTUALLY LOVED THE COMPANY...
...AND IT MADE ME SAD.

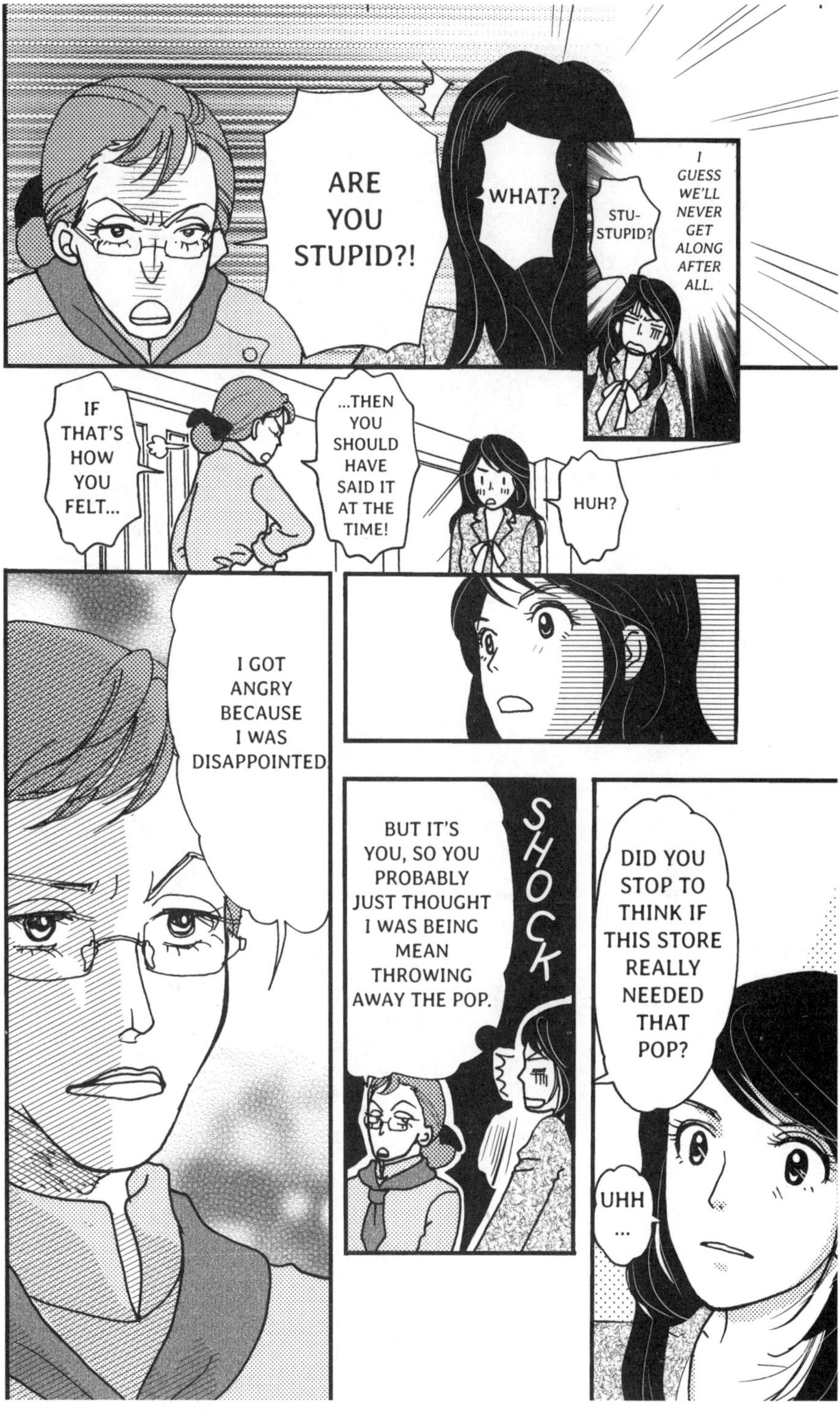
ARE YOU STUPID?!
WHAT?
STU-STUPID?
I GUESS WE'LL NEVER GET ALONG AFTER ALL.
IF THAT'S HOW YOU FELT...
...THEN YOU SHOULD HAVE SAID IT AT THE TIME!
HUH?
I GOT ANGRY BECAUSE I WAS DISAPPOINTED
BUT IT'S YOU, SO YOU PROBABLY JUST THOUGHT I WAS BEING MEAN THROWING AWAY THE POP.
SHOCK
DID YOU STOP TO THINK IF THIS STORE REALLY NEEDED THAT POP?
UHH...

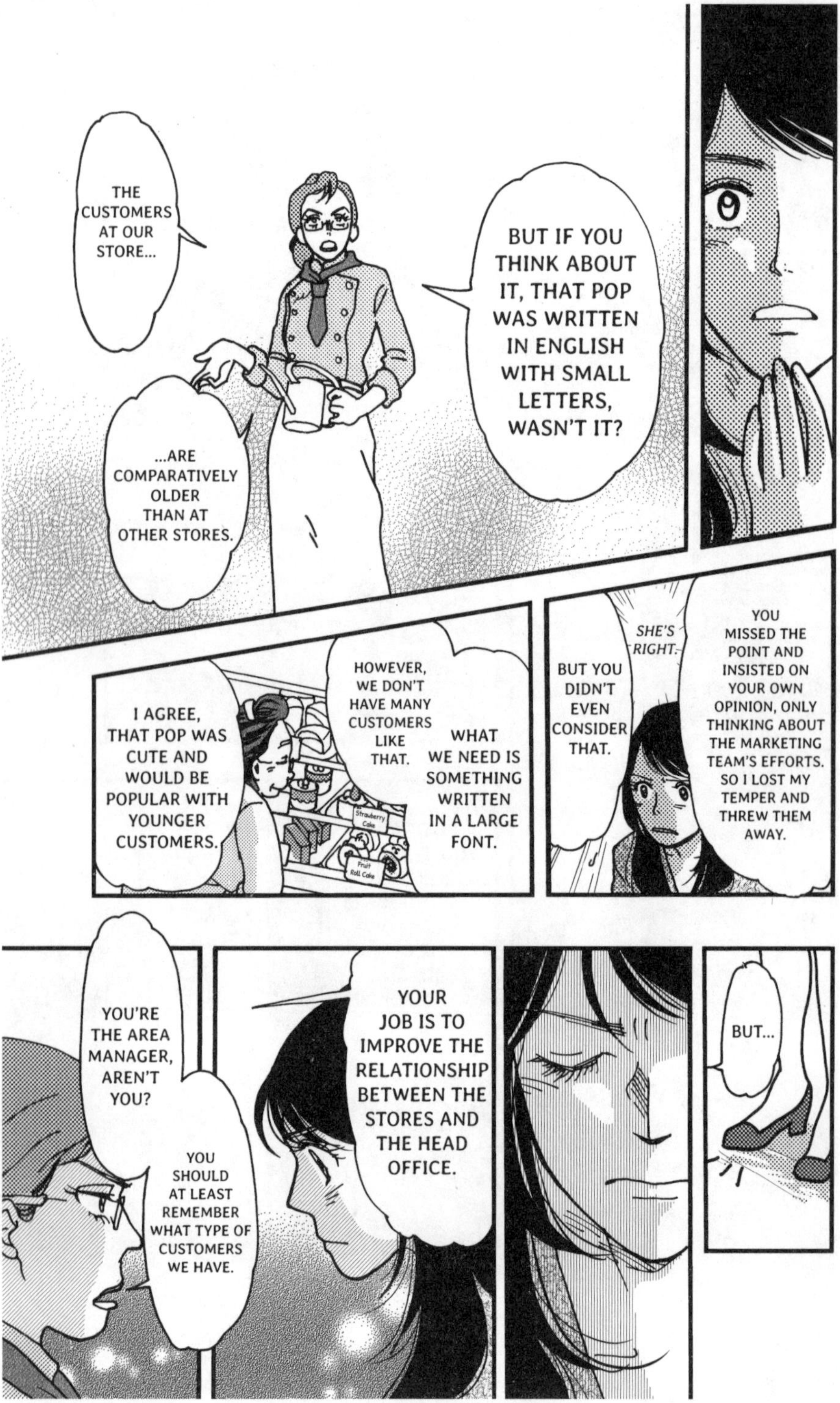
THE CUSTOMERS AT OUR STORE...
...ARE COMPARATIVELY OLDER THAN AT OTHER STORES.
BUT IF YOU THINK ABOUT IT, THAT POP WAS WRITTEN IN ENGLISH WITH SMALL LETTERS, WASN'T IT?
YOU MISSED THE POINT AND INSISTED ON YOUR OWN OPINION, ONLY THINKING ABOUT THE MARKETING TEAM'S EFFORTS. SO I LOST MY TEMPER AND THREW THEM AWAY.
SHE'S RIGHT.
BUT YOU DIDN'T EVEN CONSIDER THAT.
I AGREE, THAT POP WAS CUTE AND WOULD BE POPULAR WITH YOUNGER CUSTOMERS.
HOWEVER, WE DON'T HAVE MANY CUSTOMERS LIKE THAT.
WHAT WE NEED IS SOMETHING WRITTEN IN A LARGE FONT.
Strawberry Cake
Fruit Roll Cake
BUT...
YOUR JOB IS TO IMPROVE THE RELATIONSHIP BETWEEN THE STORES AND THE HEAD OFFICE.
YOU'RE THE AREA MANAGER, AREN'T YOU?
YOU SHOULD AT LEAST REMEMBER WHAT TYPE OF CUSTOMERS WE HAVE.

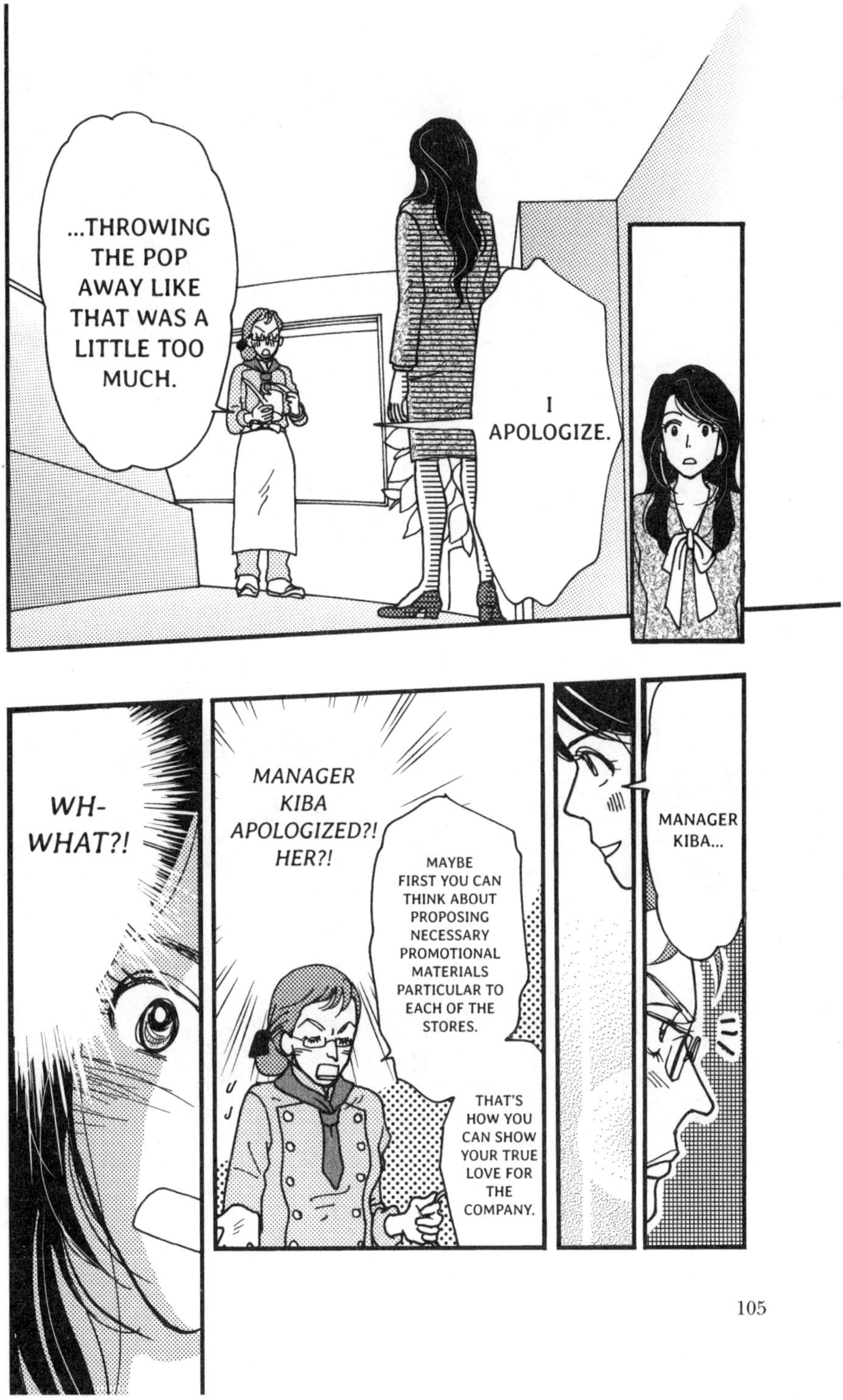
I APOLOGIZE.
...THROWING THE POP AWAY LIKE THAT WAS A LITTLE TOO MUCH.
MANAGER KIBA...
MAYBE FIRST YOU CAN THINK ABOUT PROPOSING NECESSARY PROMOTIONAL MATERIALS PARTICULAR TO EACH OF THE STORES.
THAT'S HOW YOU CAN SHOW YOUR TRUE LOVE FOR THE COMPANY.
MANAGER KIBA APOLOGIZED?! HER?!
WH- WHAT?!

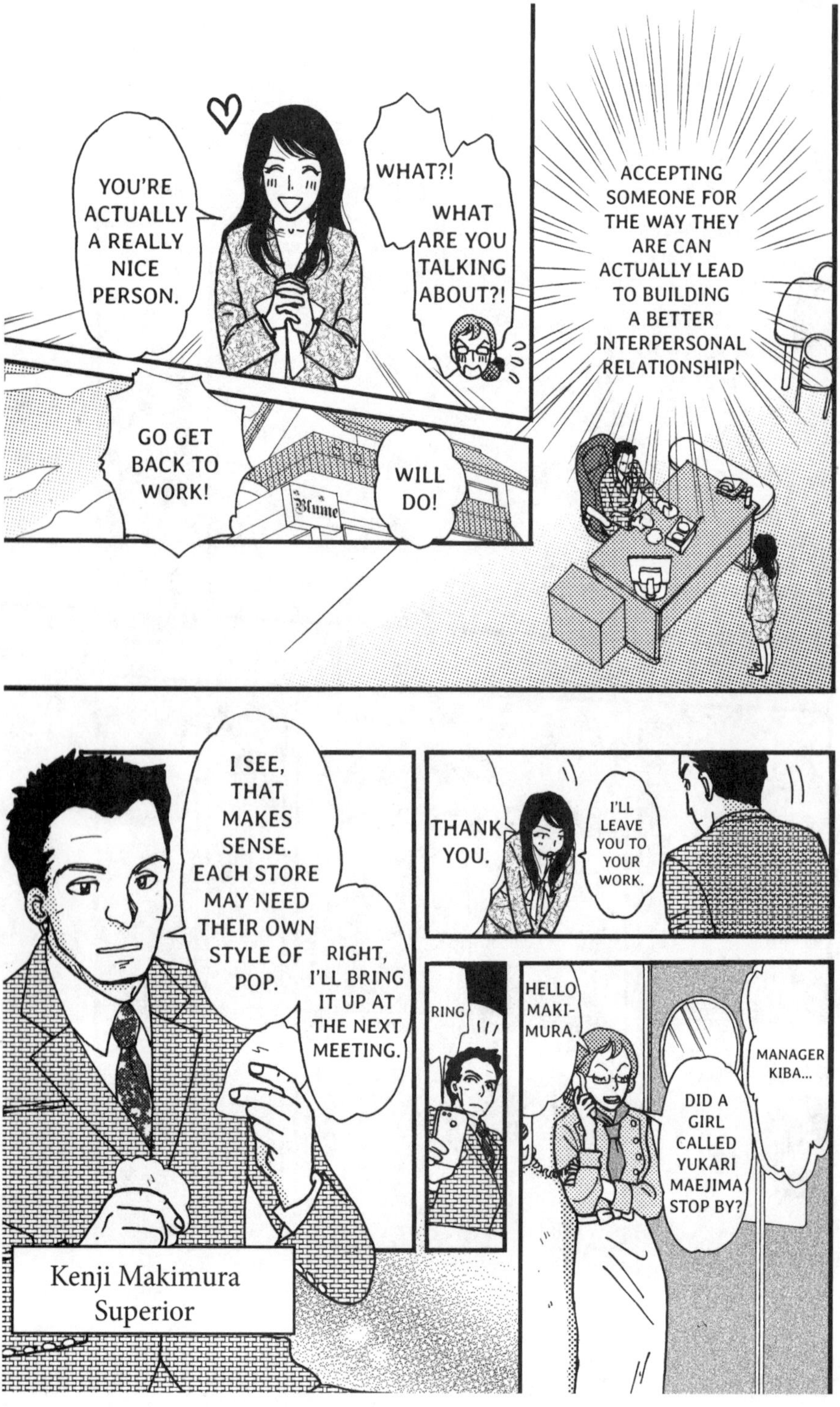
ACCEPTING SOMEONE FOR THE WAY THEY ARE CAN ACTUALLY LEAD TO BUILDING A BETTER INTERPERSONAL RELATIONSHIP!
YOU'RE ACTUALLY A REALLY NICE PERSON.
WHAT?!
WHAT ARE YOU TALKING ABOUT?!
GO GET BACK TO WORK!
WILL DO!
Blume
I SEE, THAT MAKES SENSE. EACH STORE MAY NEED THEIR OWN STYLE OF POP.
RIGHT, I'LL BRING IT UP AT THE NEXT MEETING.
Kenji Makimura
Superior
THANK YOU.
I'LL LEAVE YOU TO YOUR WORK.
RING
HELLO MAKI-MURA.
MANAGER KIBA...
DID A GIRL CALLED YUKARI MAEJIMA STOP BY?

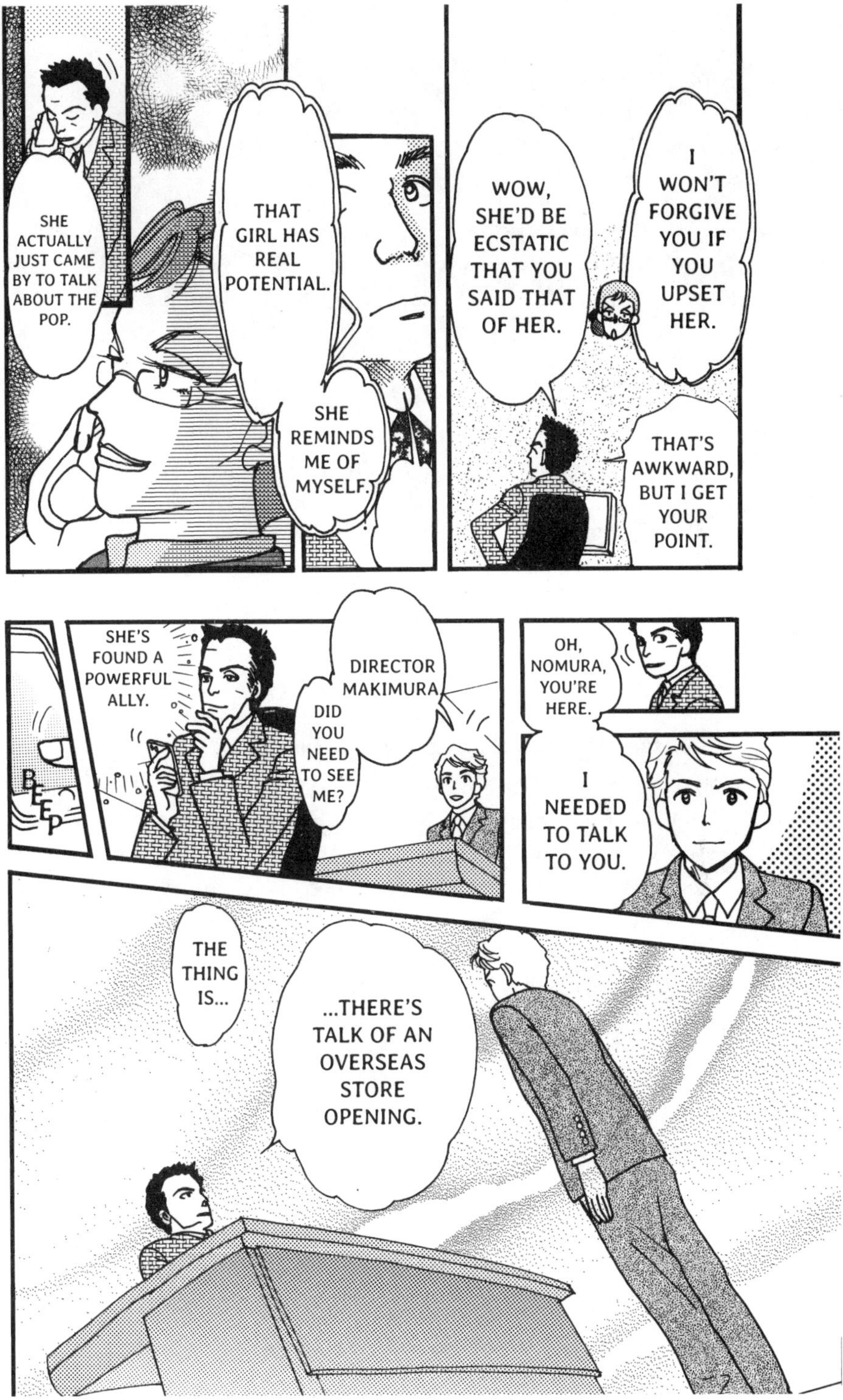
SHE ACTUALLY JUST CAME BY TO TALK ABOUT THE POP.
THAT GIRL HAS REAL POTENTIAL.
SHE REMINDS ME OF MYSELF.
WOW, SHE'D BE ECSTATIC THAT YOU SAID THAT OF HER.
I WON'T FORGIVE YOU IF YOU UPSET HER.
THAT'S AWKWARD, BUT I GET YOUR POINT.
BEEP
SHE'S FOUND A POWERFUL ALLY.
DIRECTOR MAKIMURA
DID YOU NEED TO SEE ME?
OH, NOMURA, YOU'RE HERE.
I NEEDED TO TALK TO YOU.
THE THING IS...
...THERE'S TALK OF AN OVERSEAS STORE OPENING.

Reason and Emotion

1

⇨ **The Lie Behind "I Know, But I Can't Quit"**

As explained in the Prologue, Adlerian psychology doesn't take the stance that saying "I know, but I can't quit" is simply a conflict between the conscious and subconscious or reason and emotion.

For example, "I know I'm going to pay later, but I'm going to leave my homework until the end of summer vacation," "I know I'm putting on weight, but I can't stop getting ramen noodles after going out drinking," or other such things that we feel everyday may appear at first glance to be contradictions between reason and emotion, conscious and subconscious, or body and mind, but we actually learn that these feelings are complementary.

Understanding the Role of Emotion in the Formation of Lifestyle

To understand the idea of reason and emotion complementing each other, we must first understand the role of emotion:

1) Emotion is closely related to your body, thoughts, and actions.

2) Emotion takes its share of irrational circuits as opposed to cognition's rational circuits.

Emotion isn't something that functions on its own, but is closely related to your body, thoughts, and actions. Its connection to the body is easy to see if you imagine that fresh feeling you experience after you've had plenty of sleep or the fatigue you feel from catching a cold. So how is emotion connected to your thoughts? Let's consider an example. Take the feeling of annoyance (anger) you might get when a coworker is late for a meeting. The root of that anger is a "should" belief (thought), as in "They should be here five minutes early," or a "they have to" belief as in "They have to be here on time, at least." For actions, if you imagine the feeling of panic that comes when the deadline arrives for something you've put off but that needed to be started right away, you should be able to understand this easily: inertia brings forth frustration.

Logical Circuits and Illogical Circuits

Body
Thought
Emotion
Actions
Logical Circuits
Illogical Circuits
DO NOT FORGET THAT I AM THE AREA MANAGER!
DO YOU HAVE ANY IDEA HOW HARD THEY WORKED?!
YOU WILL USE THOSE NEW DISPLAYS!
Goal

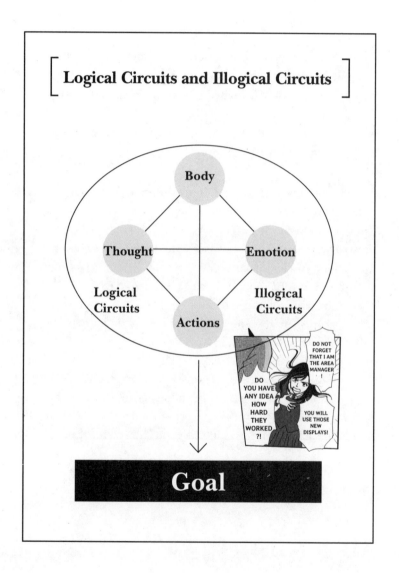

Let's think about the second aspect of emotion next. We take most of our actions after thinking about them first. When we act this way, we are following logical "circuits." Arriving at action through logical circuits can, however, be sluggish. Sometimes, in response to that sluggishness, our emotions and senses traverse illogical circuits and initiate action instantly. In her dealings with Kiba, the manager, Yukari felt that they weren't getting anywhere, so she tried to assert her authority by yelling, "Do as I say!" This is an example of illogical circuits initiating actions.

We can also use a young man in Japan as an example.* He's angry at his sales manager boss for harassing him by saying threatening things like "Jump out that window!" or "Go hang yourself!" So, at a sales meeting, when the manager utters one of his stock phrases, the young man stands up suddenly and responds, "Why don't you go die!" At the company's Compliance Committee Meeting, his boss's previous remarks are then seen as problematic and the young man escapes punishment, but you could say this outburst is an example of illogical circuits causing instant, damaging actions.

When you think about it like this, logical and illogical circuits have the same goal. In the story, for example, to get Kiba to behave the way Yukari wanted, the illogical circuits supplemented the congested logical circuits.

---

*The behavior described here would seem shocking in most organizations in the United States, but the example is illustrative nonetheless.

⇨ Anger as a Secondary Emotion

In our previous example on page 111, we touched on the emotion of anger, which is really the most dangerous of the emotions. Anger has four goals: to control, to win a struggle for leadership, to protect one's rights, and to display a sense of injustice. As was said previously, the underlying cause of this is the belief that things "should" or "have to be" a certain way.

In the story on page 92, although Yukari's anger began with the issue of Kiba's control, Kiba, not to be outdone, struggled for leadership. She may have also been trying to exhibit her sense of injustice.

As depicted in the following chart, the important issue here is that anger is the most important secondary emotion in interpersonal relationships, and it has other emotions, known as *primary emotions*, as its root. This cannot be overlooked. Nomura conveyed this to Yukari and explained that worry is often the basis for scolding children.

In addition, Yukari was able to tell Kiba that the root of her anger was sadness and that she was trying to avoid any further struggle for authority. Kiba was then able to reveal that the

[Anger as a Secondary Emotion]

Secondary Emotions
Anger
Hurt
Worry
Loneliness
Sadness
Disap-pointment
Primary Emotions
BUT I JUST COULDN'T BELIEVE THAT YOU COULD THROW AWAY THE POP LIKE THAT!
...AND IT MADE ME SAD!
I QUESTIONED WHETHER YOU ACTUALLY LOVED THE COMPANY...
I GOT ANGRY BECAUSE I WAS DISAPPOINTED.

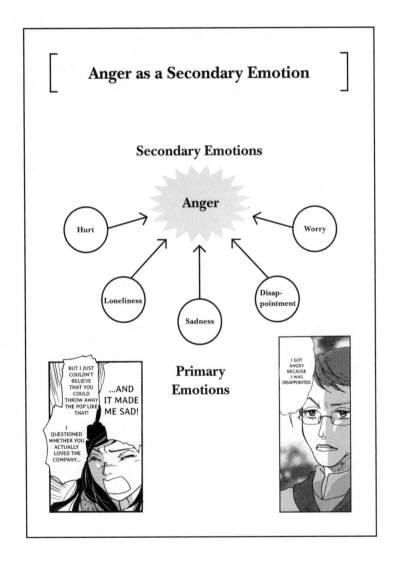

cause of her anger was the primary emotion of disappointment that she had felt. How would their second meeting have turned out if here too they ignored the primary emotions causing their anger and continued to deal with one another in an enraged way? The struggle for authority would surely have gotten out of hand and possibly ended with one of them having to leave the company.

Displaying the primary emotion of disappointment as anger is very common in the workplace, such as when a subordinate is given an important but difficult task and then their boss gets angry at them when their effort isn't up to par. In a case like this, expressing the primary emotion of disappointment instead would have induced the subordinate to self-reflect.

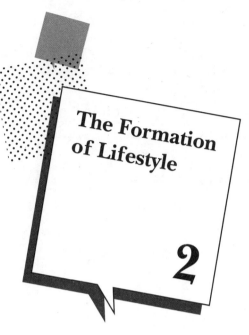

The Formation of Lifestyle

2

⇨ How Is Lifestyle Determined?

Think back to the definition of lifestyle that we learned in Part 1. It was that lifestyle is a system of beliefs about the present and the ideal states of the self in the world. So, how was this lifestyle decided?

Lifestyle is formed by self-determination; it is created by you! Even allowing for physical influences such as genetics on disposition or physical disability (damage to sensory or internal organs), the family that surrounds you, or environmental factors, the final decider of your lifestyle is your own self-determination.

Influencing factors cause the repetition and build up of trial and error so that, at some point, unconscious decisions begin to be repeated. By around the age of eight or ten, unique patterns of thought, feeling, and action are solidified and maintained. For a more detailed understanding of how influences other than the physical, such as environment and culture, affect the formation of lifestyle, let's study the following chart.

The Formation of Lifestyle

Influential Causes

1. Physical Influencers

ⓐ Genetic Disposition

ⓑ Physical Disability

2. Environment

ⓐ Genetic Disposition
- Siblings
- Birth order
- Sibling rivalry
- Family values
- Family atmosphere

ⓑ Culture
- Unique communal values and patterns of behavior

One's Own Self-Determination
(Even allowing for the trial and error caused by the influencing factors, the individual decides, solidifies, and maintains their lifestyle.)

I myself believed that lifestyle was solidified around age four or five, but modern Adlerian psychology says eight to ten.

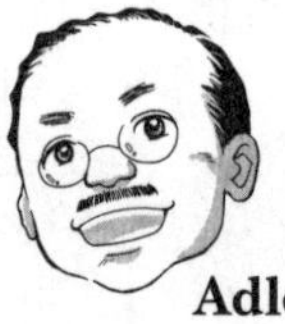

Adler

The first environmental influence is the family environment. This is the effect of birth order among siblings (what number among how many) and the existence of any sibling rivalries. Children are also influenced by the values their parents constantly represent to them (family values) and the type of atmosphere they create (family atmosphere). The family environment can be seen in married couples where each individual follows the patterns created by their own family's values and atmosphere.

The second environmental influence is the unique communal values and patterns of behavior created by where the individual lives and the character of that region. For example, in Japan, if someone from Tokyo goes to Osaka, they will experience differences not only in language but in other things as well, such as which side of the escalator to stand on. There are many things that would be obvious to a local but that might not be known to an outsider. A local, without ever doubting themselves, would conduct themselves in ways that were obvious to them.

⇨ General Personality Tendencies Based on Birth Order

Adler believed that birth order played a role in the formation of personality, as you can see in the chart below. It is important to keep in mind, however, that birth order plays a less important role than the relationship between siblings, the presence of disorders, parental expectations, and so on, even including how the individual views their position within the family. The classifications and personality traits that Adler and his successors used, such as first or second child, middle child, youngest child, only child, and so on are not always applicable.

First Child: Born first and wants to stay that way

- Wants to be the center of attention
- Believes they have to hold a position of prominence compared to their siblings
- Tends to be controlling through a sense of fairness
- Wants to treat younger siblings the same as their parents do
- Hates failing and will choose not to act if they are likely to fail
- Will take responsible actions that develop abilities
- Tries to protect and help younger siblings
- Tries to meet expectations and please those around them
- Has a sense of stability and adaptability
- Has a high level of pride (concerned with saving face)
- Becomes jealous when someone threatens their position

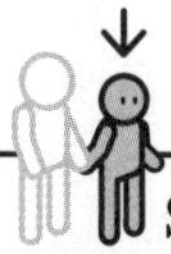

Second Child: Desperately running to catch up

- Doesn't bask in the attention of their parents or those around them
- Feels rivalry with other siblings who have more advantages
- Tries to catch and then supersede their older sibling
- Plays the part of either the good or bad child in opposition to how the older sibling is
- Tries to develop abilities that the older sibling doesn't have
- Feels uncertain about their own abilities when the older sibling succeeds
- Feels squeezed when younger siblings are born
- Tries to drag down other siblings

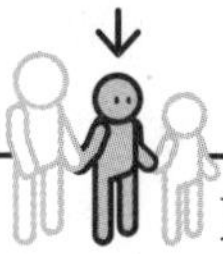

Middle Child: Tendency to push people aside their whole life

- Doesn't have the benefits of their older or younger siblings
- Often feels things are unfair and can become cynical
- Feels like their parents don't love them, that they are being uncaring

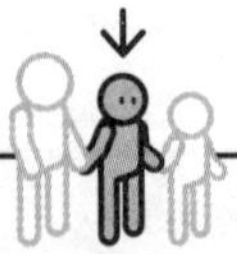

- Feels like they can't move between their siblings, that they are beset on all sides
- Feels they don't have their own place in the family
- Gets discouraged and becomes a problem child or pushes their siblings aside to better their own positions
- Highly adaptable from being skilled at acting between older and younger siblings

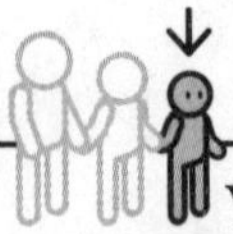

Youngest Child: Born as the baby, won't lose this throne

- Acts like an only child
- Thinks everyone else has more ability than they do
- Anticipating the actions of those above them, makes decisions and can let others take the responsibility
- Feels they are the smallest and the weakest
- Doesn't take things seriously
- Gets special treatment from others, gets their way, and becomes the boss of the family
- Develops an inferiority complex and can become threatening to older siblings
- Acts like a baby to receive special treatment from others

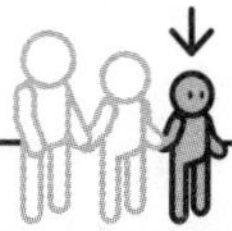

- In a three-child family, forms an alliance with the older sibling with the middle child as the common enemy

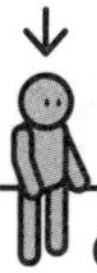

Only Child: A small person in a world of giants

- Is spoiled but lonely
- Becomes the center of attention and grows accustomed to it
- Feels they are special
- Is overprotected and expects to get what they want
- Does things at their own pace
- Looks forward to doing what they want
- Has high expectations
- Finds it difficult to have relationships with people the same age, but is good with older or younger people
- Has a strong sense of responsibility
- Has tendency to either make an effort like a first child or be dependent like a youngest child

Besides birth order, there's one more influence from siblings that affects the formation of lifestyle: the rivalry between them. Siblings are also rivals for their parents' attention. They try to stand out by setting themselves apart. They have a tendency to avoid competing in areas where their older or younger siblings excel, and instead develop their own abilities in areas where they can succeed.

For example, two brothers who graduated together from Tokyo University of the Arts are working as performers. Only two years apart, the brothers attended the same violin school as children. Years later, the younger brother began to play better and better, eventually surpassing his older brother. When the older brother entered middle school, he switched to wind instruments. The younger brother continued with the violin. They occasionally perform together, playing different parts in the same orchestra. Sibling rivalry like this, especially when accompanied by strong parental expectations, can lead to siblings staying in the same fields. Former sumo wrestlers and brothers Wakanohana and Takanohana, as well as the three boxing Kameda brothers, are good examples of this.

⇨ Jockeying for Power

Let's analyze Yukari with respect to her birth order. She is sandwiched between her capable older brother raised by their parents' expectations and her astute younger sister. Yukari's

birth order should give her the personality characteristics of
a second child and a middle child, possessing the merits and
demerits of both. She has an especially strong tendency to
enter struggle-for-authority mode. She has a tendency to bristle
against authority and finds it unacceptable to be under others'
control. Yukari jockeys for power not only within her family but
also at work, creating problems in both spaces. It's easy to see
how her personality, which is prone to these types of struggles
for authority, has influenced her.

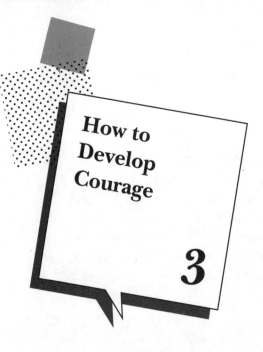

How to Develop Courage

3

⇒ Four Points in Developing Courage

In his writings, Adler frequently used the term *courage.* Courage means "the strength to overcome difficulties." In the story, Adler acts as a mentor to Yukari, encouraging her in each aspect of her life. Starting with interpersonal relationships, even the timid can develop courage. But how? Four steps can get you started on your way:

1) Base interpersonal relationships on respect and trust.
2) Recognize differences in personality.
3) Turn weaknesses into strengths.
4) Allow occasional confrontation.

Even if you want to build a good interpersonal relationship with someone, it's impossible if there is no respect or trust between you. For that reason, you should respect and trust others without setting conditions on how they are or what they do. To do that, you need to recognize that everyone is different and accept their different personalities.

Even if parents or superiors exert influence on their children or subordinates, they can't mold them into a copy of themselves. The things that they may see as a weakness, to that person might be part of their individuality. If you want to develop a weakness into a strength, look at the chart on page 126.

Returning to our story, Yukari developed courage and faced her older veteran subordinate. This type of stance is called *confrontation.* It is necessary to occasionally have confrontations between superiors and subordinates. Confrontation means to face a common goal, as two individuals, without one looking down on the other, but rather with respect and trust, accepting the differences in each other's personality.

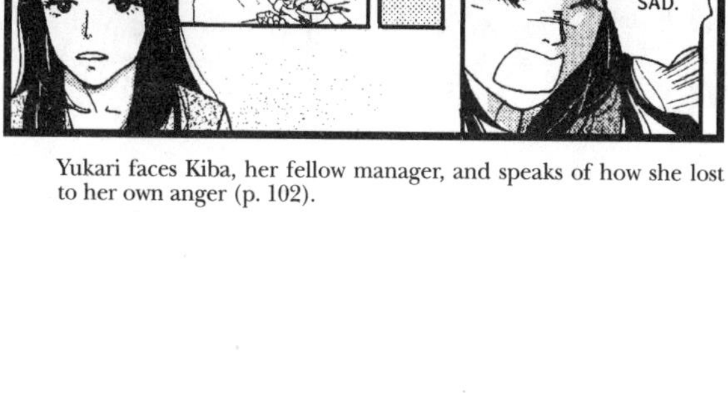
WHEN I SEE YOUR ATTITUDE AND APPROACH TO WORK...
...I CAN REALLY SEE HOW REAL YOUR LOVE FOR THE COMPANY IS.
SO I JUST COULDN'T BELIEVE THAT YOU COULD THROW AWAY THE POP LIKE THAT!
I QUESTIONED WHETHER YOU ACTUALLY LOVED THE COMPANY...
...AND IT MADE ME SAD.

Yukari faces Kiba, her fellow manager, and speaks of how she lost to her own anger (p. 102).

Examples of Turning Weaknesses into Strengths

Weakness	Strength
Short-tempered	Can directly express their thoughts
Dispirited	Tranquil
Indecisive	Doesn't make decision lightly
Flighty	Can change gears quickly
Poor concentration	Can multi-task
Overbearing	Has leadership qualities
Stubborn	Believes in themself
Doesn't have energy	Is recharging
Can't say no	Cares about others
Bad at talking	Good at listening
Lacks independence	Good follower
Brash	Gets their thoughts across
Verbose	Good at conveying information

When Kiba had her confrontation with Yukari, she was able to express what she was really thinking. She was also able to admit fault for discarding the POP right in front of Yukari. Through this interaction, Yukari was able to grow as a person and polish her leadership skills.

In his book *The Education of Children*, Adler said the following:

"It is important to teach people that to have courage, endurance, confidence, and not be discouraged by your failures, is an important task to take up."

Reading this sentence, Yukari would be able to see her momentary failure as a need for self-training and then take up that task.

Yukari's battle continues.

Adler, Who Began a New Era

While Adler was practicing psychology, he was invited to become the first member of the Wednesday Psychology Society (now known as the Vienna Psychoanalytic Society) created by Freud, the founder of psychoanalysis. In 1910, he became the chairman of the Vienna Psychoanalysis Society and co-editor of its journal, but he would eventually grow to disagree with Freud's thinking.

At the time, Freud believed that the root motivation of all human activity could be attributed to sexual drive (which he referred to as the *libido*). Freud also insisted that any psychiatric treatment required thoroughly analyzing the depths of the patient's mind. Adler, however, insisted that the source of motivation was the seeking of power and superiority. The result of this disagreement was an irreparable rift between the two men, leading Adler to leave the society in 1911 and begin his own activities.

People in Freud's camp refer to Adler as the "backstabbing disciple," but even if he was a collaborator, he was not a disciple. Adler never attended a lecture by Freud, nor was he ever psychoanalyzed, which was a necessary step to becoming a Freudian analyst.

Adler took his parting from Freud as an opportunity to leap into his own work, especially after Austria sustained a defeat in the First World War (1914–1918), opening his first Child Consultation Center and having his psychology incorporated into school education. In this way, he engaged in education and counseling in an open atmosphere rather than treating people individually. In the latter half of the 1920s in particular, he gained a lot of followers, having gone to America, where his theories were widely accepted.

Part 3

From the World of Assumptions to Common Sense

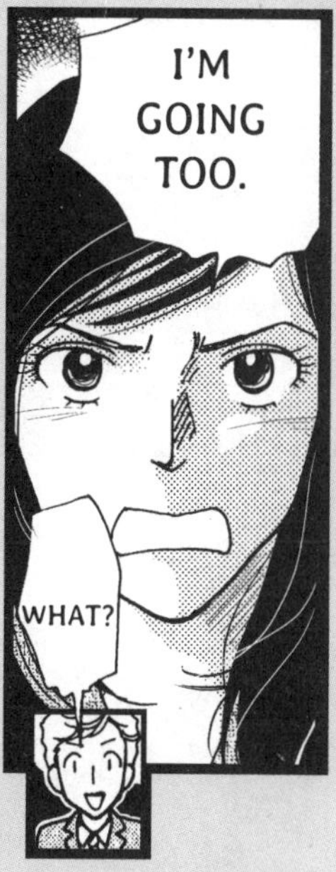
I'M GOING TOO.
WHAT?

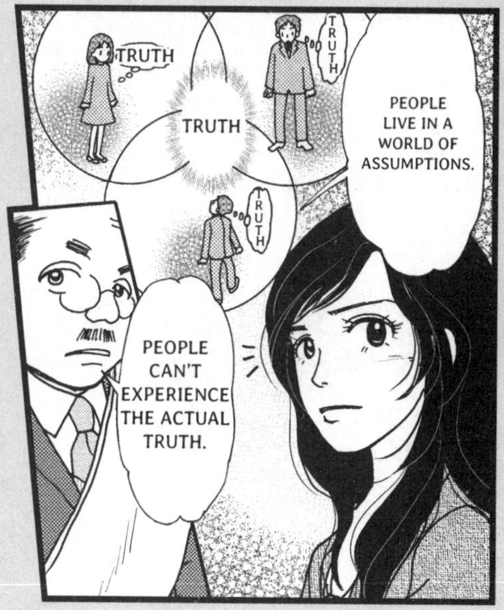
TRUTH
TRUTH
TRUTH
TRUTH
PEOPLE LIVE IN A WORLD OF ASSUMPTIONS.
PEOPLE CAN'T EXPERIENCE THE ACTUAL TRUTH.

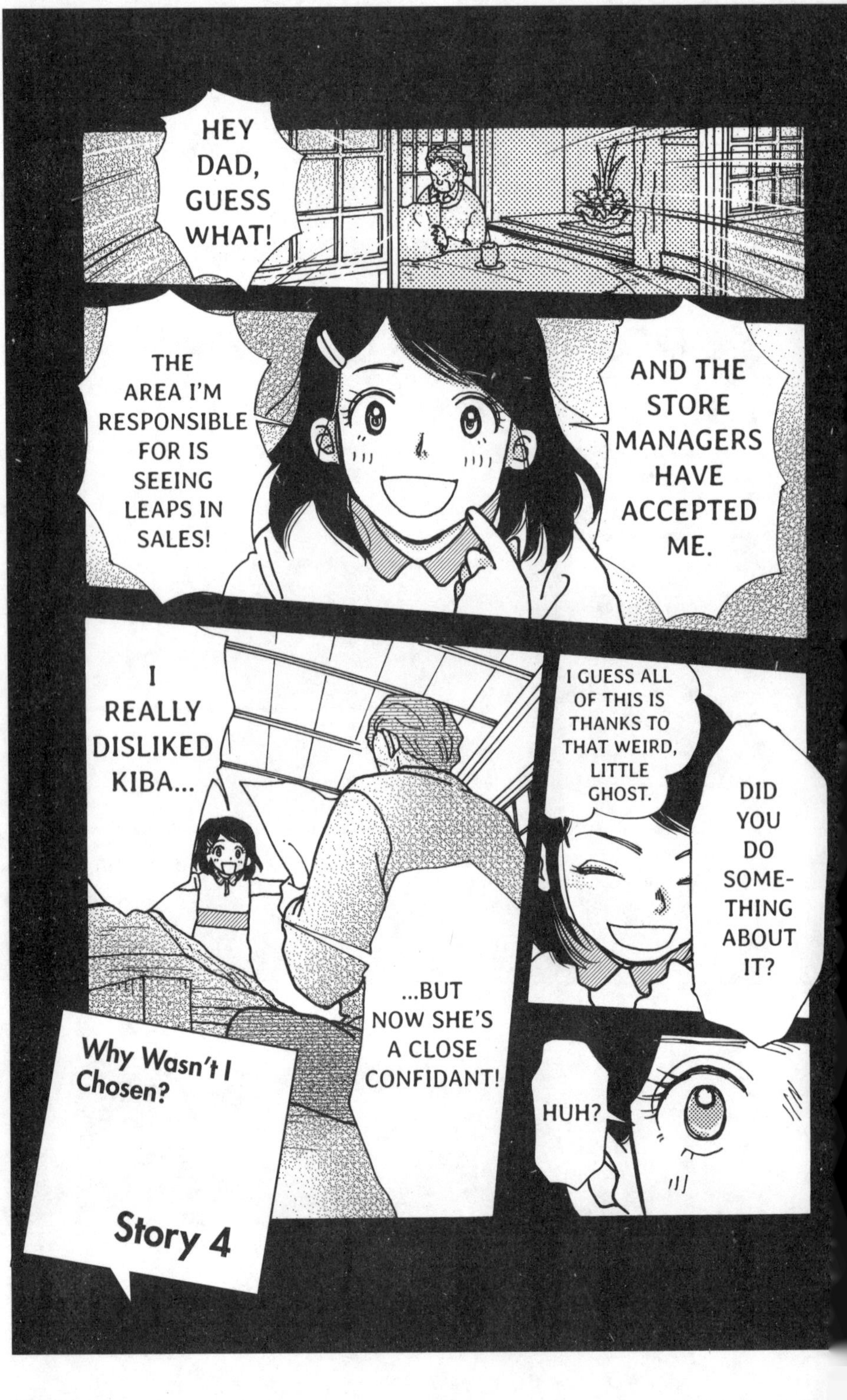
HEY DAD, GUESS WHAT!
THE AREA I'M RESPONSIBLE FOR IS SEEING LEAPS IN SALES!
AND THE STORE MANAGERS HAVE ACCEPTED ME.
I REALLY DISLIKED KIBA...
...BUT NOW SHE'S A CLOSE CONFIDANT!
I GUESS ALL OF THIS IS THANKS TO THAT WEIRD, LITTLE GHOST.
DID YOU DO SOME-THING ABOUT IT?
HUH?
Why Wasn't I Chosen?
Story 4

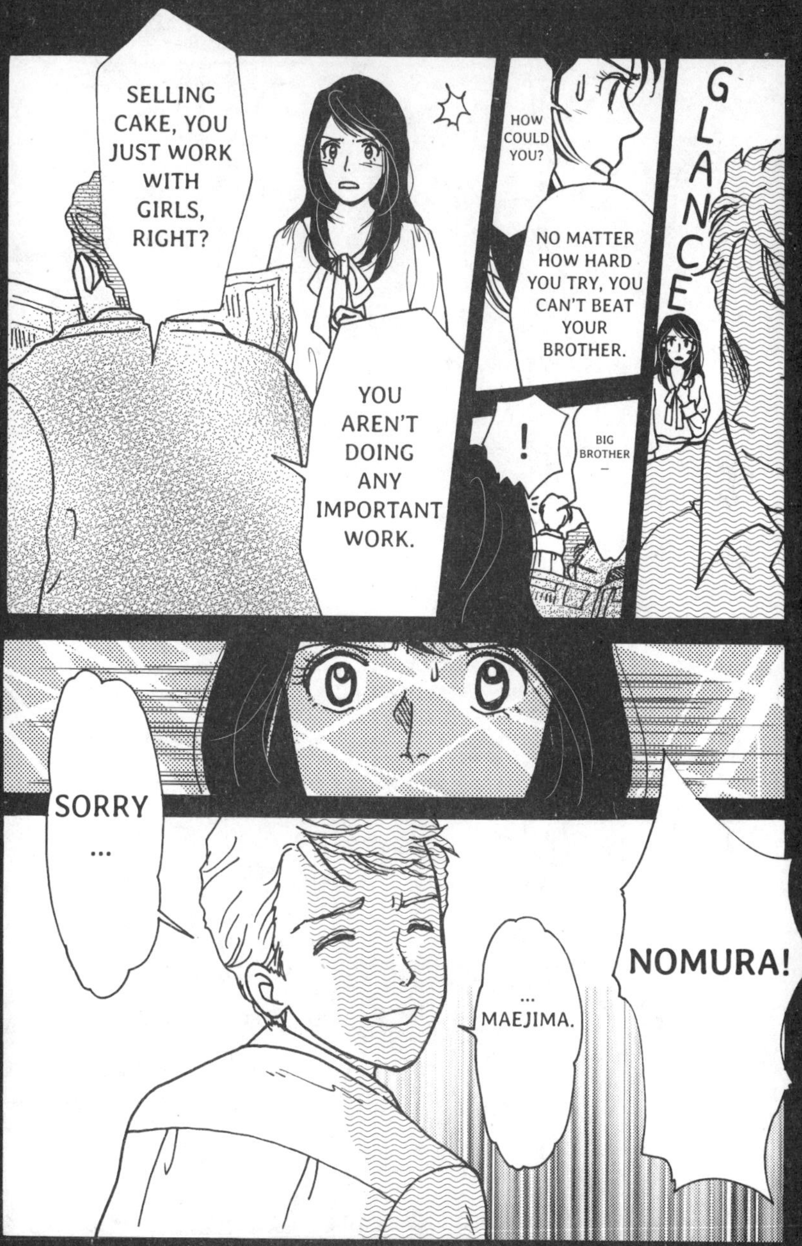
SELLING CAKE, YOU JUST WORK WITH GIRLS, RIGHT?
YOU AREN'T DOING ANY IMPORTANT WORK.
HOW COULD YOU?
NO MATTER HOW HARD YOU TRY, YOU CAN'T BEAT YOUR BROTHER.
GLANCE
!
BIG BROTHER —
SORRY ...
NOMURA!
... MAEJIMA.

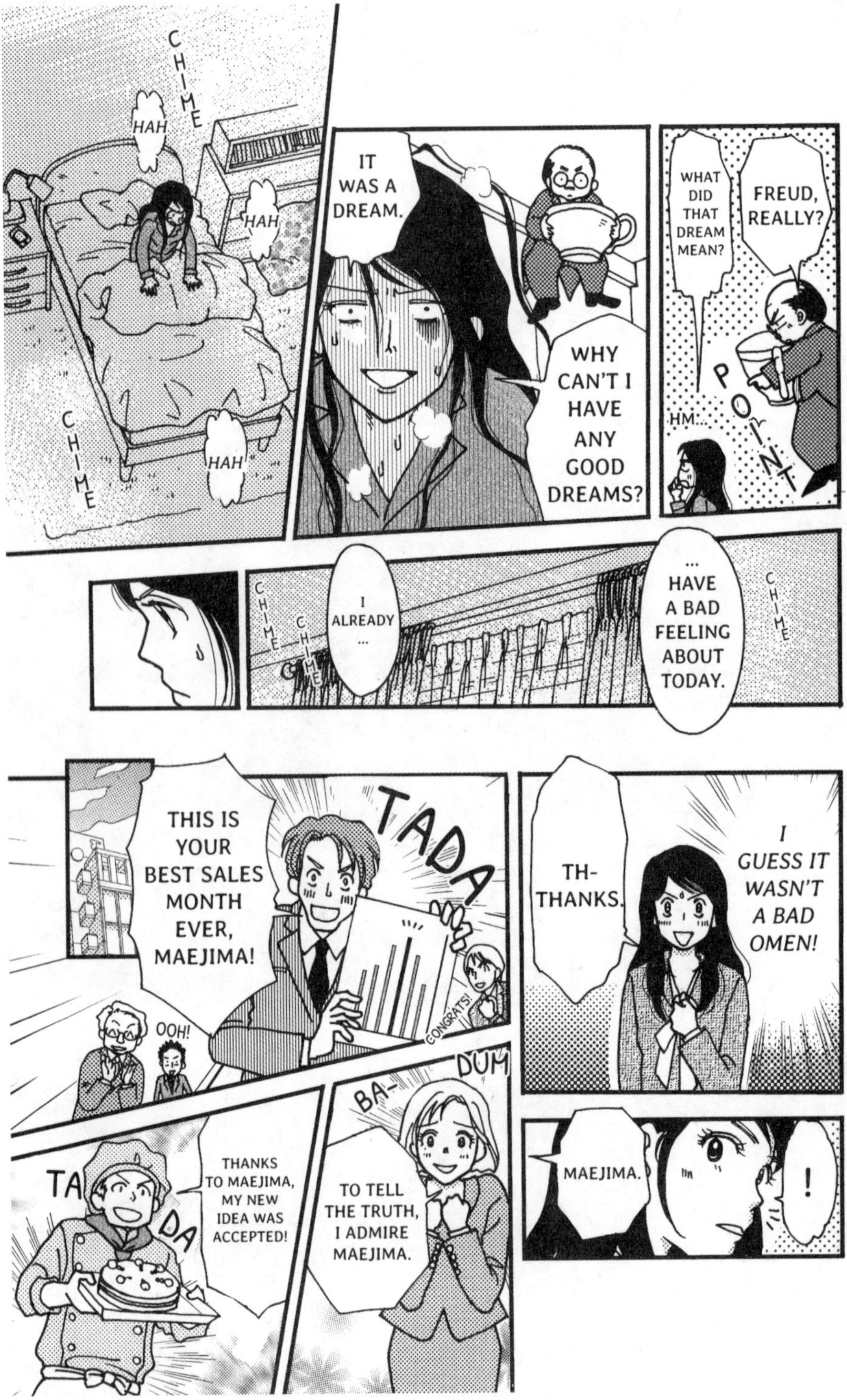
CHIME
HAH
HAH
HAH
CHIME
IT WAS A DREAM.
WHY CAN'T I HAVE ANY GOOD DREAMS?
FREUD, REALLY?
WHAT DID THAT DREAM MEAN?
POINT
HM...
... HAVE A BAD FEELING ABOUT TODAY.
I ALREADY ...
CHIME
CHIME
CHIME
TADA
THIS IS YOUR BEST SALES MONTH EVER, MAEJIMA!
OOH!
CONGRATS!
I GUESS IT WASN'T A BAD OMEN!
TH- THANKS.
BA-DUM
TO TELL THE TRUTH, I ADMIRE MAEJIMA.
TA DA
THANKS TO MAEJIMA, MY NEW IDEA WAS ACCEPTED!
!
MAEJIMA.

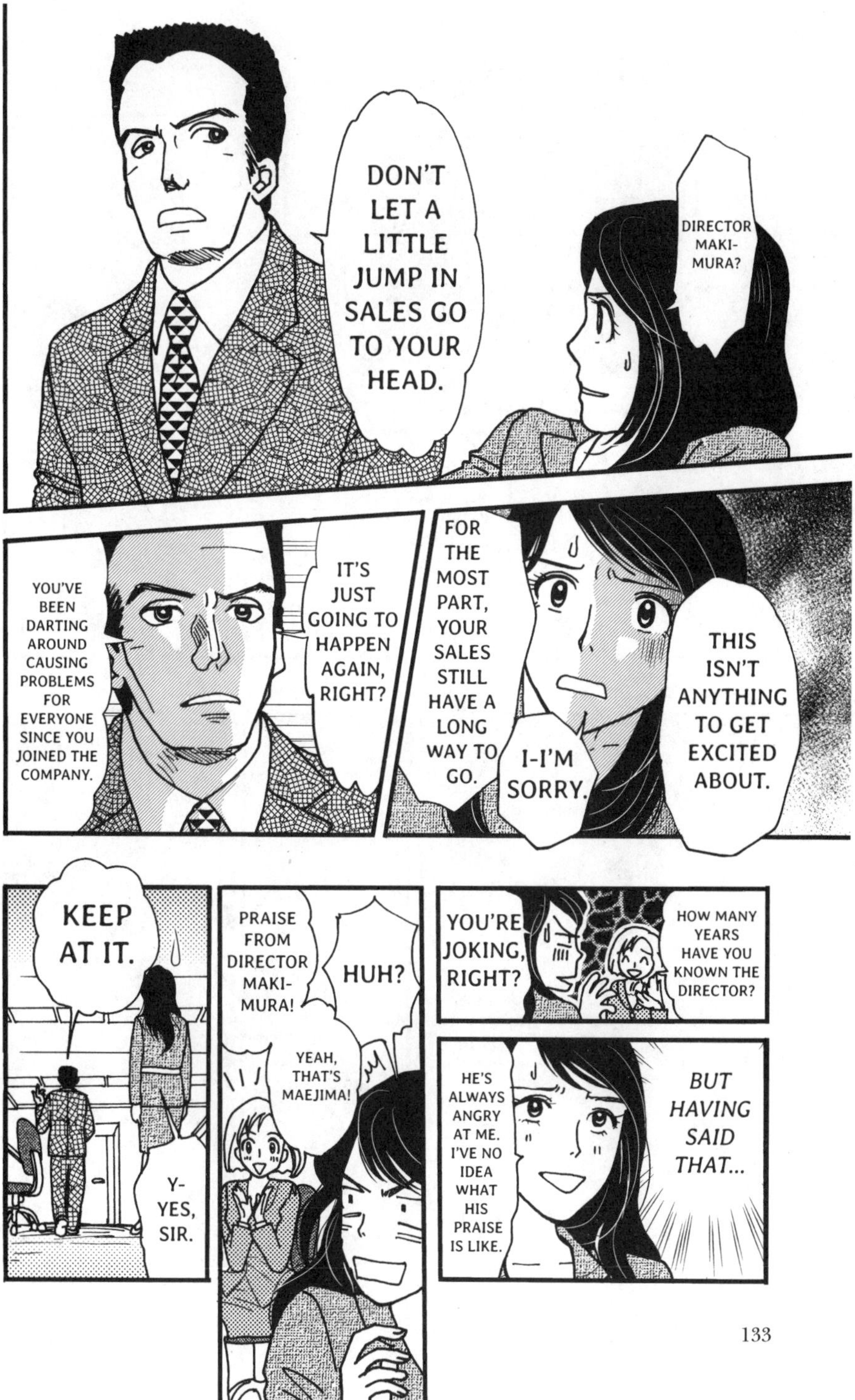
DIRECTOR MAKI-MURA?
DON'T LET A LITTLE JUMP IN SALES GO TO YOUR HEAD.
THIS ISN'T ANYTHING TO GET EXCITED ABOUT.
I-I'M SORRY.
FOR THE MOST PART, YOUR SALES STILL HAVE A LONG WAY TO GO.
IT'S JUST GOING TO HAPPEN AGAIN, RIGHT?
YOU'VE BEEN DARTING AROUND CAUSING PROBLEMS FOR EVERYONE SINCE YOU JOINED THE COMPANY.
KEEP AT IT.
Y-YES, SIR.
HUH?
PRAISE FROM DIRECTOR MAKI-MURA!
YEAH, THAT'S MAEJIMA!
HOW MANY YEARS HAVE YOU KNOWN THE DIRECTOR?
YOU'RE JOKING, RIGHT?
BUT HAVING SAID THAT...
HE'S ALWAYS ANGRY AT ME. I'VE NO IDEA WHAT HIS PRAISE IS LIKE.

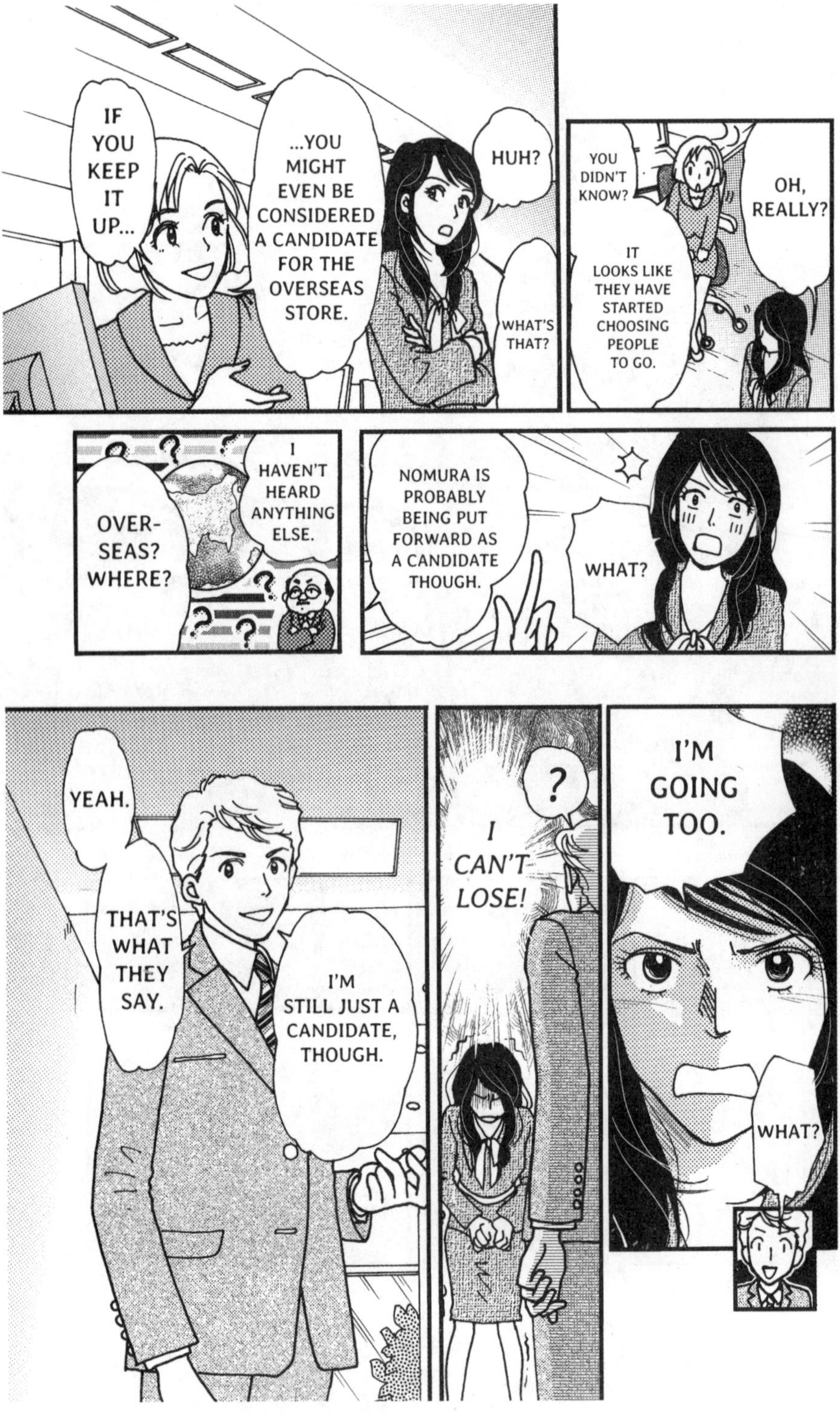

IF YOU KEEP IT UP...
...YOU MIGHT EVEN BE CONSIDERED A CANDIDATE FOR THE OVERSEAS STORE.
HUH?
WHAT'S THAT?
YOU DIDN'T KNOW?
OH, REALLY?
IT LOOKS LIKE THEY HAVE STARTED CHOOSING PEOPLE TO GO.
OVER-SEAS? WHERE?
I HAVEN'T HEARD ANYTHING ELSE.
NOMURA IS PROBABLY BEING PUT FORWARD AS A CANDIDATE THOUGH.
WHAT?
YEAH.
THAT'S WHAT THEY SAY.
I'M STILL JUST A CANDIDATE, THOUGH.
?
I CAN'T LOSE!
I'M GOING TOO.
WHAT?

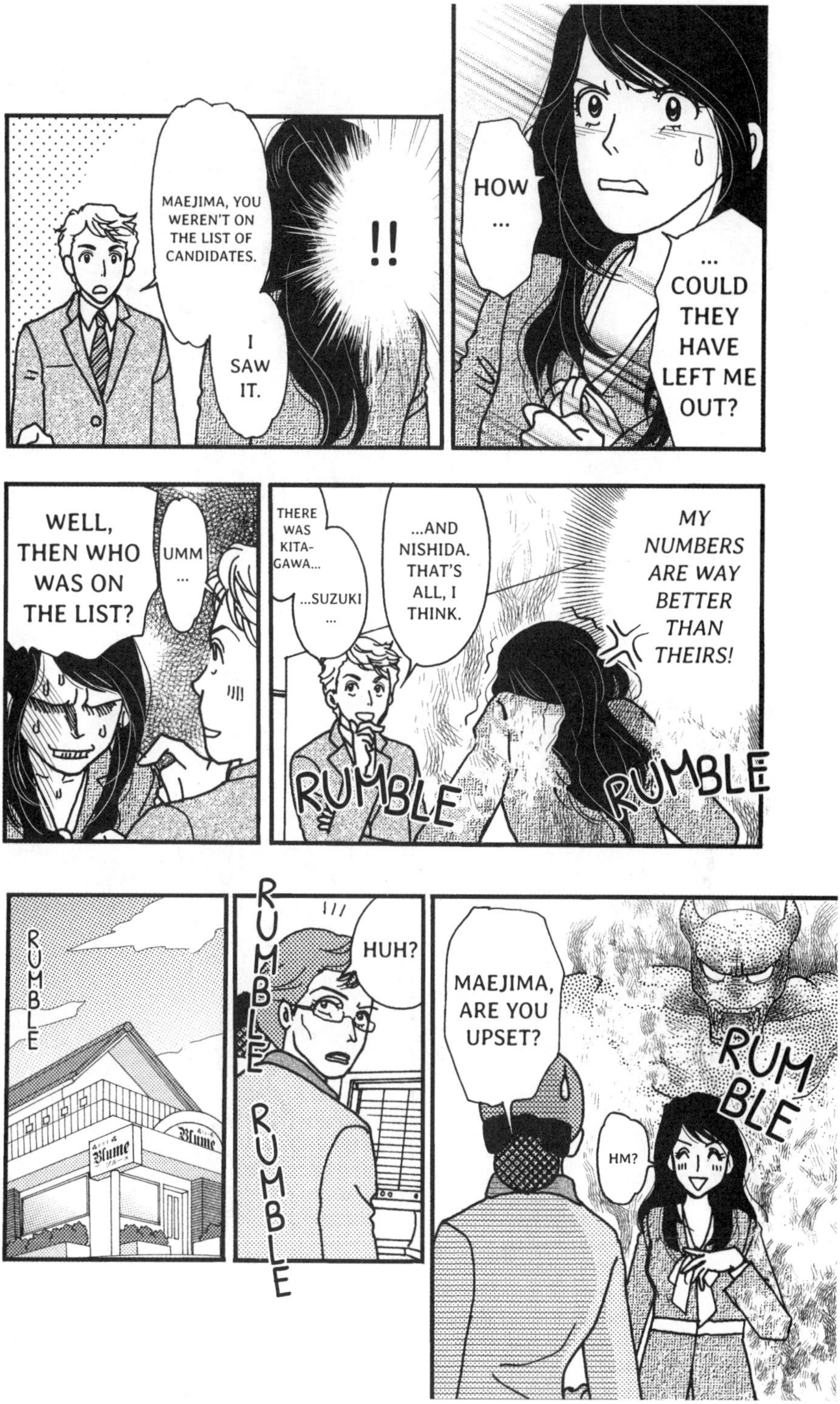
MAEJIMA, YOU WEREN'T ON THE LIST OF CANDIDATES.
I SAW IT.
!!
HOW ...
... COULD THEY HAVE LEFT ME OUT?
WELL, THEN WHO WAS ON THE LIST?
UMM ...
THERE WAS KITA-GAWA...
...SUZUKI ...
...AND NISHIDA. THAT'S ALL, I THINK.
MY NUMBERS ARE WAY BETTER THAN THEIRS!
RUMBLE
RUMBLE
RUMBLE
Blume
RUMBLE
RUMBLE
HUH?
MAEJIMA, ARE YOU UPSET?
HM?
RUMBLE

SQUISH

I'M SORRY, IS IT THAT OBVIOUS?

YOU'VE GOT AN AURA.

ACTUALLY...

I SEE.

THAT'S ODD, THOUGH.

I'D HAVE THOUGHT YOU WOULD'VE BEEN INCLUDED ON THE LIST.

YOU'RE THE BEST AREA MANAGER I'VE WORKED WITH.

I'M NO GOOD, RIGHT? I KNEW IT.

"I KNEW IT"?

IT'S ALWAYS BEEN LIKE THIS.

MY OLDER BROTHER CAN DO ANYTHING.

I COULD NEVER BEAT HIM NO MATTER HOW I TRIED.

I THINK BECAUSE OF THAT, MY DAD NEVER REALLY NOTICED ME.

SELLING CAKE, YOU JUST WORK WITH GIRLS, RIGHT?

YOU AREN'T DOING ANY IMPORTANT WORK.

I'M SURE IT'S BECAUSE I'M STILL NOT TRYING HARD ENOUGH.

136

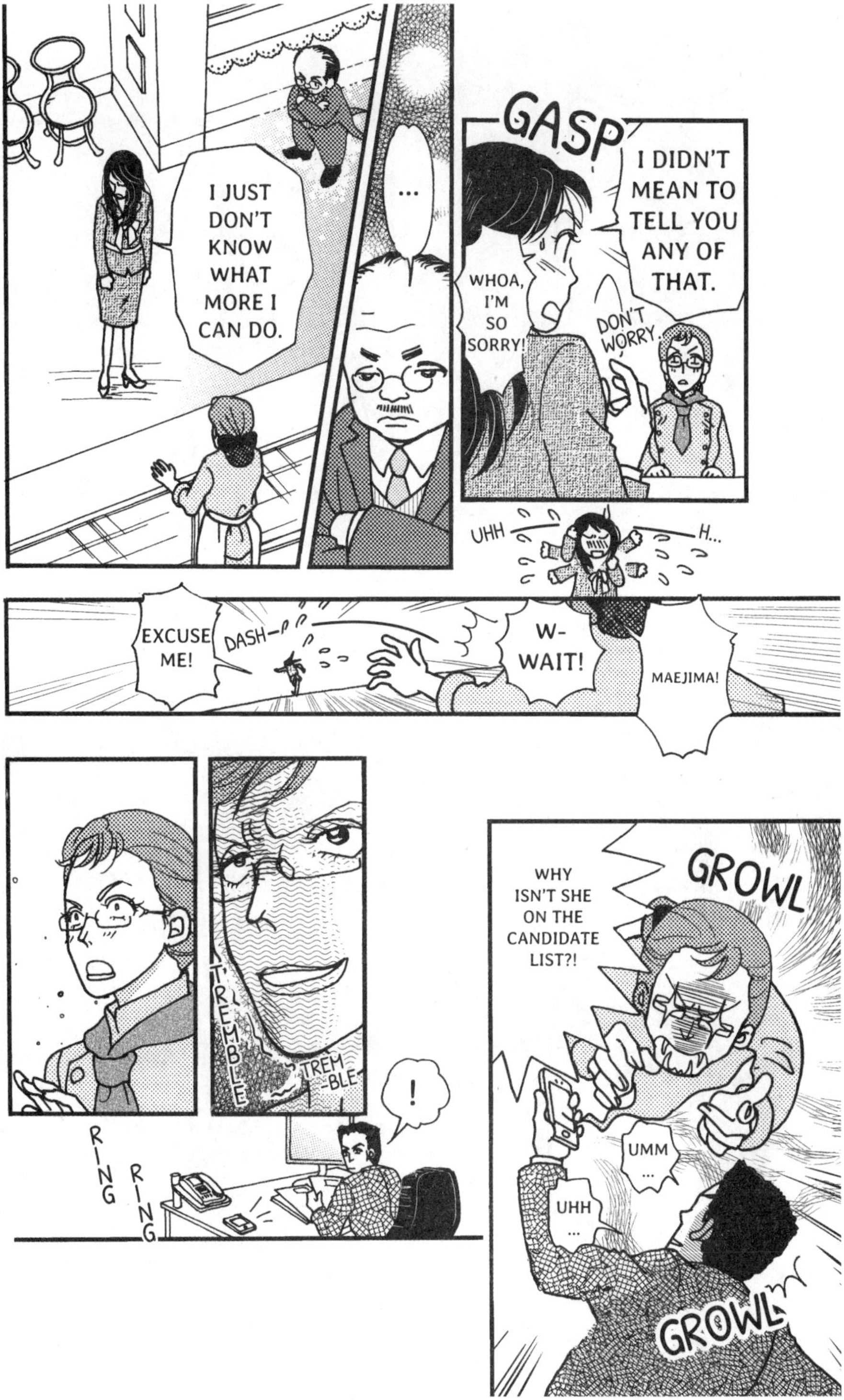
I JUST DON'T KNOW WHAT MORE I CAN DO.
...
GASP
I DIDN'T MEAN TO TELL YOU ANY OF THAT.
WHOA, I'M SO SORRY!
DON'T WORRY.
UHH—H...
EXCUSE ME!
DASH—
W-WAIT!
MAEJIMA!
TREMBLE
TREMBLE
RING RING
!
WHY ISN'T SHE ON THE CANDIDATE LIST?!
GROWL
UMM ...
UHH ...
GROWL

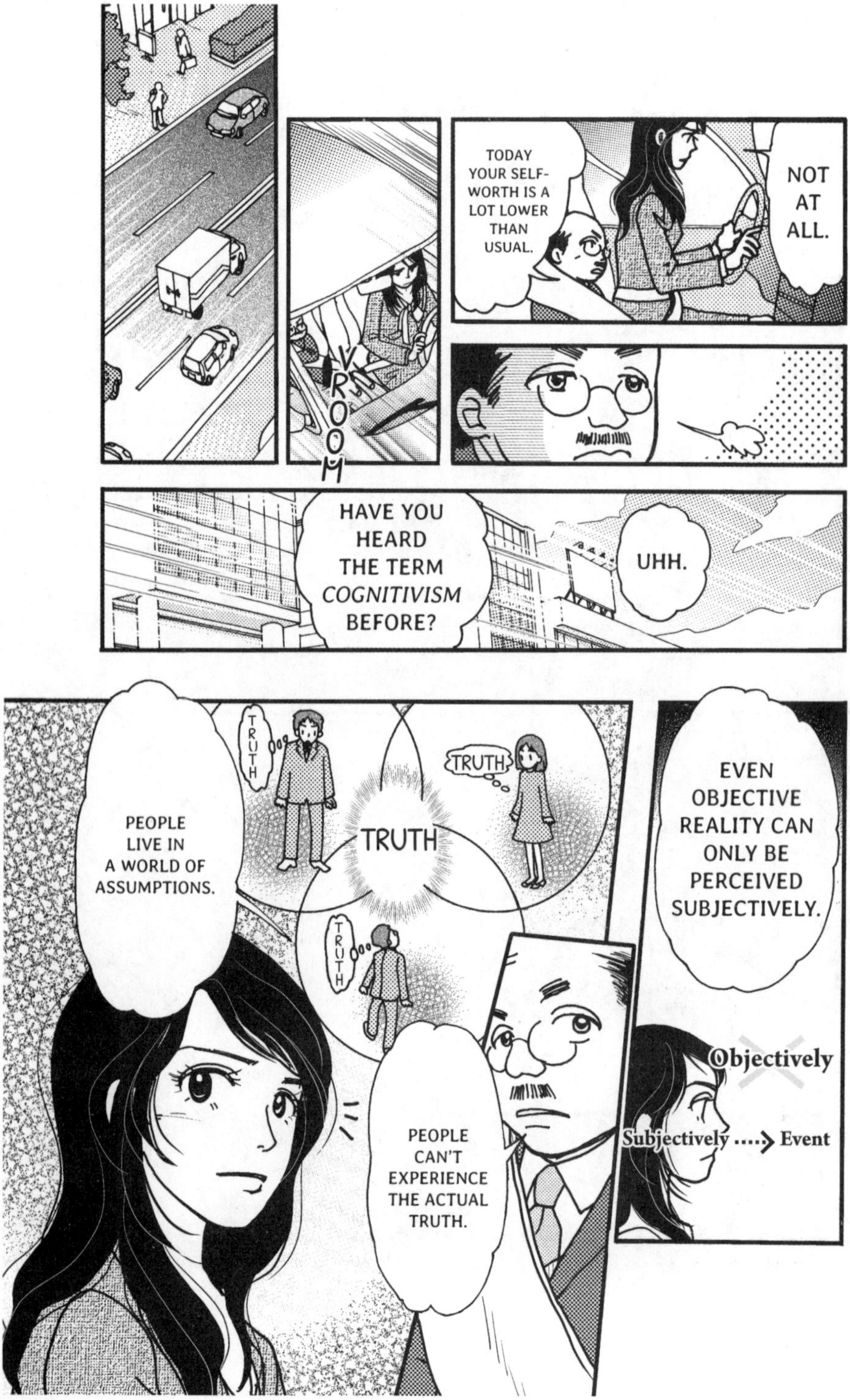
VROOM
TODAY YOUR SELF-WORTH IS A LOT LOWER THAN USUAL.
NOT AT ALL.
HAVE YOU HEARD THE TERM *COGNITIVISM* BEFORE?
UHH.
PEOPLE LIVE IN A WORLD OF ASSUMPTIONS.
TRUTH
TRUTH
TRUTH
TRUTH
PEOPLE CAN'T EXPERIENCE THE ACTUAL TRUTH.
EVEN OBJECTIVE REALITY CAN ONLY BE PERCEIVED SUBJECTIVELY.
Objectively
Subjectively ····> Event

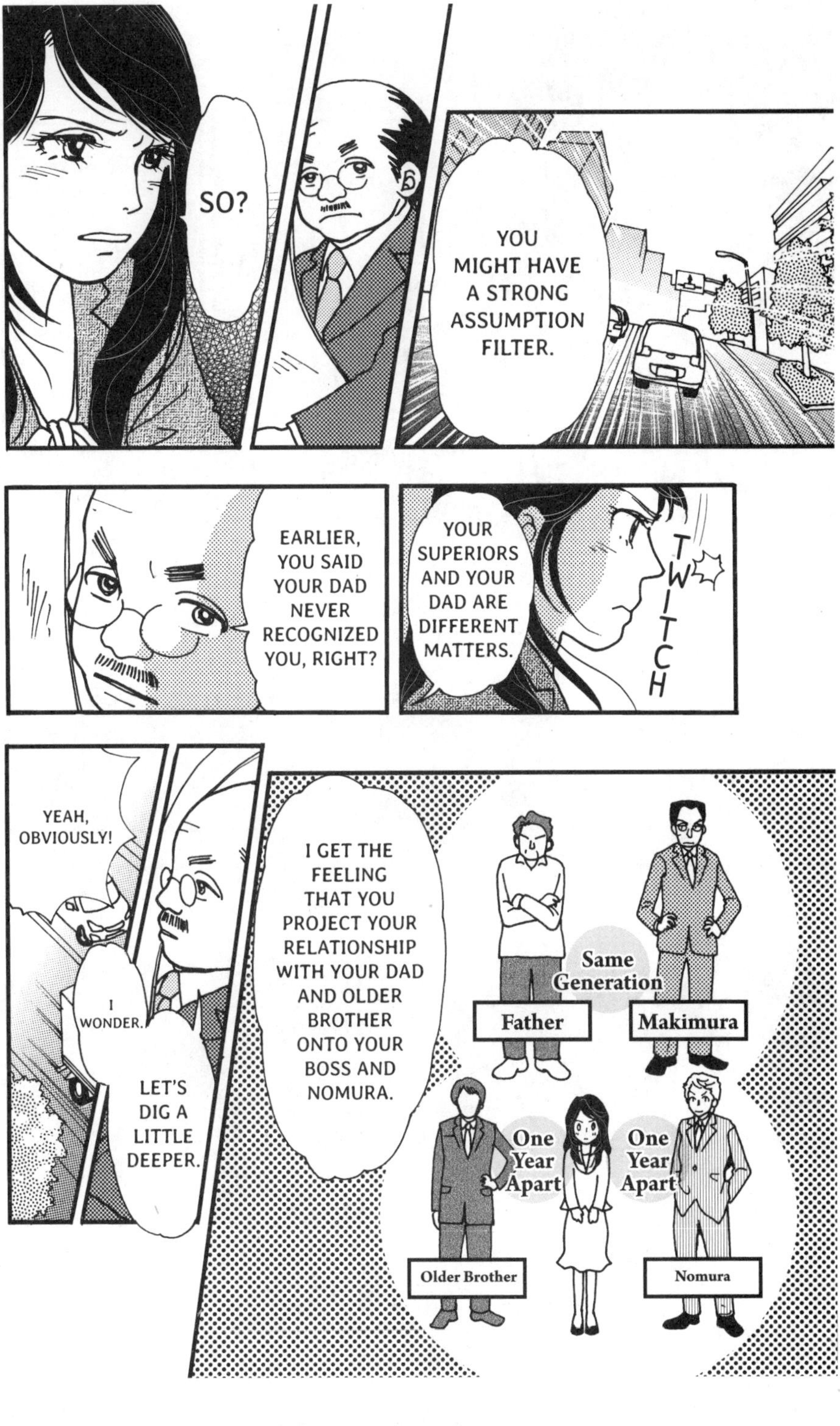
SO?
YOU MIGHT HAVE A STRONG ASSUMPTION FILTER.
EARLIER, YOU SAID YOUR DAD NEVER RECOGNIZED YOU, RIGHT?
YOUR SUPERIORS AND YOUR DAD ARE DIFFERENT MATTERS.
TWITCH
YEAH, OBVIOUSLY!
I WONDER.
LET'S DIG A LITTLE DEEPER.
I GET THE FEELING THAT YOU PROJECT YOUR RELATIONSHIP WITH YOUR DAD AND OLDER BROTHER ONTO YOUR BOSS AND NOMURA.
Same Generation
Father
Makimura
One Year Apart
One Year Apart
Older Brother
Nomura

PUSH

I'M NOT DOING THAT!

I WONDER.

YOU'RE TAKING YOUR FEELING OF NOT BEING NOTICED BY YOUR DAD...

...AND APPLYING IT TO YOUR BOSS.

SO SOMEWHERE IN YOUR MIND, YOU THINK "I CAN'T WIN" AND "I'M NOT TRYING ENOUGH," AND THEN YOU UNDERVALUE YOURSELF.

SQUEEZE

I AM NOT.

YOU'RE DOING IT A LOT.

...

WHATEVER YOU SAY, IT'S ALREADY DECIDED.

MAEJIMA, YOU WEREN'T ON THE LIST OF CANDIDATES.

I WASN'T CHOSEN.

YOU REALLY DON'T KNOW HOW THE WORLD WORKS.

MIND YOUR OWN BUSINESS.

BUT...

...WHY DON'T YOU THINK ABOUT IT AGAIN?

AGAIN?

WHY DO YOU THINK DIRECTOR MAKIMURA DIDN'T PUT YOU ON THE CANDIDATE LIST?

IT'S BECAUSE YOU'VE BEEN TIED TOGETHER AS BOSS AND SUBORDINATE FOR SO LONG.

THINKING OF THAT TIME AND EXPERIENCE, PUT YOURSELF IN HIS SHOES. THEN, THINK ABOUT THE SITUATION AGAIN.

HUH?

WHAT'S THE POINT OF THAT?

IN ADLERIAN PSYCHOLOGY, WE EMPATHIZE.

Empathize

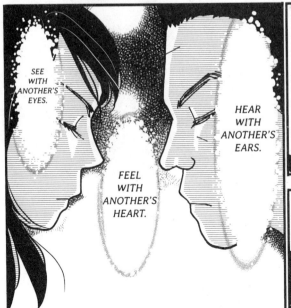

SEE WITH ANOTHER'S EYES.

FEEL WITH ANOTHER'S HEART.

HEAR WITH ANOTHER'S EARS.

I MEAN, TRY TO BECOME DIRECTOR MAKIMURA.

ME, BECOME HIM?!

!!

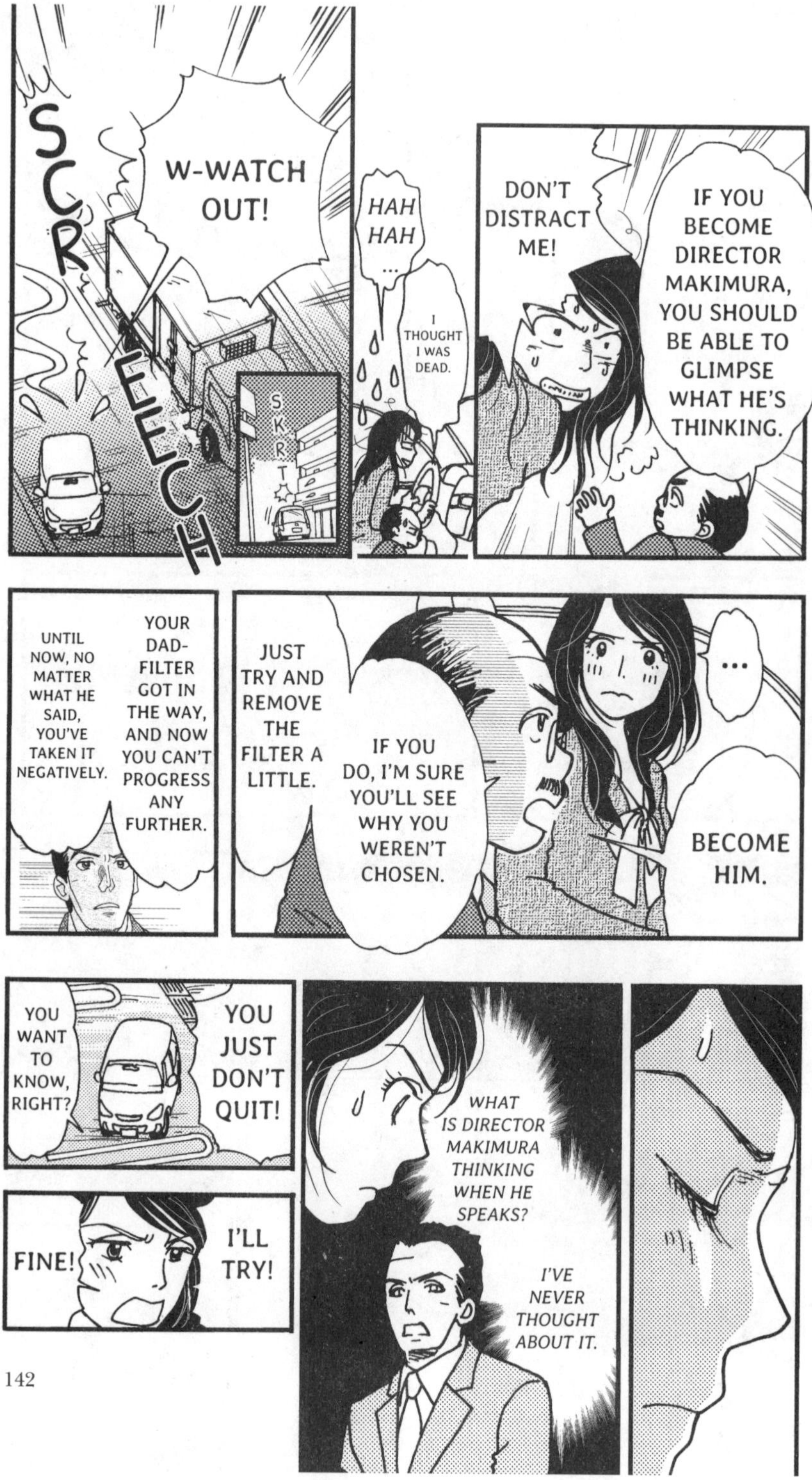
SCREEECH
W-WATCH OUT!
SKRT
HAH HAH ...
I THOUGHT I WAS DEAD.
DON'T DISTRACT ME!
IF YOU BECOME DIRECTOR MAKIMURA, YOU SHOULD BE ABLE TO GLIMPSE WHAT HE'S THINKING.
UNTIL NOW, NO MATTER WHAT HE SAID, YOU'VE TAKEN IT NEGATIVELY.
YOUR DAD-FILTER GOT IN THE WAY, AND NOW YOU CAN'T PROGRESS ANY FURTHER.
JUST TRY AND REMOVE THE FILTER A LITTLE.
IF YOU DO, I'M SURE YOU'LL SEE WHY YOU WEREN'T CHOSEN.
...
BECOME HIM.
YOU WANT TO KNOW, RIGHT?
YOU JUST DON'T QUIT!
FINE!
I'LL TRY!
WHAT IS DIRECTOR MAKIMURA THINKING WHEN HE SPEAKS?
I'VE NEVER THOUGHT ABOUT IT.

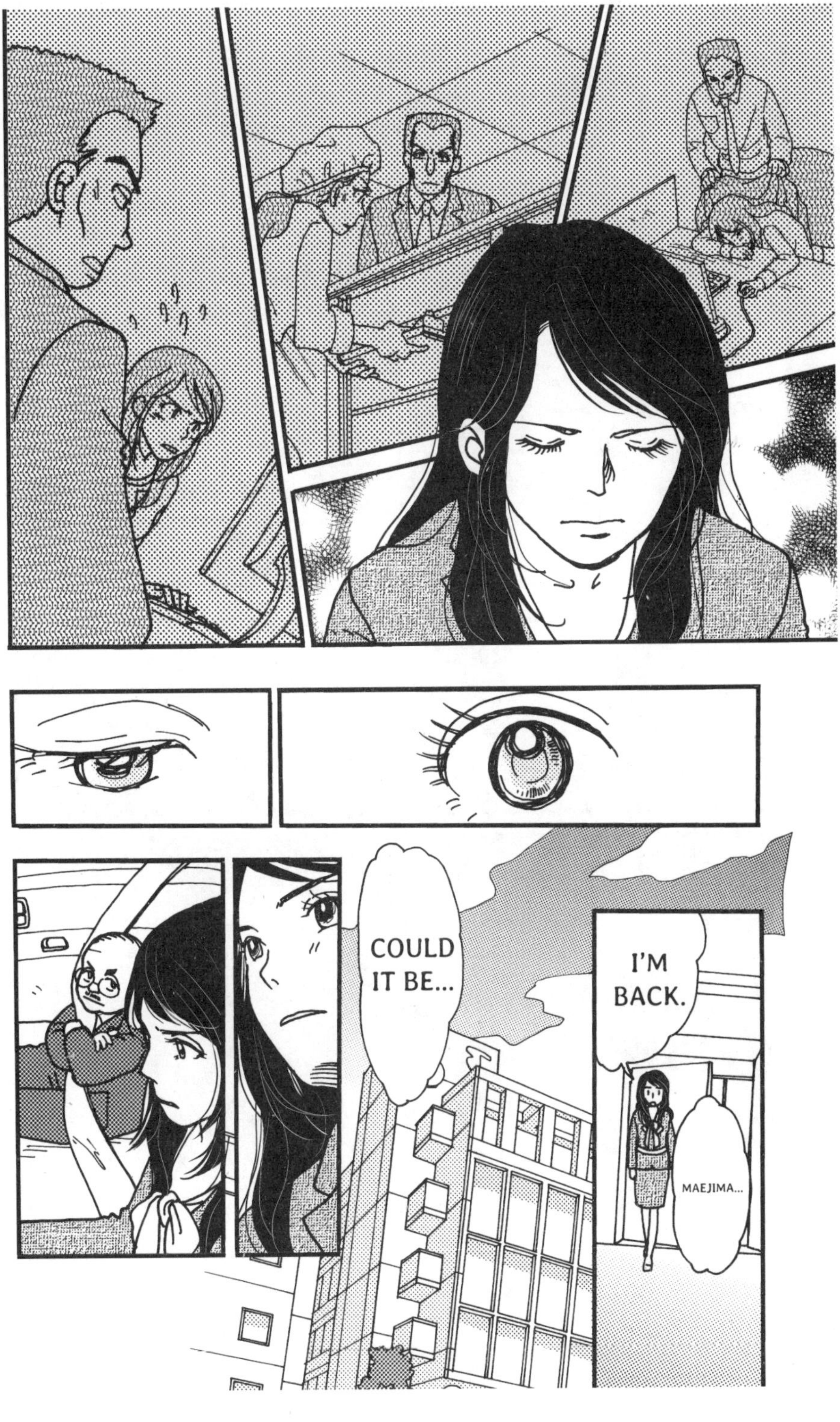
I'M BACK.
MAEJIMA...
COULD IT BE...

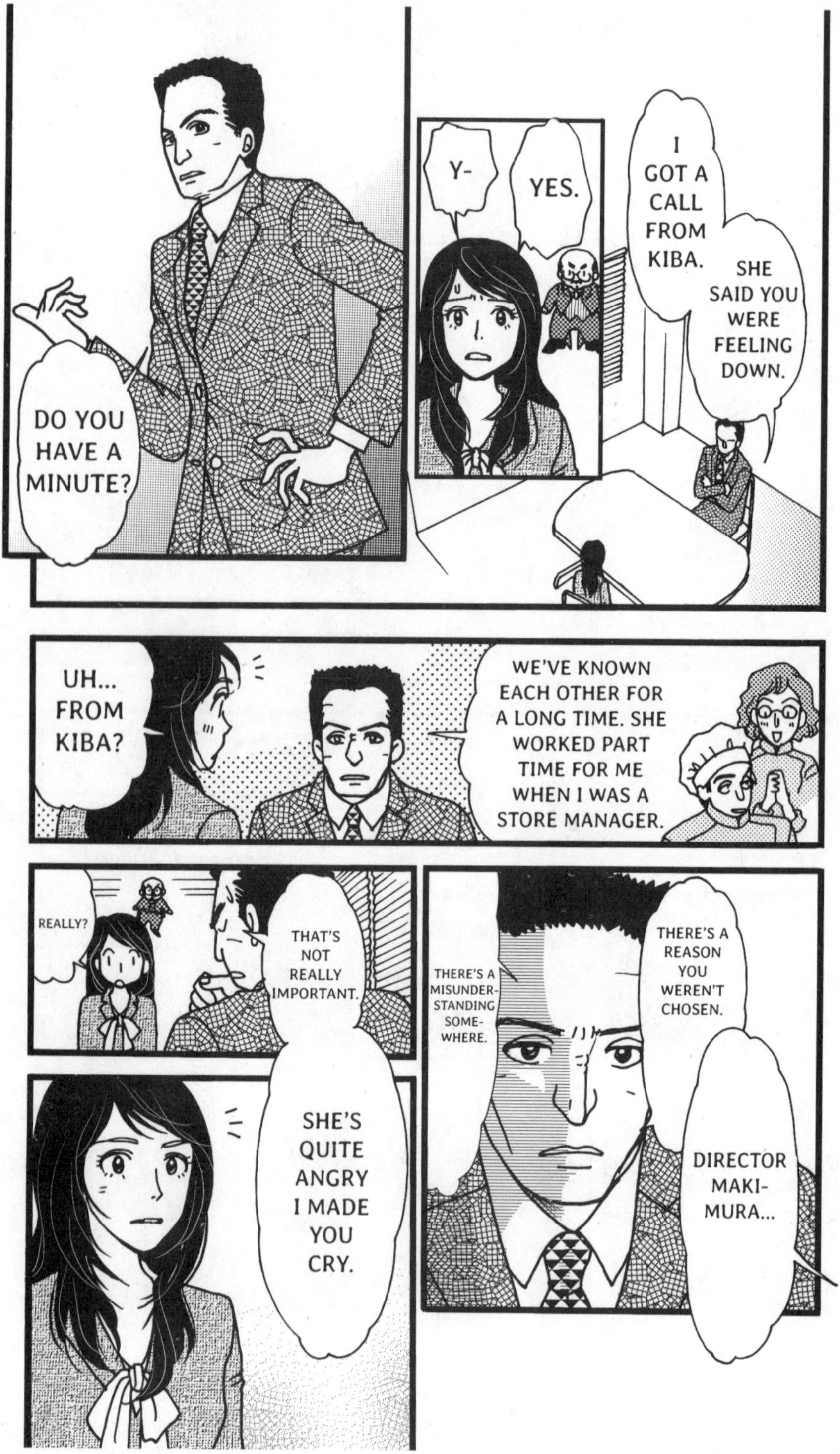
DO YOU HAVE A MINUTE?
Y-
YES.
I GOT A CALL FROM KIBA.
SHE SAID YOU WERE FEELING DOWN.
UH... FROM KIBA?
WE'VE KNOWN EACH OTHER FOR A LONG TIME. SHE WORKED PART TIME FOR ME WHEN I WAS A STORE MANAGER.
REALLY?
THAT'S NOT REALLY IMPORTANT.
SHE'S QUITE ANGRY I MADE YOU CRY.
THERE'S A MISUNDER-STANDING SOME-WHERE.
THERE'S A REASON YOU WEREN'T CHOSEN.
DIRECTOR MAKI-MURA...

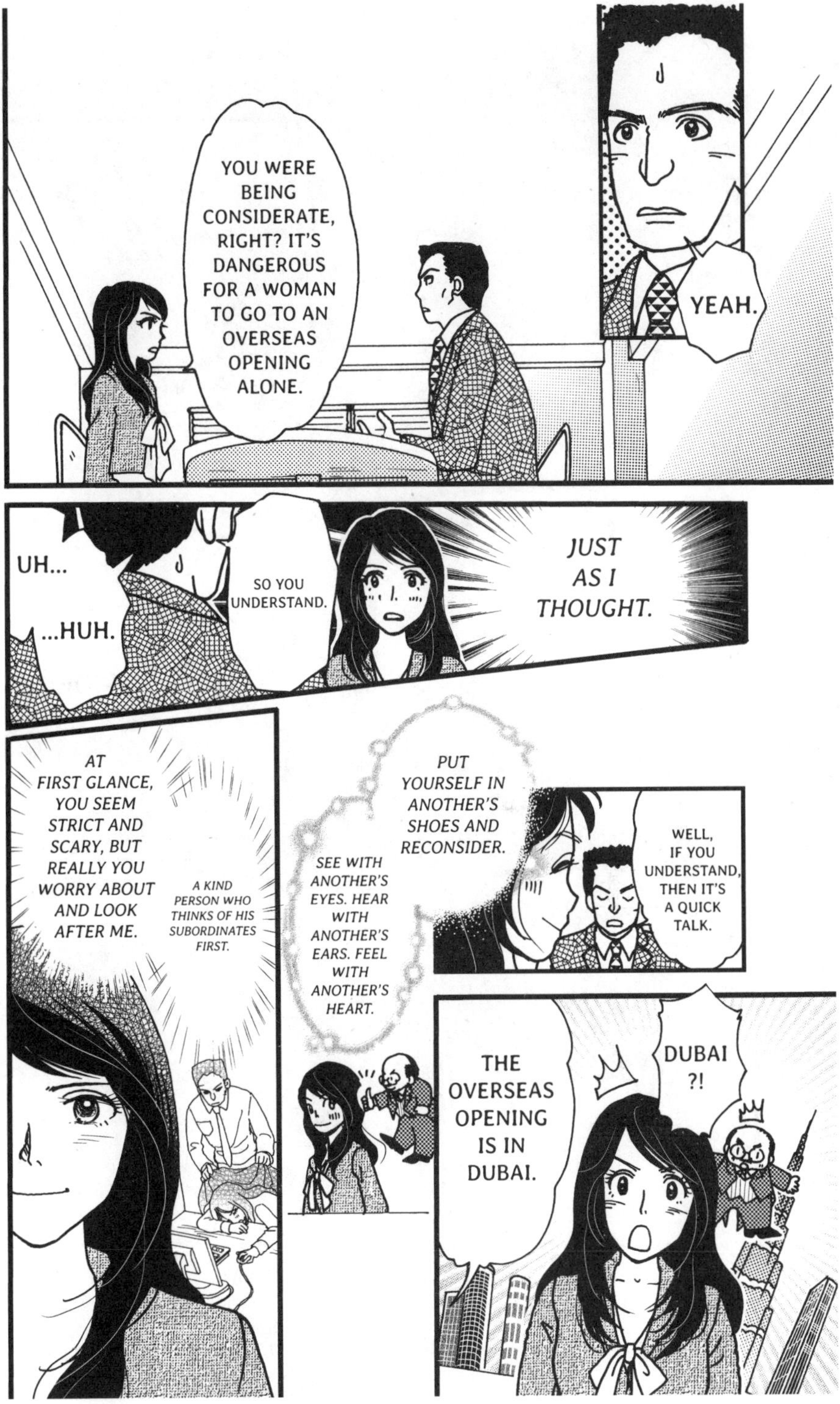
YOU WERE BEING CONSIDERATE, RIGHT? IT'S DANGEROUS FOR A WOMAN TO GO TO AN OVERSEAS OPENING ALONE.
YEAH.
JUST AS I THOUGHT.
SO YOU UNDERSTAND.
UH...
...HUH.
AT FIRST GLANCE, YOU SEEM STRICT AND SCARY, BUT REALLY YOU WORRY ABOUT AND LOOK AFTER ME.
A KIND PERSON WHO THINKS OF HIS SUBORDINATES FIRST.
PUT YOURSELF IN ANOTHER'S SHOES AND RECONSIDER.
SEE WITH ANOTHER'S EYES. HEAR WITH ANOTHER'S EARS. FEEL WITH ANOTHER'S HEART.
WELL, IF YOU UNDERSTAND, THEN IT'S A QUICK TALK.
THE OVERSEAS OPENING IS IN DUBAI.
DUBAI ?!

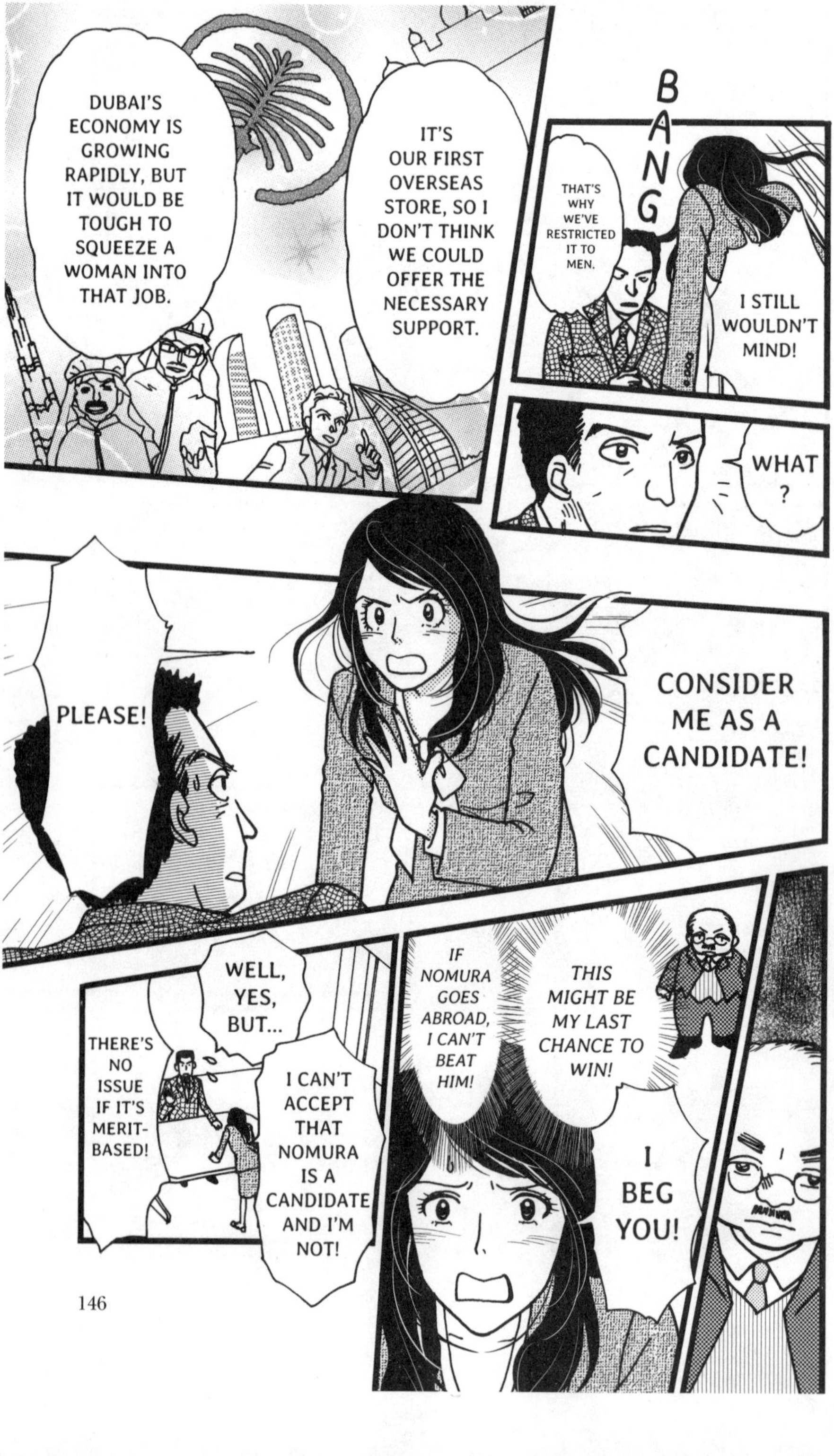
DUBAI'S ECONOMY IS GROWING RAPIDLY, BUT IT WOULD BE TOUGH TO SQUEEZE A WOMAN INTO THAT JOB.
IT'S OUR FIRST OVERSEAS STORE, SO I DON'T THINK WE COULD OFFER THE NECESSARY SUPPORT.
THAT'S WHY WE'VE RESTRICTED IT TO MEN.
BANG
I STILL WOULDN'T MIND!
WHAT?
PLEASE!
CONSIDER ME AS A CANDIDATE!
WELL, YES, BUT...
THERE'S NO ISSUE IF IT'S MERIT-BASED!
I CAN'T ACCEPT THAT NOMURA IS A CANDIDATE AND I'M NOT!
IF NOMURA GOES ABROAD, I CAN'T BEAT HIM!
THIS MIGHT BE MY LAST CHANCE TO WIN!
I BEG YOU!

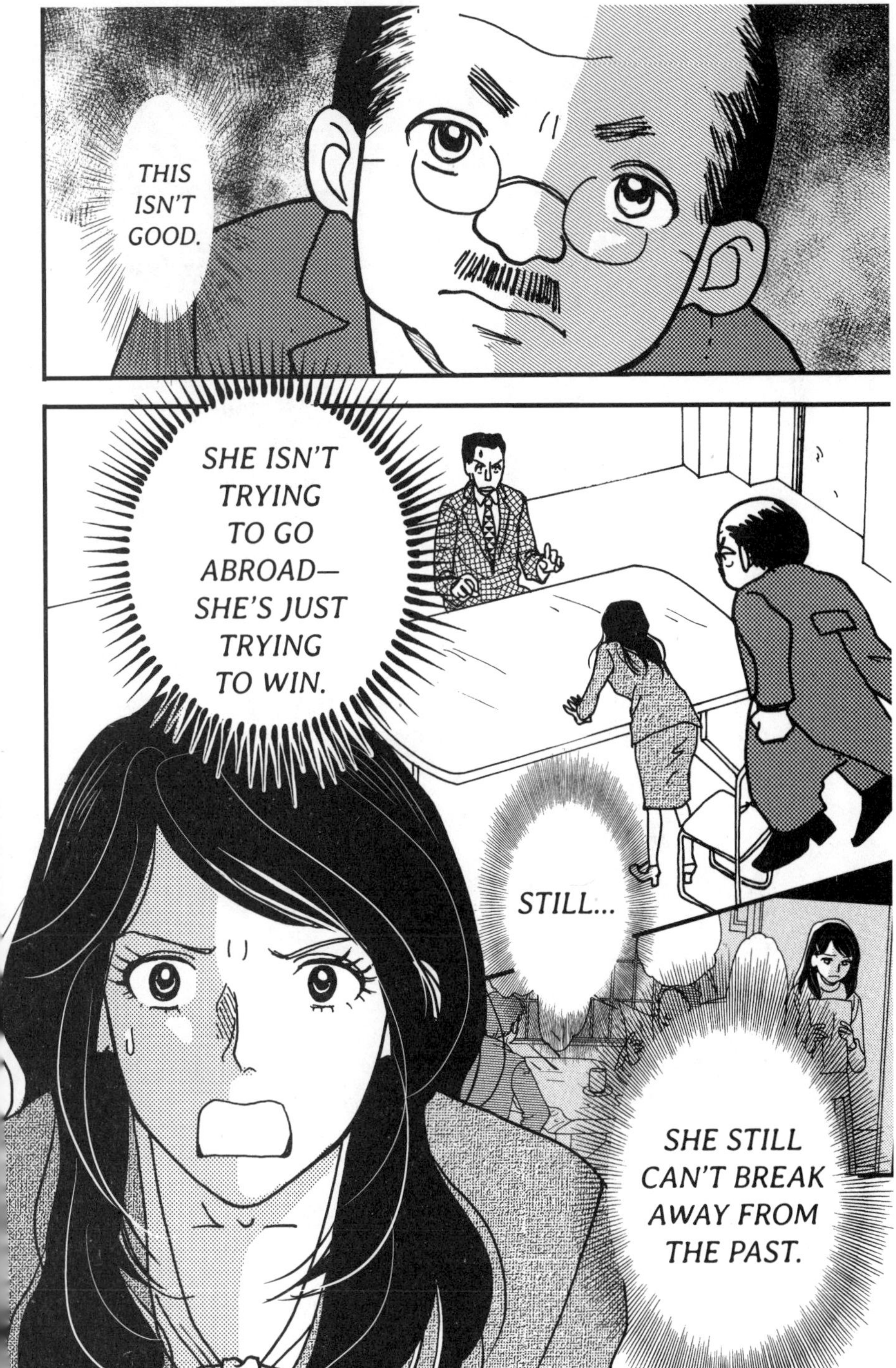
THIS ISN'T GOOD.
SHE ISN'T TRYING TO GO ABROAD—SHE'S JUST TRYING TO WIN.
STILL...
SHE STILL CAN'T BREAK AWAY FROM THE PAST.

What Is Cognitivism?

1

⇨ Everything Is a World of Assumptions

Before we touch on the point of cognitivism, remember what we learned in Chapter 3 of Part 1, page 74. The individual's unique viewpoint, way of thinking, and valuation of themselves and the world (both humanity as a whole and other individuals) are called *private logic* in Adlerian psychology. This *private logic* can create non-constructive (and occasionally destructive) interpretations, making life more difficult and causing friction with one's surroundings. These warped perceptions and self-defeating thoughts are known as *basic mistakes*.

In this way, people do not perceive events in an objective way as they really are, but rather see them subjectively through their own cognition and in their own unique way as an individual reality. Adlerians refer to the framework of understanding this reality as *cognitivism*.

From the World of Assumptions to Common Sense

In the opening section of *What Life Should Mean to You,* Adler himself wrote, "People live in a realm of meaning. We don't experience things the way they are. We only experience things that have meaning to people." He continued with the following: "People cannot escape meaning. We are always experiencing reality through the meaning we attach to it."

For example, even if ten people experience the same event, they are going to have ten different interpretations of that event. Truly, there are as many opinions as there are people. Each person takes the experience in a different way. Some might say it was miserable, while others might say it was a valuable experience. There might be another person who said it was neither miserable nor a valuable experience, but rather an utterly normal one. Each person, according to their own experiences and knowledge, has a unique interpretation and experiences things in their own way.

From the point of view of cognitivism, people's memories are not always accurate. When asked many times by a counselor if they were abused by their parents when they were young or if their parents' poor relationship is still affecting them in the present, some children who are suspected of having problems with their parents begin talking about how they were beaten by their father or how their mother kept taking them back to her parents' house, even when these events may not have actually happened.

According to Adler, "People make memories." Objectively, what actually happened is also important, but finding out how the person remembers it will provide some insight into the person.

In Yukari's case, she conflated her father and Director Makimura as well as her one-year-older brother and Nomura in a cognitive distortion because of her childhood history. She also showed her tendency to make assumptions by thinking that she was deliberately being left out of consideration for the overseas opening. These actions show that, as Adler put it, "People can't experience the actual truth. They live in a world of assumptions." In the manga, the ghost of Adler also informed Yukari that she had strong assumptions through which she filtered everything.

From the perspective of cognitivism, you can understand that everyone lives in a world of assumptions and that understanding the pattern of their assumptions is the key to understanding people. In addition, the bridge to leaving the world of assumptions and crossing over to ordinary, healthy common sense is empathy.

[How People See Things]

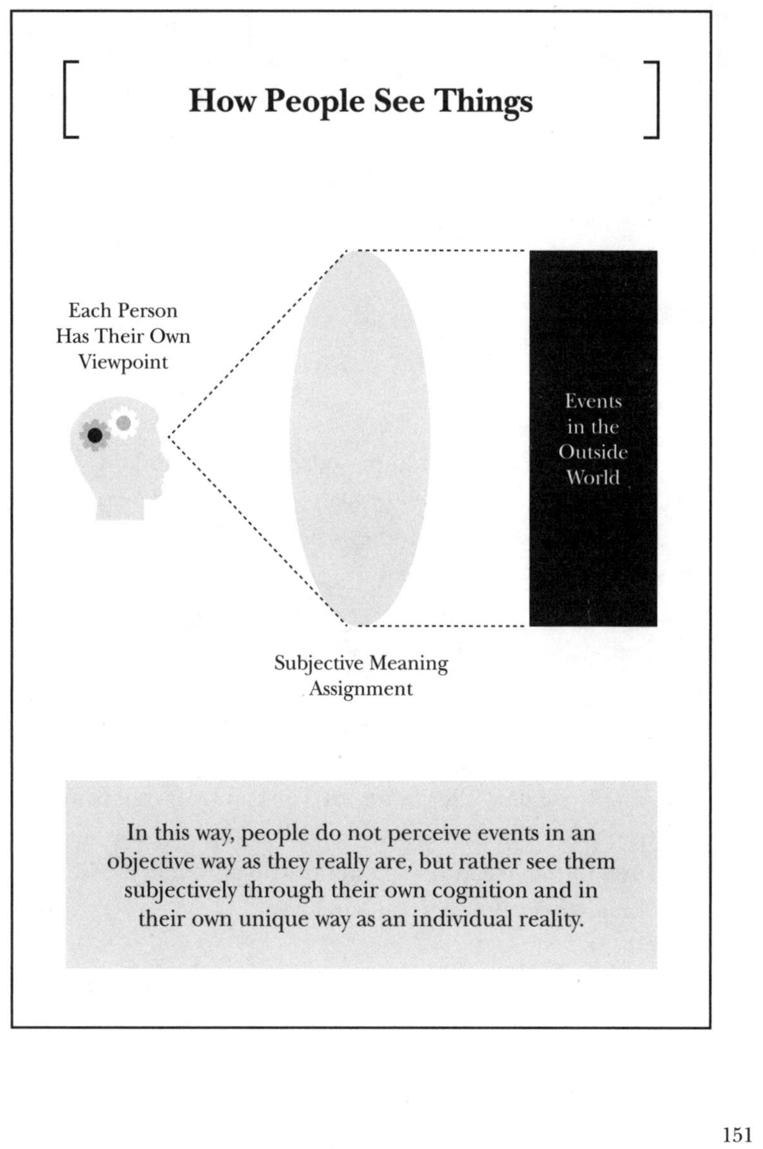
Each Person
Has Their Own
Viewpoint
Events
in the
Outside
World
Subjective Meaning
Assignment

In this way, people do not perceive events in an objective way as they really are, but rather see them subjectively through their own cognition and in their own unique way as an individual reality.

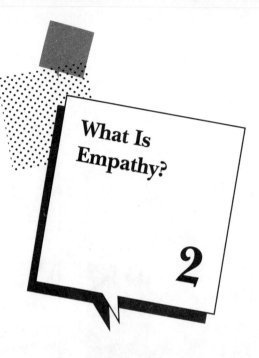

What Is Empathy?

2

⇨ Caring About Your Partner's Thoughts, Feelings, and Current Situation

Empathy is having an open heart toward others' emotions, thoughts, and conditions. In Part 1, we touched lightly on how an attitude of empathy is necessary to develop common sense when we studied how Adler often said, "Look with another's eyes. Hear with another's ears. Feel with another's heart." In Part 3's story, Adler advised Yukari to empathize by becoming Makimura, saying, "See with your partner's eyes, hear with your partner's ears, and feel with your partner's heart."

When you read Adler's books, you can see that he liked this expression, often using the word *partner* to mean others or children. If you use Adler's pattern, you can treat others with empathy. See yourself as elderly when dealing with the elderly, as a patient when treating patients as a doctor, or as a customer when helping customers as an employee.

With that in mind, this is how I define empathy: Empathy is having an open heart for others' emotions, thoughts, and conditions.

⇒ The Difference Between Empathy and Sympathy

Some people may believe that feeling sympathy for others is the same as having empathy for them, but in Adlerian psychology, these are not the same. The chart below highlights the differences. As you can see, sympathy can bring about unwanted effects.

Differences Between Empathy and Sympathy

	Empathy	Sympathy
Base	Respect and trust	Dominance
Open heart	Partner	Self
Emotions	Begins with trust and tends to be controllable	Begins with pity and tends to be uncontrollable

Sympathy can sometimes have undesirable side-effects.

As you can see in the first row of the chart, sympathy is about doing something from a position of power for a weaker partner in a domineering manner, whereas empathy is about respect and trust for your partner. The second row shows that empathy is about having an open heart for your partner's true feelings, while you just act on what's in your heart once you've entered sympathy mode. In the third row, empathy has good self-control, but with sympathy, your compassion for your partner takes prominence and you may lose control of your emotions.

Before I studied Adlerian psychology, I had the following experience. There was a person crossing an intersection using a white cane. They were crossing a large intersection while relying on sound. Eventually, the signal began to flash, so I placed my hands on their shoulders and guided them to the median. But instead of expressing gratitude for my kindness, the person acted like they were going to hit me with their cane. I felt that my kindness had been for nothing. After the fact, I learned that the blind person was most likely accustomed to crossing to that median. They were probably trying to cross while relying on sound and counting their steps with their cane, so they had likely gotten angry at me for interfering.

I had acted on sympathetic feelings without really seeing how that person was or trying to understand them. I just put my hands on their shoulders and made a mess of things. I had fallen, I fell under the three negative effects of sympathy: I tried to do something for a weaker partner from a position of strength, I didn't think about their feelings and acted only on

my own, and I lost control of my emotions. I doubt I am the
only one who has had this kind of experience. Many people
have likely found themselves in a similar situation. It's very
easy to feel sympathy. Empathy, however, occasionally requires
patience and tolerance—not just respect and trust. In this way,
empathy and sympathy are different.

The key to preserving a rich interpersonal relationship is
empathy that does not flow into sympathy.

⇒ Methods to Train Your Empathy

How do we sustain ourselves in empathy mode to avoid falling
into sympathy mode, forgetting ourselves, ending up causing
problems for our partner, and regretting our actions?

I first recommend *employing your self-monitoring system when
dealing with your partner.* It might be good to think of this
as a television monitor that you can use to check your own
behaviors as well as your partner's actions. As I said in the
section on common sense in Part 1, seize the moment and use
it to stop yourself one step before falling into the sympathy
danger zone.

The second method is to *train yourself to see things with a
different private logic.* We perceive things in the outside world

subjectively, but our glasses are all warped in different ways. This should be easy to understand if you remember the happenings between Yukari and Kiba over the POP in Part 2. Even though Yukari as area manager was trying to push the same POP on all of her stores, Kiba was thinking of her predominantly elderly customers and refused the small font POP, needing the menu written in larger type. When the two of them got into a struggle for authority, it would have been best to calmly take a step back and review things from their partner's private logic. And not only from the point of view of their partner—even a third party would be fine. If you can step away from your own private logic and view things, you might discover points that you wouldn't have thought of.

The third method is to *use meta-cognition*. The *meta* in meta-cognition means to transcend or surpass, so meta-cognition is borrowing a concept from the most recent cognitive psychology. Meta-cognition is said to be seeing things from one step above your own cognition. In the manga, the ghost of Adler is trying to manage Yukari's meta-cognition. At this point, its existence is helping Yukari to correct the distortions in her own cognition, but even if Dr. Adler disappears, she'll be able to grow into a more empathic person who can view things from a step above, using her own cognitive activities and correcting her own mistakes.

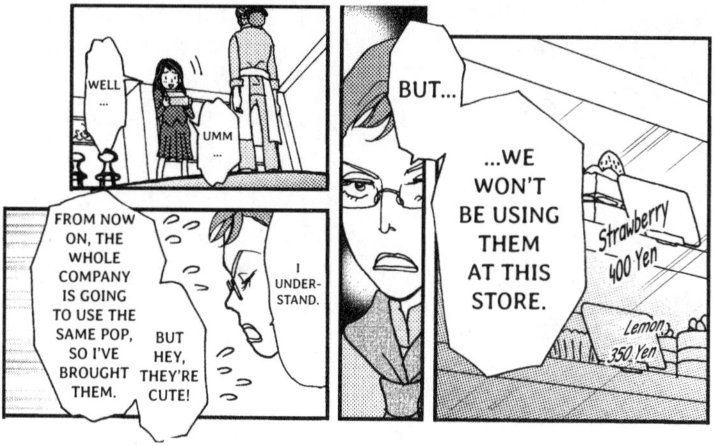
WELL ...
UMM ...
FROM NOW ON, THE WHOLE COMPANY IS GOING TO USE THE SAME POP, SO I'VE BROUGHT THEM.
BUT HEY, THEY'RE CUTE!
I UNDER-STAND.
BUT...
...WE WON'T BE USING THEM AT THIS STORE.
Strawberry 400 Yen
Lemon 350 Yen

Kiba curtly refuses the POP that Yukari brought for all of the stores.

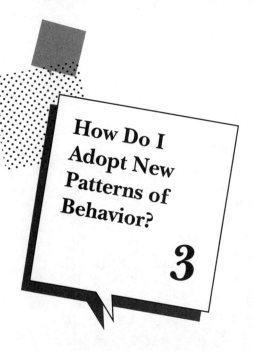

How Do I Adopt New Patterns of Behavior?

3

⇨ The Three Cycles

In the story from Part 1 to Part 3, Yukari has grown by training herself to look at things through a different private logic while using her self-monitoring system and training her empathy with Dr. Adler's instruction on meta-cognition. However, at the end of Part 3's manga, she's unintentionally shown the common second child tendency to see things as win-lose. In this chapter, I'll provide the know-how to adopt new patterns of behavior. As illustrated in the chart below, there are three cycles in the development of new patterns.

The Three Cycles of Adopting New Patterns

Mastery
Capability
Understanding
Decision
Implementation
Continuance
① Unconsciously Skillful
② Consciously Unskillful
③ Consciously Skillful

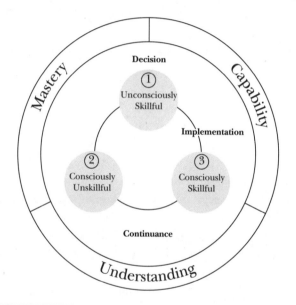

① At this stage, you can do your past patterns unconsciously.

② At this stage, you consciously try new patterns, but can only do them unskillfully.

③ While continuing your new patterns, you can do them consciously and skillfully.

Let's look at them in order.

The first cycle is going from understanding to capability to mastery. No matter how much someone else explains how to do something, if you can't understand it logically, then you won't decide to do it.

Next is actually trying something to see how much you can do. At this stage, if the goal is too high, you might get discouraged and lose the will to keep trying. The final stage is repeating the behavior over and over until mastery is achieved.

The second cycle is going from decision to implementation to continuance. The first step in this cycle is deciding to give something a try. Next is the actual trying. At this stage, it is not important to be perfect—even a half-hearted attempt is all right. After that is continuance. Even at this step, it is okay to fall off the wagon. Even if you take a few days off, if you begin again, you will eventually have spent enough days in a year doing the new activity, and that is a great thing. My recommendation is when you fall down, which you will, pick yourself up and keep going. It's important not to give up even if you take a break.

The third cycle is going from unconsciously skillful to consciously unskillful to consciously skillful. Before trying something new, you may be good at a certain pattern, but unconsciously so. This is unconsciously skillful. From this stage, if you attempt a new pattern, it will feel strange. For example, if you had a habit of locking your fingers together, but you tried to lock them backward, you won't be unable to do it, but it will feel off. This is consciously unskilled. But if you continue this new pattern, it will become familiar. This is consciously skillful.

⇒ How to Overcome Being Consciously Unskilled

Now, let's take a look at your habits. A *habit* is an unconsciously skillful action that has turned into a pattern. Drinking alcohol, smoking, fast eating, impulse buying, staying up late, sleeping in, and so on are all just actions that you started repeating without realizing it. In a comfortable environment, if an action is unconscious and skillful, it will become a pattern of behavior.

At some point, you will realize that your habits need to change. As shown in the chart, when you decide to behave differently amid feelings of discomfort and strangeness, the consciously unskilled step will be waiting for you. You will have to consciously observe every aspect of yourself while encouraging improvement in your unskilled areas as you continue to try and conquer your previously held patterns.

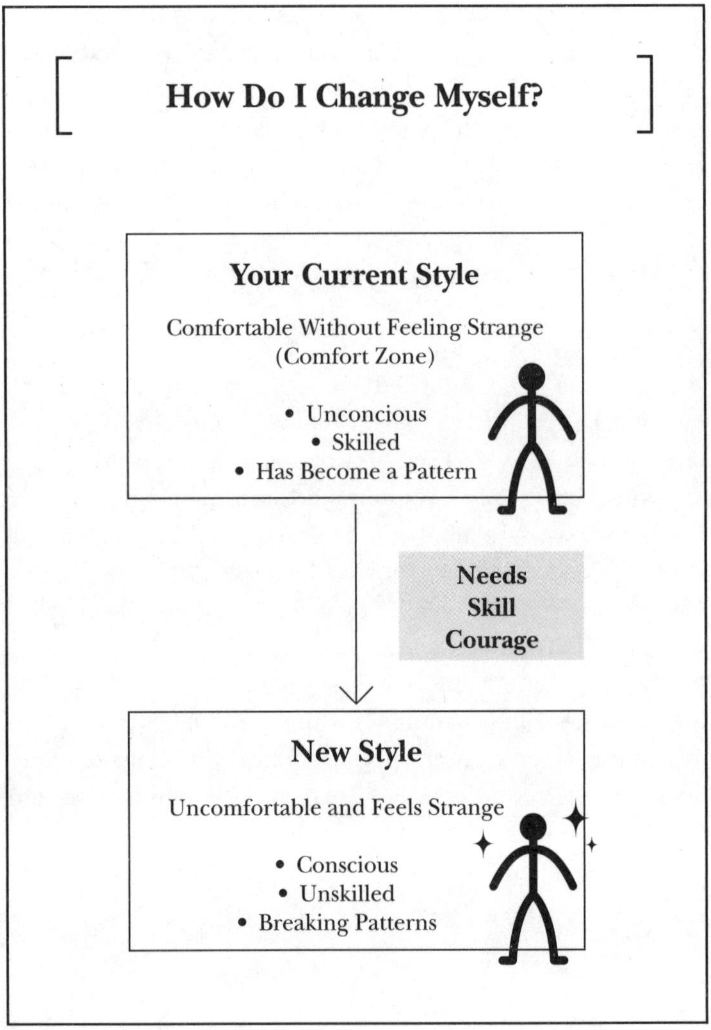
How Do I Change Myself?
Your Current Style
Comfortable Without Feeling Strange
(Comfort Zone)
• Unconcious
• Skilled
• Has Become a Pattern
Needs
Skill
Courage
New Style
Uncomfortable and Feels Strange
• Conscious
• Unskilled
• Breaking Patterns

Changing yourself is like replacing your old worn-in shoes with new ones, but then getting blisters. Many people would think, "Well, if it's this strange and uncomfortable, then I'll just stick with my old comfy shoes." Individuals in the process of change often revert to their comfort zone. But if they feel a strong need to change their current habits, have a concrete skill, and have the courage to overcome difficulties, they can take up their new style knowing that a difficult and uncomfortable stage is part of the process.

Let's take for example a person who has decided to go on a diet in preparation for the summer. This person's needs are a slim, shapely body. In order to lose fifteen pounds in three months, they decide to burn calories by going to the gym three times a week and walking as much as they can. They start eating more vegetables and cut their intake of rice and other carbohydrates in half, deciding to reduce their daily intake by 300 calories. They also decide to lay off the sweets and chew gum if they feel a craving. They also cut the intake of their beloved beer in half. They know that doing this in secret might cause trouble for the people around them, so they let everyone know about the diet.

After keeping this up for a month, there was little change in their body weight. But after the second month, the difference was easily noticeable.

At this point, they feel a sense of accomplishment, like "Hey, I really can do this!" and it becomes easy to continue. This is when they enter the consciously skilled phase. It is the same feeling of self-confidence and courage you get when you go from not being able to do something to being able to do it well, like learning to ride a bike. In this way, as a challenge becomes second nature and you decide to take up new challenges and begin trying new things one after another, you'll grow content not only with your actions, but also with your emotions and your thoughts.

⇒ How to Avoid the Contingency Trap

You will need to consider one more thing when adopting a new pattern of behavior: the *contingency trap*. Contingency is when an action or happening becomes intertwined with another action or happening. You need to know that previous actions that have become patterns can end up changing into other patterns. For example, drinking alcohol often becomes intertwined with eating, stress relief, communication, and ceremonies and may even become necessary to fall asleep.

People who drink alcohol with breakfast are extremely rare, but there are many people who have a beer with dinner. In this case, drinking beer is connected with stress relief and acts as a diversion, so even if you don't drink beer, having a beer-flavored drink and saying, "Job well done!" to yourself may be enough to accomplish the same goal.

As another example, you may meet friends at a bar after work to chit-chat. You may feel elated, and you might say things you normally wouldn't, livening up the communication. However, if work communication is the point, it should be done at the office. You wouldn't want to speak your mind and say something that you would later regret. At ceremonies such as weddings, you could toast, have just a little alcohol, and then switch to coffee or tea.

In order to escape the contingency trap that may exist when you consume alcohol, you should ask yourself why you are drinking alcohol and then switch to another drink or activity. Adlerian psychology teaches that *you are not controlled by your environment or habits—rather, you shape and control them.*

Adler, the Encourager

In *Alfred Adler: As We Remember Him,* I was introduced to an unforgettable episode of Adler's. It happened when Adler was invited by his wife to the house of an acquaintance, Mrs. F. The three of them were going to the city together, but decided to have a light meal first. When they left, Mrs. F's five-year-old son bid them farewell. When they came back, the living room floor was covered in toys. The acquaintance's son had taken out so many toys that there wasn't any place to step. Mrs. F. was so angry she was visibly shaking and was turning red, but when she seemed about to unleash her anger, Adler approached the son and said kindly, "You did a great job spreading these toys out. Can you do a great job cleaning them up?" In less than a minute, all of the toys had been cleaned up and returned to their place.

Some psychologists might have approached the child and said, "Little boy, you were lonely, right? An older man took your mom, so you got angry, right?" and then taught them that it still wasn't okay to do that. But standing in the place of the child, having faith in the child's abilities, accepting the situation, and having the ability to look with a child's eyes, hear with their ears, and feel with their heart, Adler—with his strong sense of empathy, even though he had just met the child—was able to draw out the child's ability to resolve the situation without anyone getting hurt by simply saying, "You did a great job spreading these toys out. Can you do a great job cleaning them up?" This, to me, is the perfect example of encouragement.

Part 4

Interpersonal Relationships and Emotions

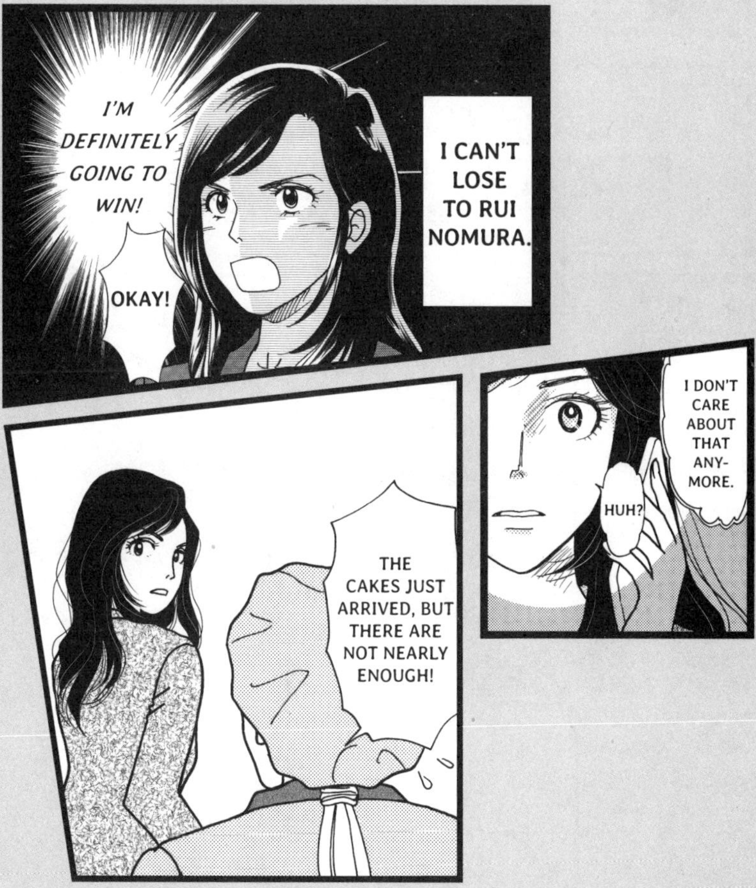
I'M DEFINITELY GOING TO WIN!
OKAY!
I CAN'T LOSE TO RUI NOMURA.
THE CAKES JUST ARRIVED, BUT THERE ARE NOT NEARLY ENOUGH!
I DON'T CARE ABOUT THAT ANY-MORE.
HUH?

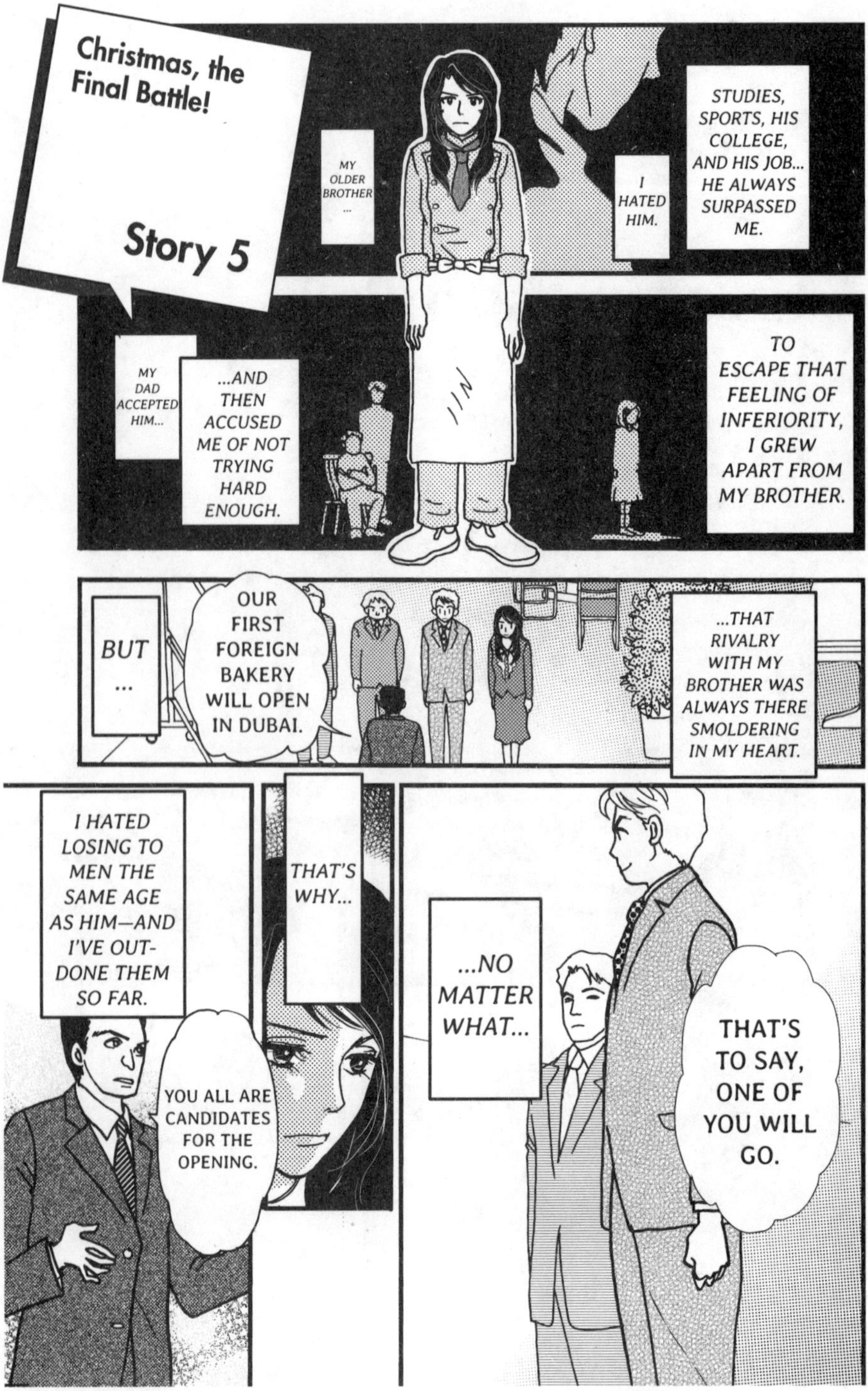

Christmas, the Final Battle!
Story 5
MY OLDER BROTHER ...
I HATED HIM.
STUDIES, SPORTS, HIS COLLEGE, AND HIS JOB... HE ALWAYS SURPASSED ME.
MY DAD ACCEPTED HIM...
...AND THEN ACCUSED ME OF NOT TRYING HARD ENOUGH.
TO ESCAPE THAT FEELING OF INFERIORITY, I GREW APART FROM MY BROTHER.
BUT ...
OUR FIRST FOREIGN BAKERY WILL OPEN IN DUBAI.
...THAT RIVALRY WITH MY BROTHER WAS ALWAYS THERE SMOLDERING IN MY HEART.
I HATED LOSING TO MEN THE SAME AGE AS HIM—AND I'VE OUT-DONE THEM SO FAR.
THAT'S WHY...
YOU ALL ARE CANDIDATES FOR THE OPENING.
...NO MATTER WHAT...
THAT'S TO SAY, ONE OF YOU WILL GO.

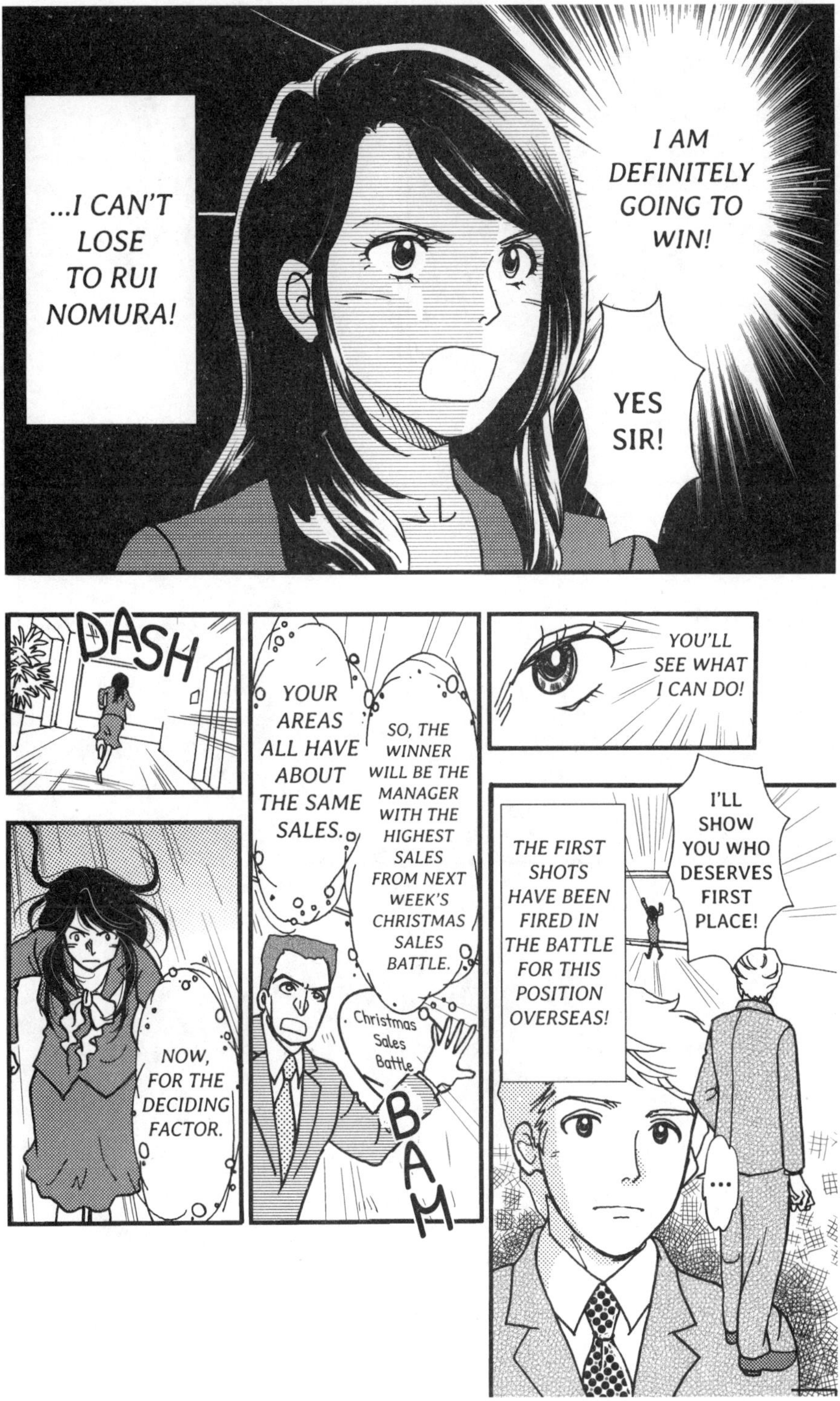

...I CAN'T LOSE TO RUI NOMURA!
YES SIR!
I AM DEFINITELY GOING TO WIN!
DASH
YOUR AREAS ALL HAVE ABOUT THE SAME SALES.
SO, THE WINNER WILL BE THE MANAGER WITH THE HIGHEST SALES FROM NEXT WEEK'S CHRISTMAS SALES BATTLE.
NOW, FOR THE DECIDING FACTOR.
Christmas Sales Battle
BAM
YOU'LL SEE WHAT I CAN DO!
THE FIRST SHOTS HAVE BEEN FIRED IN THE BATTLE FOR THIS POSITION OVERSEAS!
I'LL SHOW YOU WHO DESERVES FIRST PLACE!
...

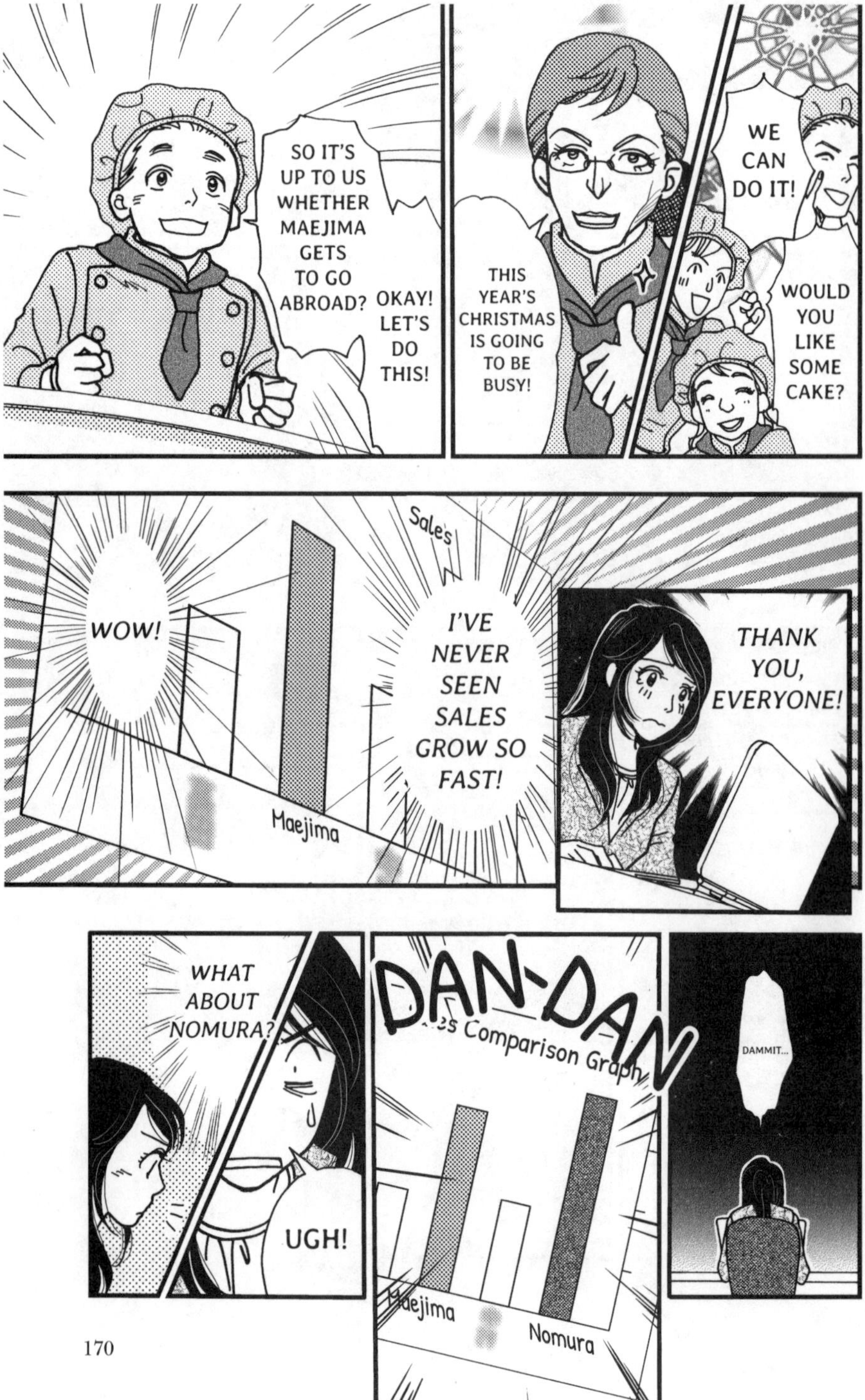
SO IT'S UP TO US WHETHER MAEJIMA GETS TO GO ABROAD?
OKAY! LET'S DO THIS!
THIS YEAR'S CHRISTMAS IS GOING TO BE BUSY!
WE CAN DO IT!
WOULD YOU LIKE SOME CAKE?
Sale's
WOW!
I'VE NEVER SEEN SALES GROW SO FAST!
Maejima
THANK YOU, EVERYONE!
WHAT ABOUT NOMURA?
UGH!
DAN-DAN
Comparison Graph
Maejima
Nomura
DAMMIT...

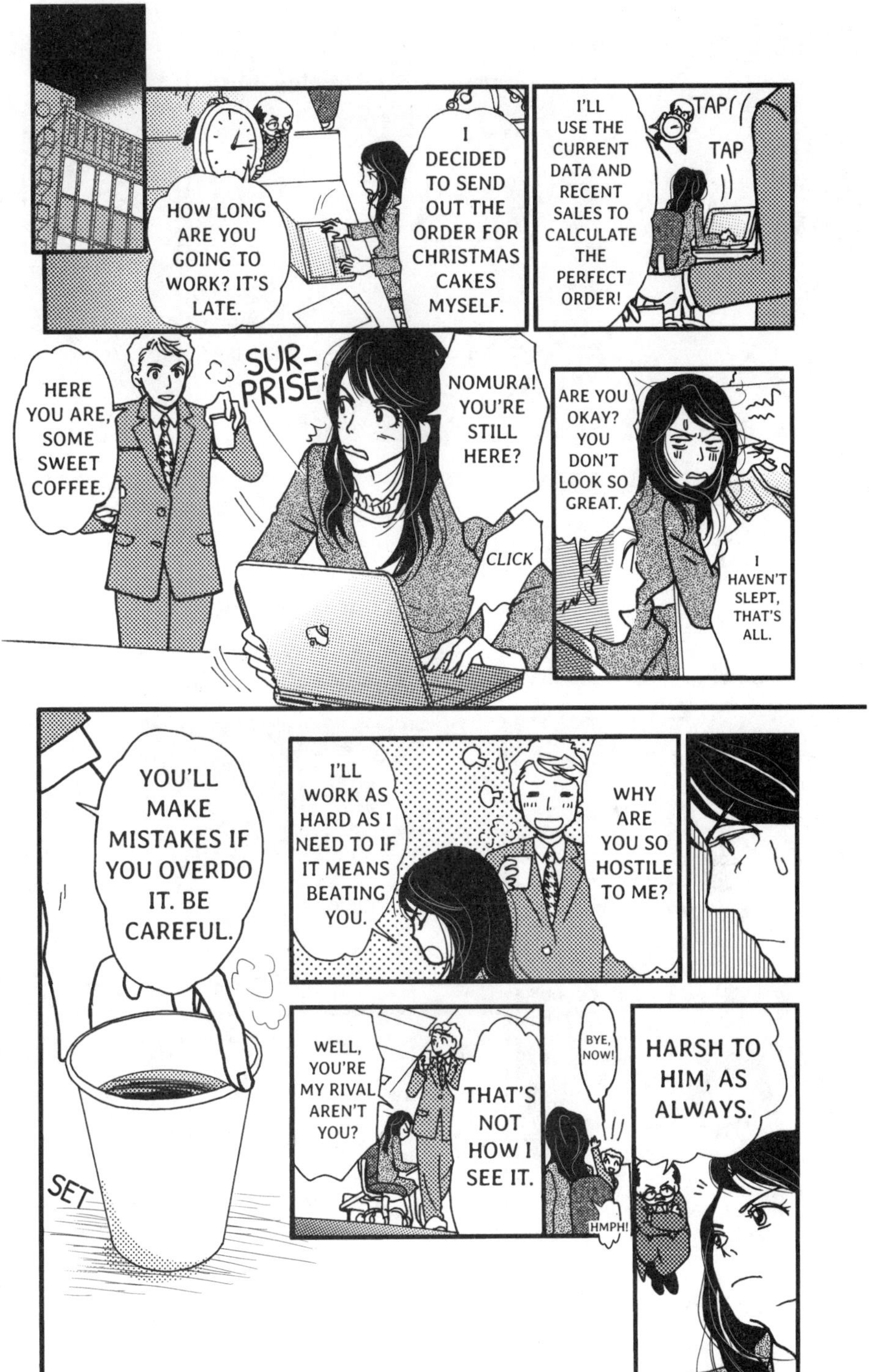
HOW LONG ARE YOU GOING TO WORK? IT'S LATE.
I DECIDED TO SEND OUT THE ORDER FOR CHRISTMAS CAKES MYSELF.
I'LL USE THE CURRENT DATA AND RECENT SALES TO CALCULATE THE PERFECT ORDER!
TAP
TAP
HERE YOU ARE, SOME SWEET COFFEE.
SUR-PRISE
NOMURA! YOU'RE STILL HERE?
CLICK
ARE YOU OKAY? YOU DON'T LOOK SO GREAT.
I HAVEN'T SLEPT, THAT'S ALL.
YOU'LL MAKE MISTAKES IF YOU OVERDO IT. BE CAREFUL.
SET
I'LL WORK AS HARD AS I NEED TO IF IT MEANS BEATING YOU.
WHY ARE YOU SO HOSTILE TO ME?
WELL, YOU'RE MY RIVAL AREN'T YOU?
THAT'S NOT HOW I SEE IT.
BYE, NOW!
HMPH!
HARSH TO HIM, AS ALWAYS.

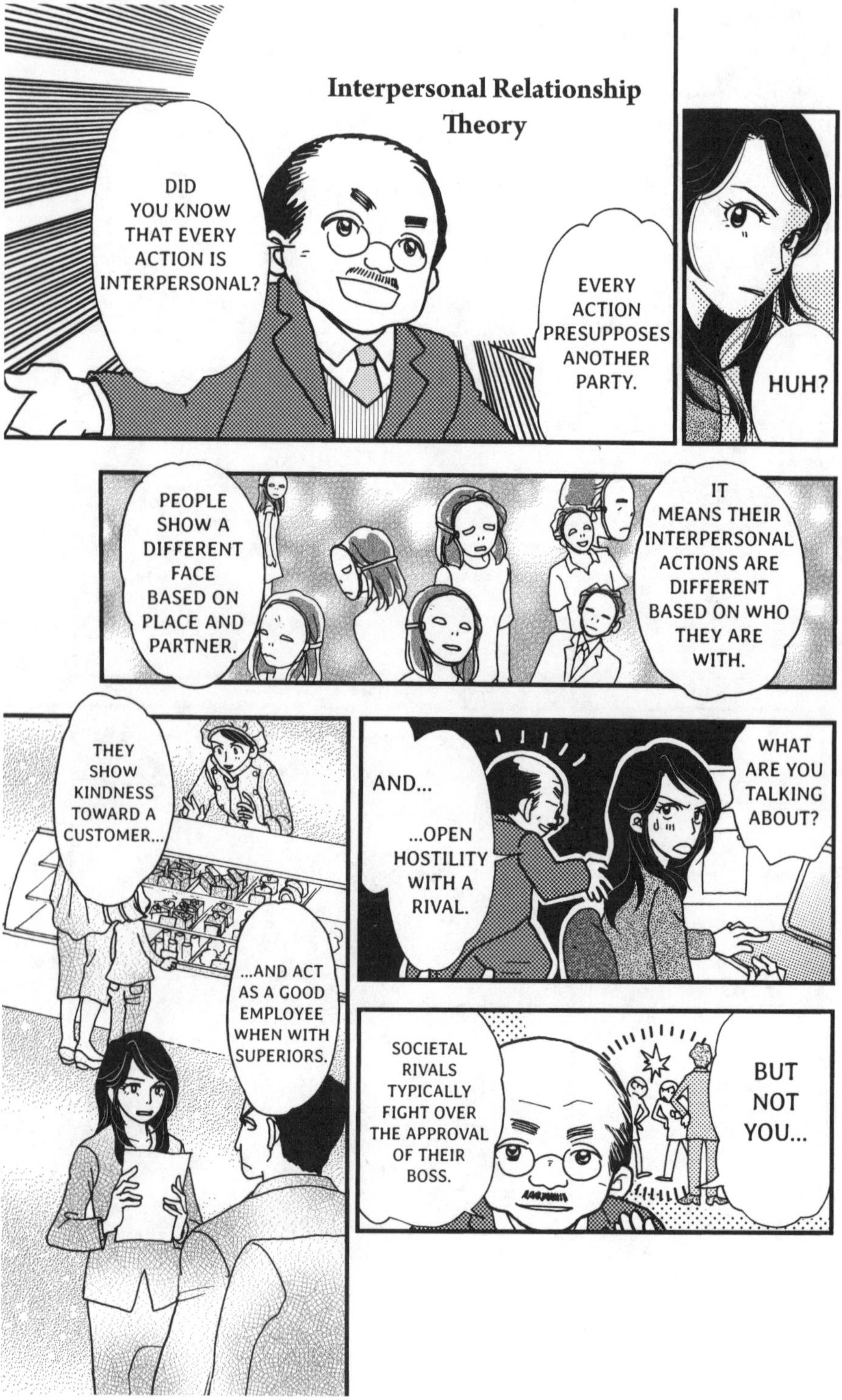
Interpersonal Relationship Theory
DID YOU KNOW THAT EVERY ACTION IS INTERPERSONAL?
EVERY ACTION PRESUPPOSES ANOTHER PARTY.
HUH?
PEOPLE SHOW A DIFFERENT FACE BASED ON PLACE AND PARTNER.
IT MEANS THEIR INTERPERSONAL ACTIONS ARE DIFFERENT BASED ON WHO THEY ARE WITH.
THEY SHOW KINDNESS TOWARD A CUSTOMER...
...AND ACT AS A GOOD EMPLOYEE WHEN WITH SUPERIORS.
AND...
...OPEN HOSTILITY WITH A RIVAL.
WHAT ARE YOU TALKING ABOUT?
SOCIETAL RIVALS TYPICALLY FIGHT OVER THE APPROVAL OF THEIR BOSS.
BUT NOT YOU...

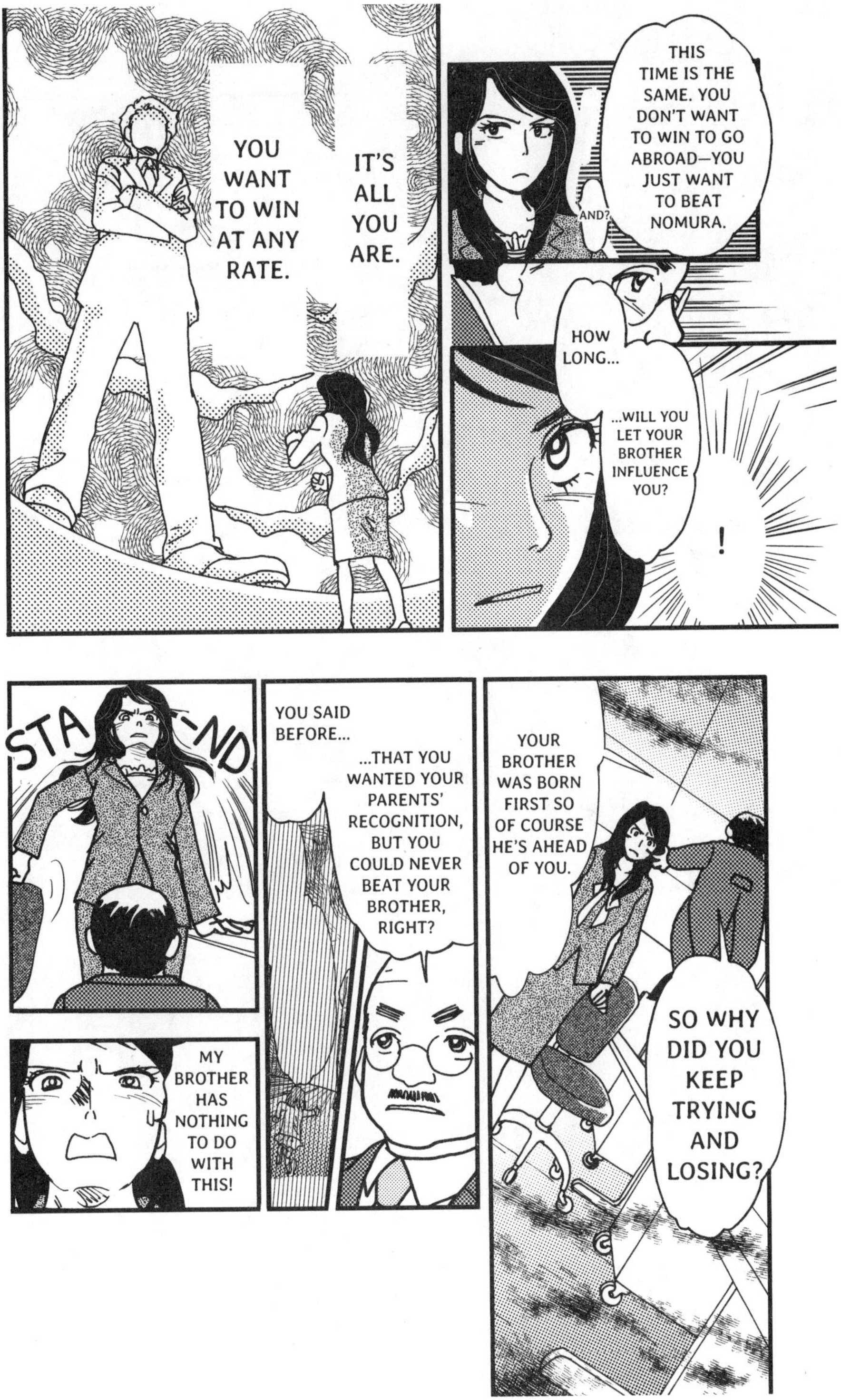
YOU WANT TO WIN AT ANY RATE.
IT'S ALL YOU ARE.
THIS TIME IS THE SAME. YOU DON'T WANT TO WIN TO GO ABROAD—YOU JUST WANT TO BEAT NOMURA.
AND?
HOW LONG...
...WILL YOU LET YOUR BROTHER INFLUENCE YOU?
!
STA-ND
YOU SAID BEFORE...
...THAT YOU WANTED YOUR PARENTS' RECOGNITION, BUT YOU COULD NEVER BEAT YOUR BROTHER, RIGHT?
YOUR BROTHER WAS BORN FIRST SO OF COURSE HE'S AHEAD OF YOU.
SO WHY DID YOU KEEP TRYING AND LOSING?
MY BROTHER HAS NOTHING TO DO WITH THIS!

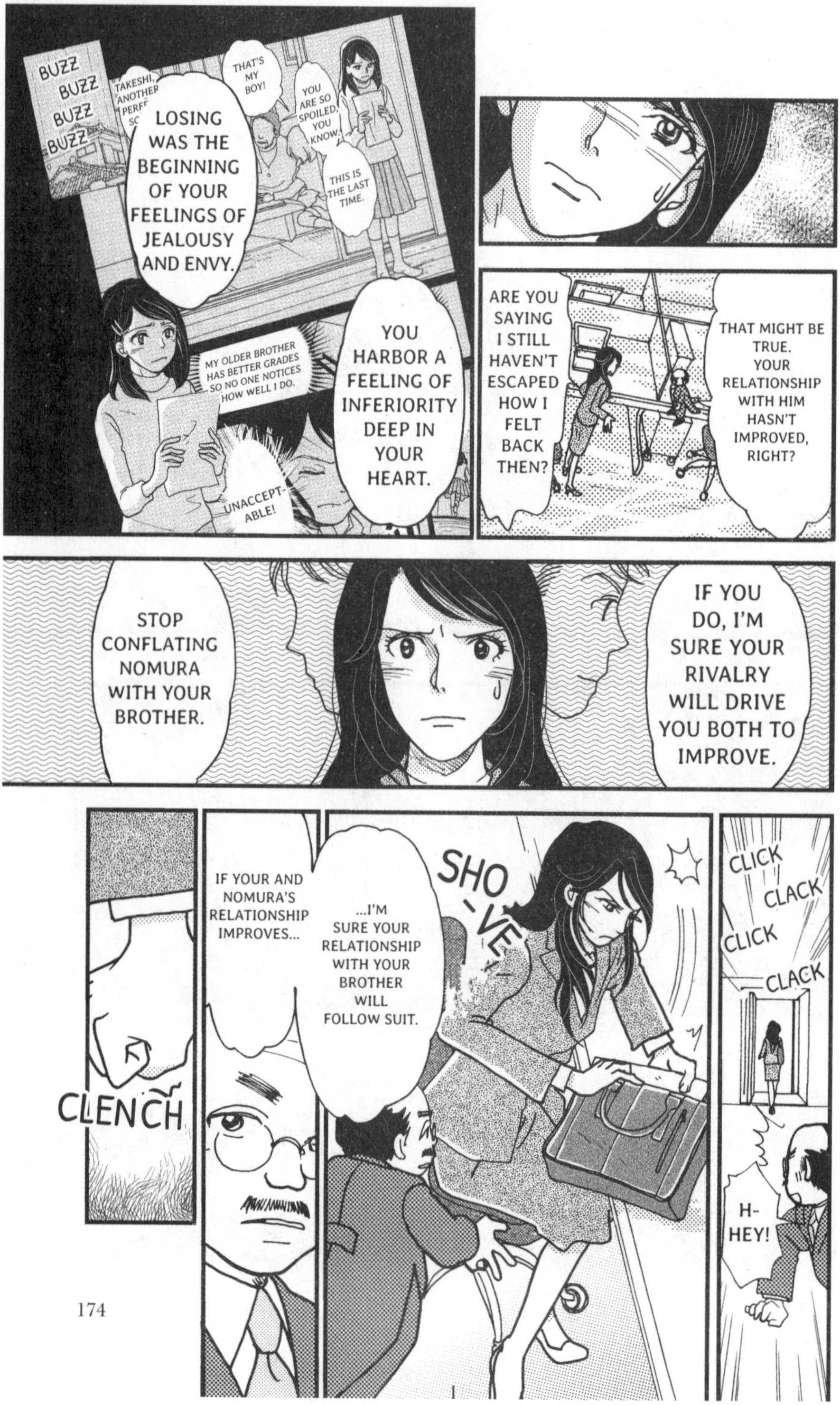
BUZZ BUZZ BUZZ BUZZ
TAKESHI, ANOTHER PERF
THAT'S MY BOY!
YOU ARE SO SPOILED, YOU KNOW.
THIS IS THE LAST TIME.
LOSING WAS THE BEGINNING OF YOUR FEELINGS OF JEALOUSY AND ENVY.
MY OLDER BROTHER HAS BETTER GRADES SO NO ONE NOTICES HOW WELL I DO.
UNACCEPT-ABLE!
YOU HARBOR A FEELING OF INFERIORITY DEEP IN YOUR HEART.
ARE YOU SAYING I STILL HAVEN'T ESCAPED HOW I FELT BACK THEN?
THAT MIGHT BE TRUE. YOUR RELATIONSHIP WITH HIM HASN'T IMPROVED, RIGHT?
STOP CONFLATING NOMURA WITH YOUR BROTHER.
IF YOU DO, I'M SURE YOUR RIVALRY WILL DRIVE YOU BOTH TO IMPROVE.
CLENCH
IF YOUR AND NOMURA'S RELATIONSHIP IMPROVES...
...I'M SURE YOUR RELATIONSHIP WITH YOUR BROTHER WILL FOLLOW SUIT.
SHO-VE
CLICK CLACK CLICK CLACK
H-HEY!

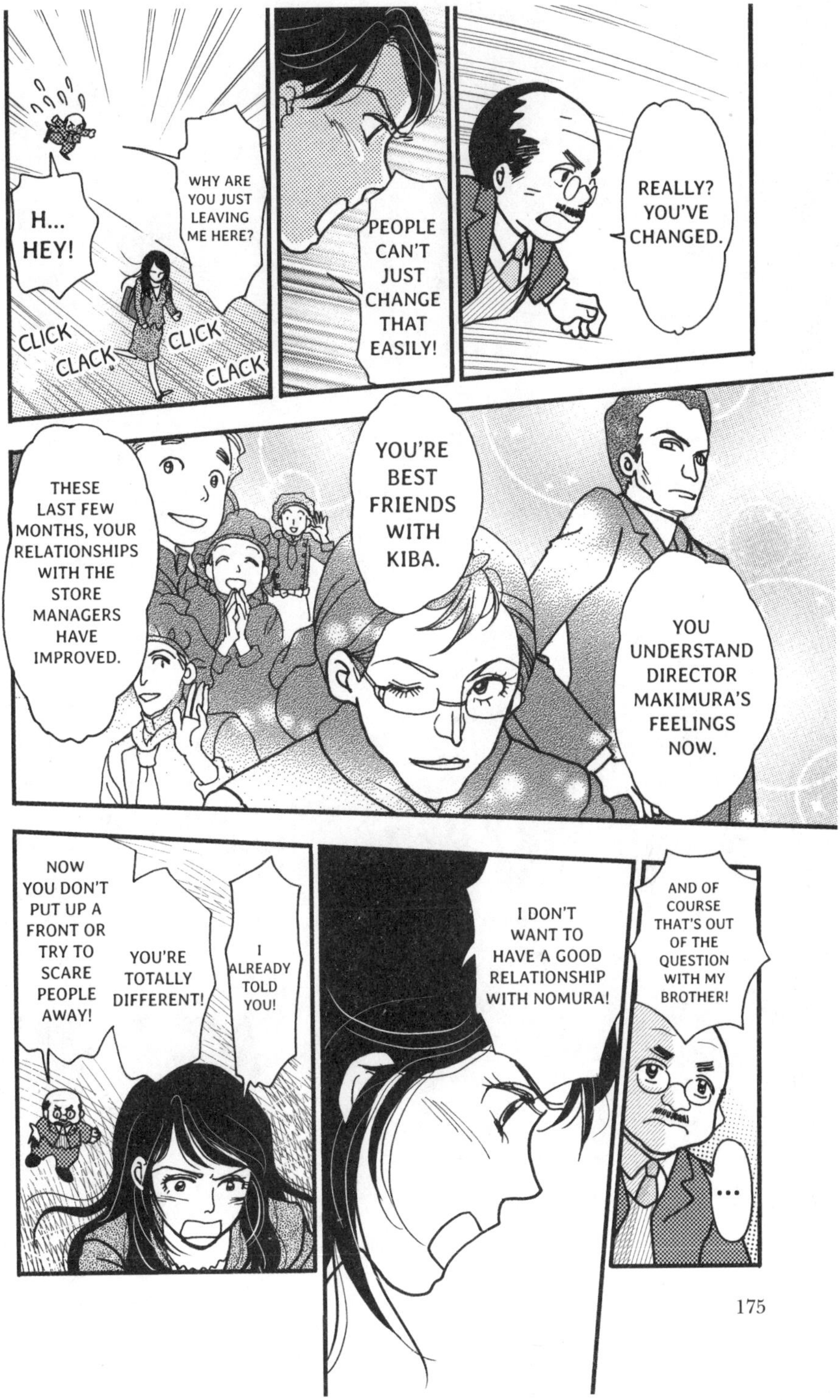
H... HEY!
WHY ARE YOU JUST LEAVING ME HERE?
CLICK CLACK CLICK CLACK
PEOPLE CAN'T JUST CHANGE THAT EASILY!
REALLY? YOU'VE CHANGED.
THESE LAST FEW MONTHS, YOUR RELATIONSHIPS WITH THE STORE MANAGERS HAVE IMPROVED.
YOU'RE BEST FRIENDS WITH KIBA.
YOU UNDERSTAND DIRECTOR MAKIMURA'S FEELINGS NOW.
NOW YOU DON'T PUT UP A FRONT OR TRY TO SCARE PEOPLE AWAY!
YOU'RE TOTALLY DIFFERENT!
I ALREADY TOLD YOU!
I DON'T WANT TO HAVE A GOOD RELATIONSHIP WITH NOMURA!
AND OF COURSE THAT'S OUT OF THE QUESTION WITH MY BROTHER!
...

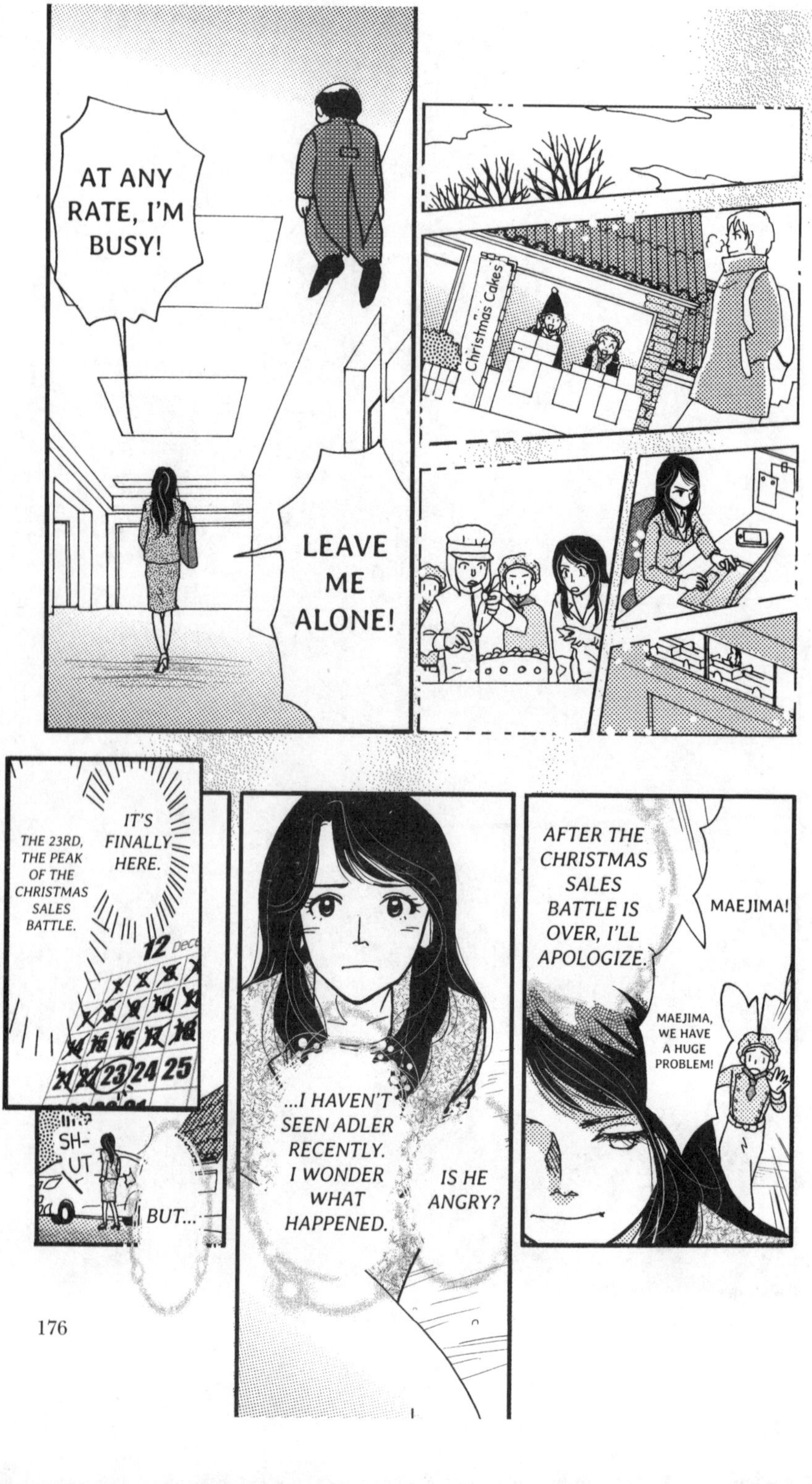
AT ANY RATE, I'M BUSY!
LEAVE ME ALONE!
Christmas Cakes
THE 23RD, THE PEAK OF THE CHRISTMAS SALES BATTLE.
IT'S FINALLY HERE.
12 Dece
14 15 16 17 18
21 22 23 24 25
SH-UT
BUT...
...I HAVEN'T SEEN ADLER RECENTLY. I WONDER WHAT HAPPENED.
IS HE ANGRY?
AFTER THE CHRISTMAS SALES BATTLE IS OVER, I'LL APOLOGIZE.
MAEJIMA!
MAEJIMA, WE HAVE A HUGE PROBLEM!

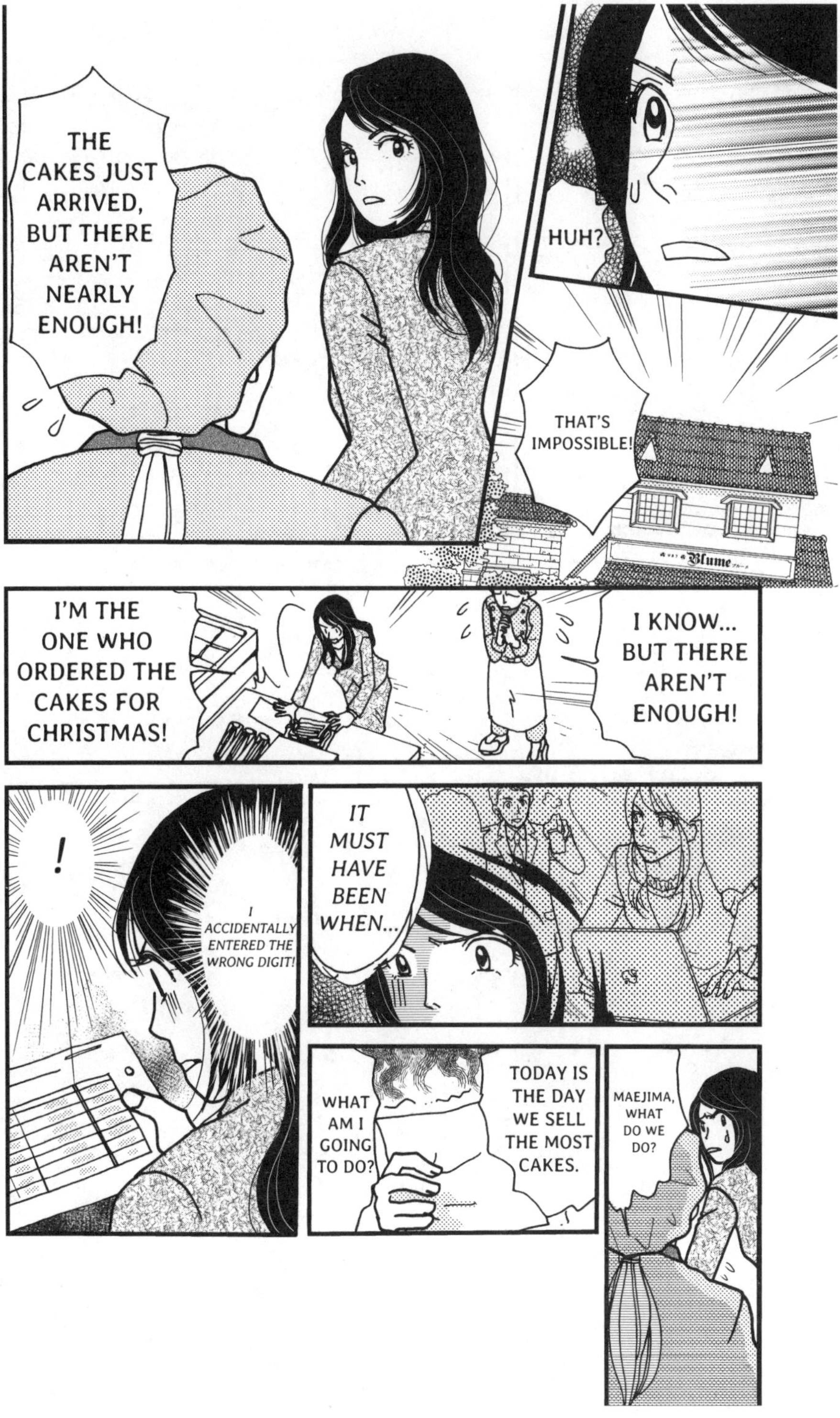
THE CAKES JUST ARRIVED, BUT THERE AREN'T NEARLY ENOUGH!
HUH?
THAT'S IMPOSSIBLE!
Blume
I'M THE ONE WHO ORDERED THE CAKES FOR CHRISTMAS!
I KNOW... BUT THERE AREN'T ENOUGH!
!
I ACCIDENTALLY ENTERED THE WRONG DIGIT!
IT MUST HAVE BEEN WHEN...
WHAT AM I GOING TO DO?
TODAY IS THE DAY WE SELL THE MOST CAKES.
MAEJIMA, WHAT DO WE DO?

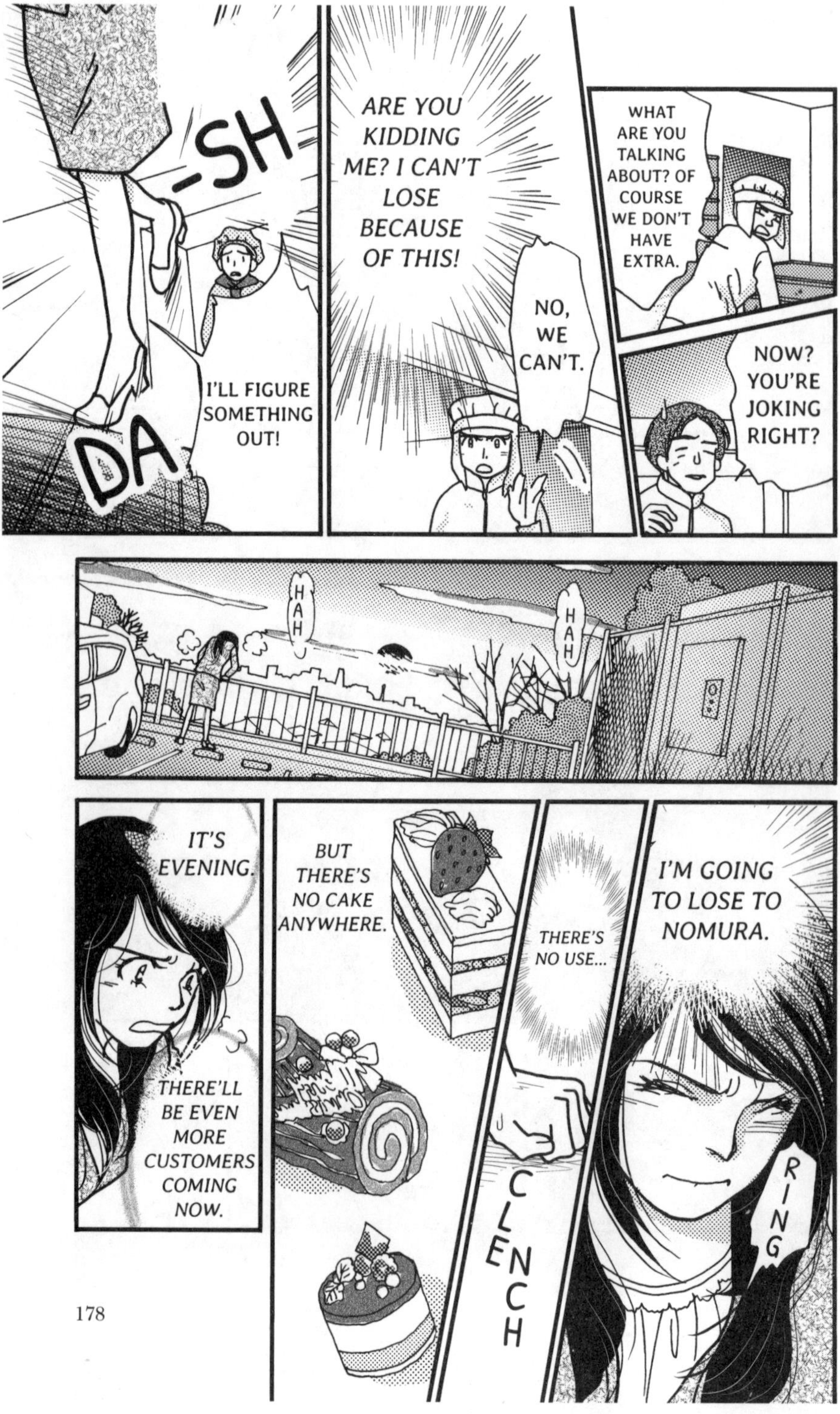
DA-SH
I'LL FIGURE SOMETHING OUT!
ARE YOU KIDDING ME? I CAN'T LOSE BECAUSE OF THIS!
NO, WE CAN'T.
WHAT ARE YOU TALKING ABOUT? OF COURSE WE DON'T HAVE EXTRA.
NOW? YOU'RE JOKING RIGHT?
HAH
HAH
IT'S EVENING.
THERE'LL BE EVEN MORE CUSTOMERS COMING NOW.
BUT THERE'S NO CAKE ANYWHERE.
THERE'S NO USE...
CLENCH
I'M GOING TO LOSE TO NOMURA.
RING

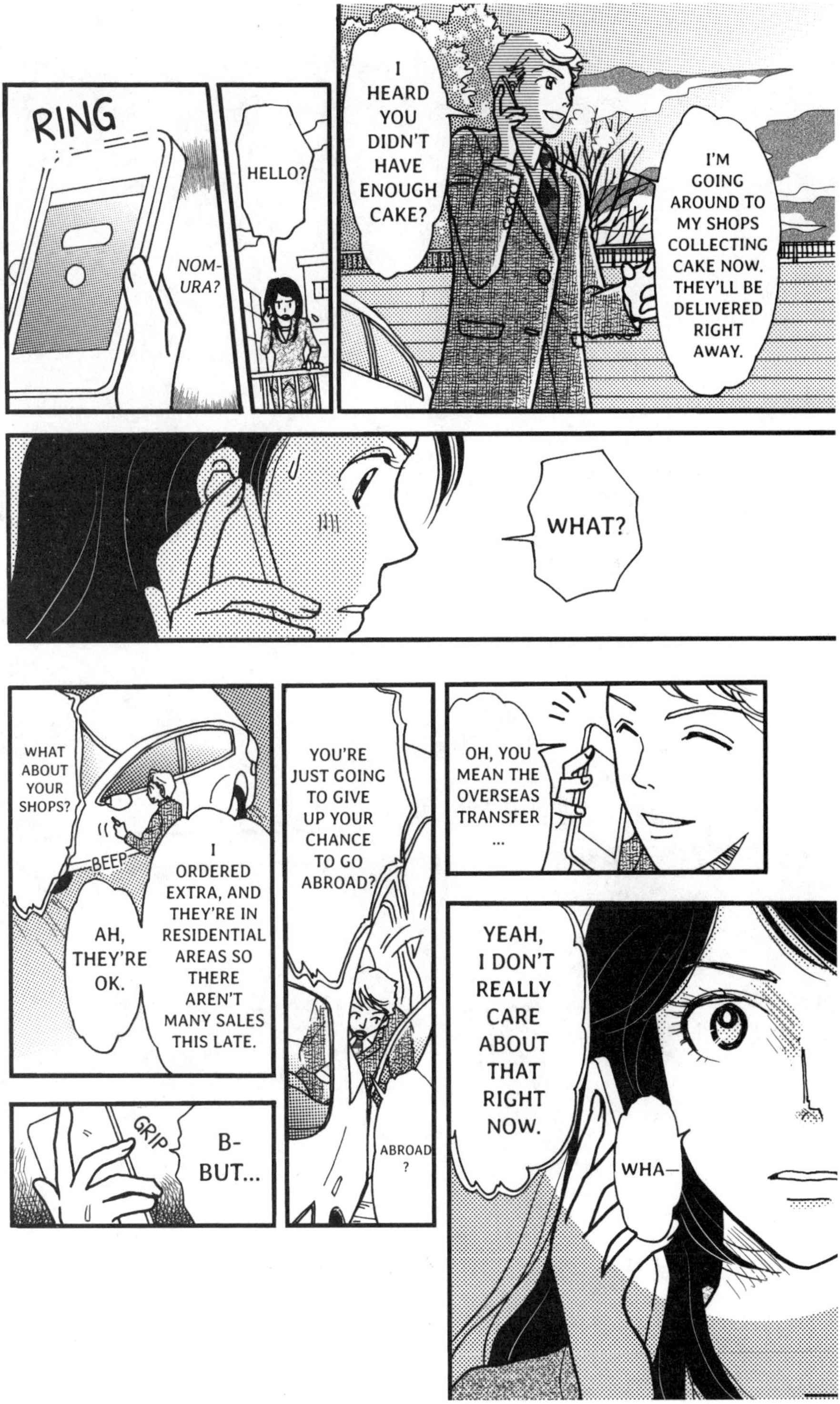
RING
NOM-URA?
HELLO?
I HEARD YOU DIDN'T HAVE ENOUGH CAKE?
I'M GOING AROUND TO MY SHOPS COLLECTING CAKE NOW. THEY'LL BE DELIVERED RIGHT AWAY.
WHAT?
OH, YOU MEAN THE OVERSEAS TRANSFER ...
YOU'RE JUST GOING TO GIVE UP YOUR CHANCE TO GO ABROAD?
WHAT ABOUT YOUR SHOPS?
BEEP
I ORDERED EXTRA, AND THEY'RE IN RESIDENTIAL AREAS SO THERE AREN'T MANY SALES THIS LATE.
AH, THEY'RE OK.
YEAH, I DON'T REALLY CARE ABOUT THAT RIGHT NOW.
WHA—
ABROAD ?
GRIP
B-BUT...

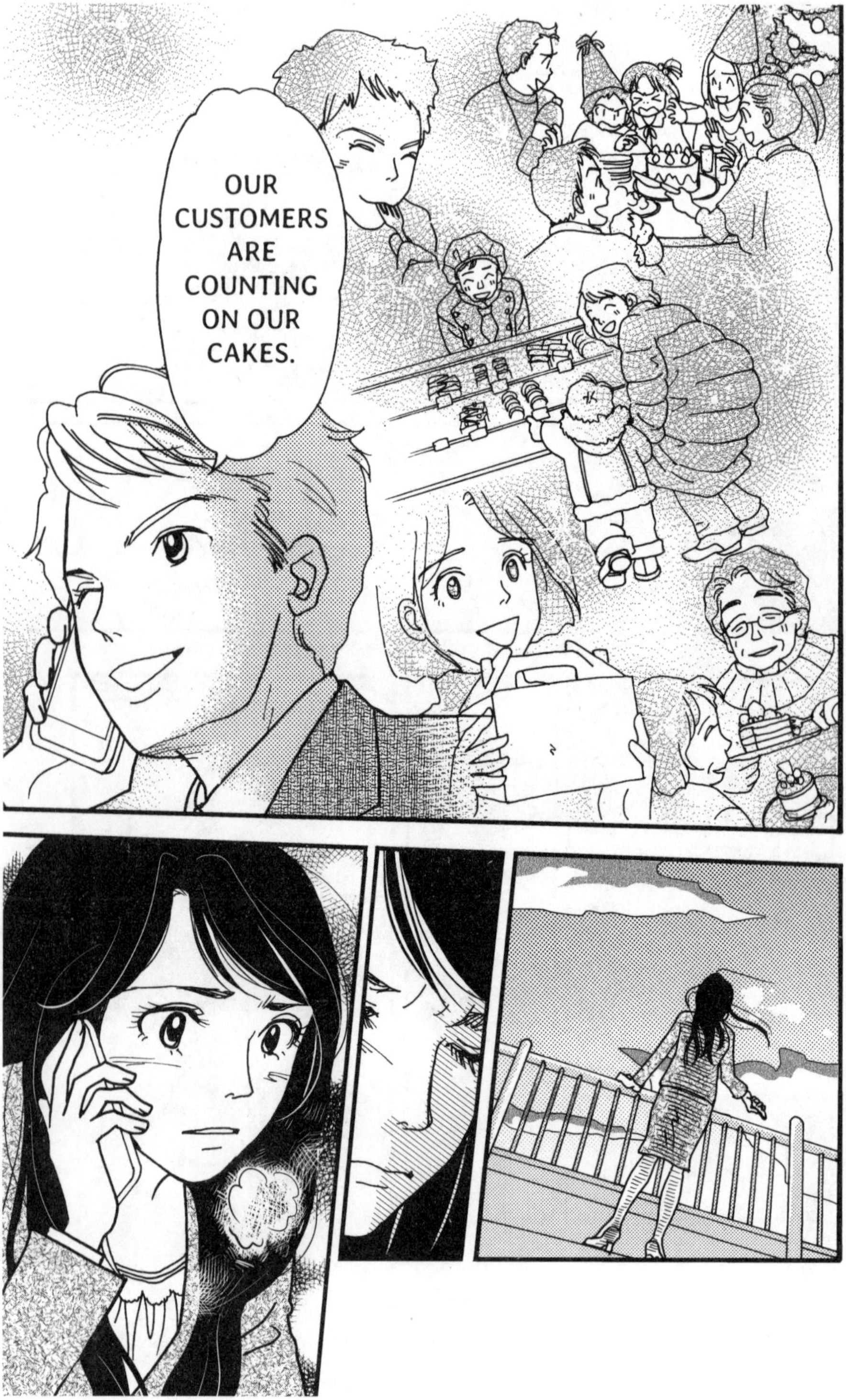
OUR CUSTOMERS ARE COUNTING ON OUR CAKES.

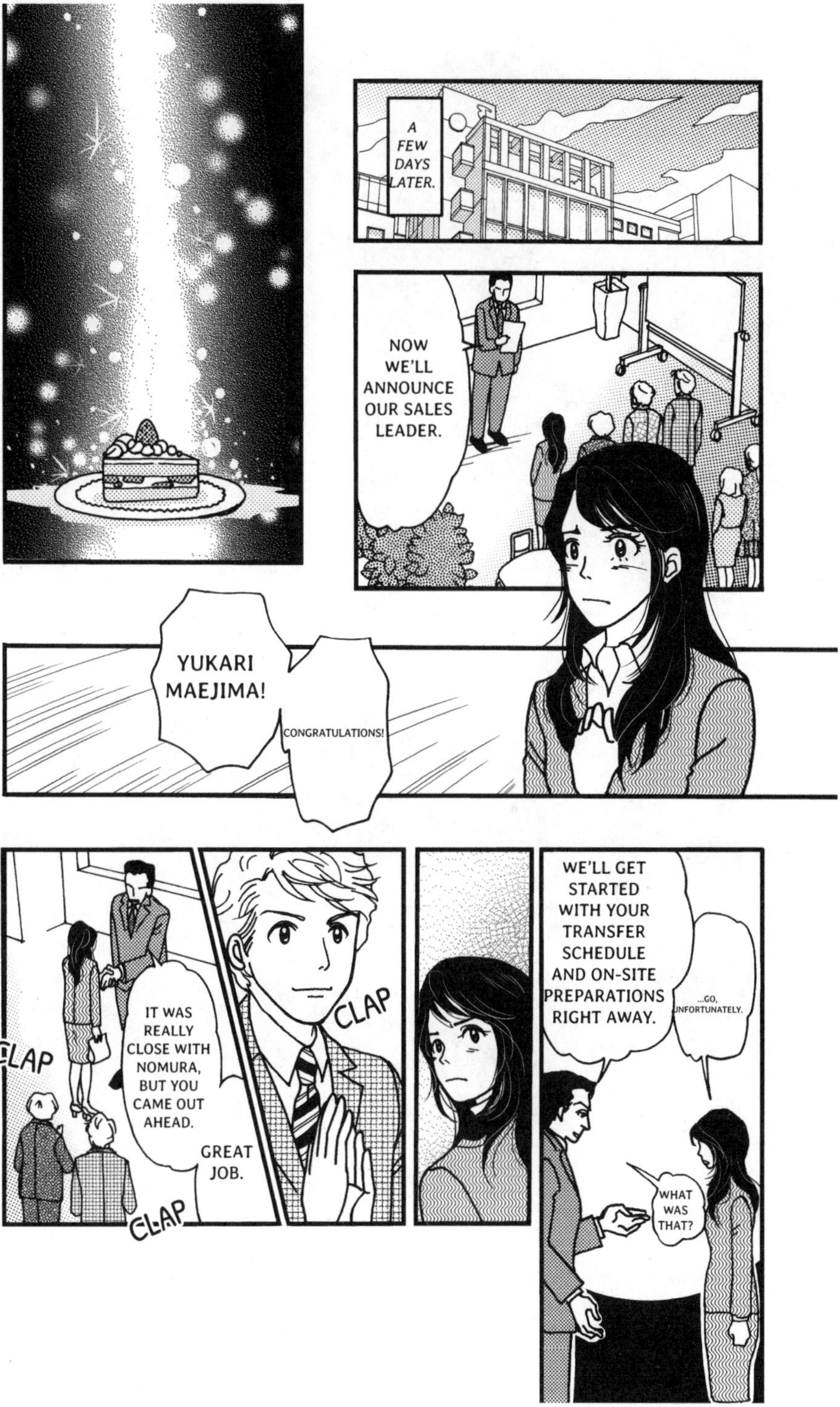
A FEW DAYS LATER.
NOW WE'LL ANNOUNCE OUR SALES LEADER.
YUKARI MAEJIMA!
CONGRATULATIONS!
CLAP
IT WAS REALLY CLOSE WITH NOMURA, BUT YOU CAME OUT AHEAD.
GREAT JOB.
CLAP
CLAP
WE'LL GET STARTED WITH YOUR TRANSFER SCHEDULE AND ON-SITE PREPARATIONS RIGHT AWAY.
...GO, UNFORTUNATELY.
WHAT WAS THAT?

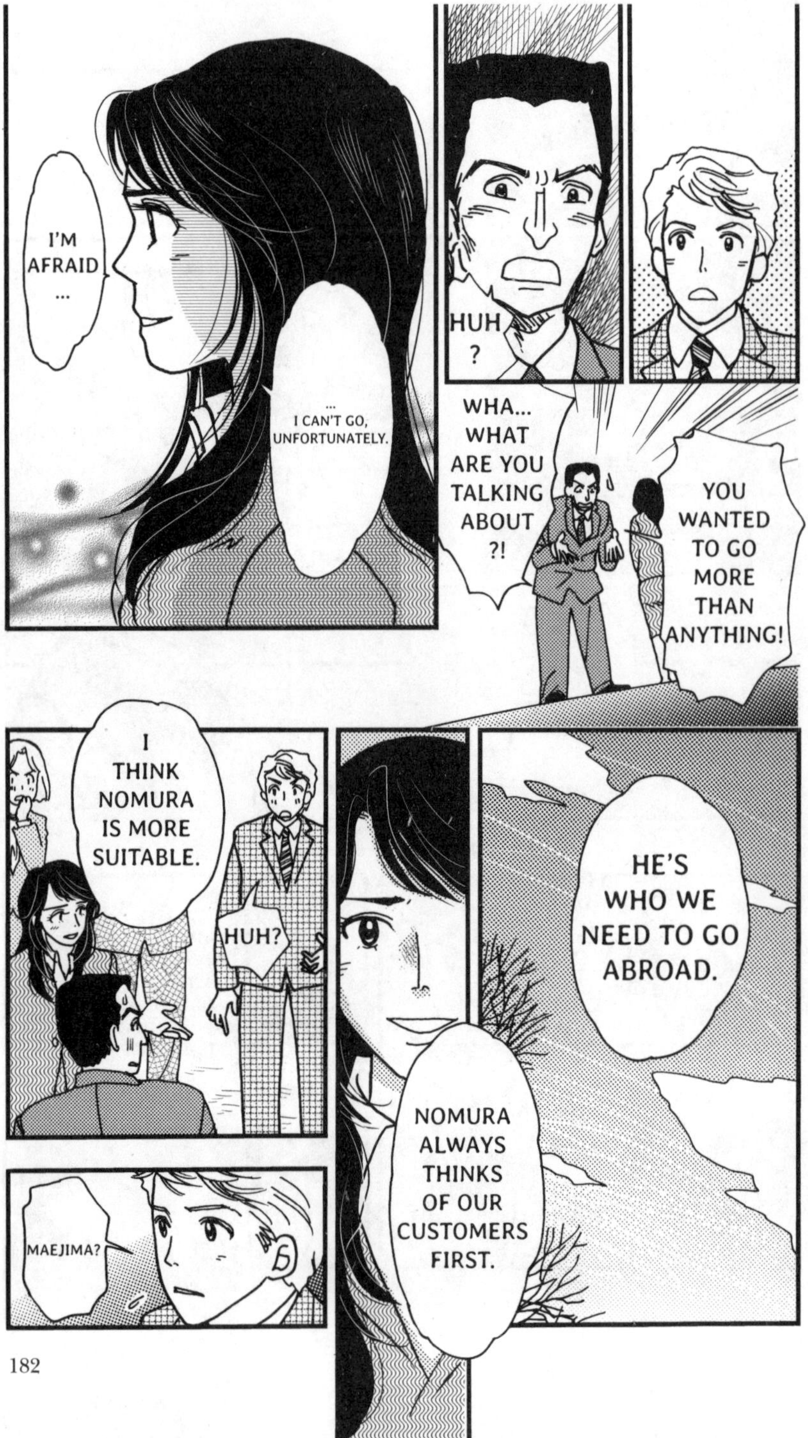
I'M AFRAID ...
... I CAN'T GO, UNFORTUNATELY.
HUH ?
WHA... WHAT ARE YOU TALKING ABOUT ?!
YOU WANTED TO GO MORE THAN ANYTHING!
I THINK NOMURA IS MORE SUITABLE.
HUH?
MAEJIMA?
HE'S WHO WE NEED TO GO ABROAD.
NOMURA ALWAYS THINKS OF OUR CUSTOMERS FIRST.

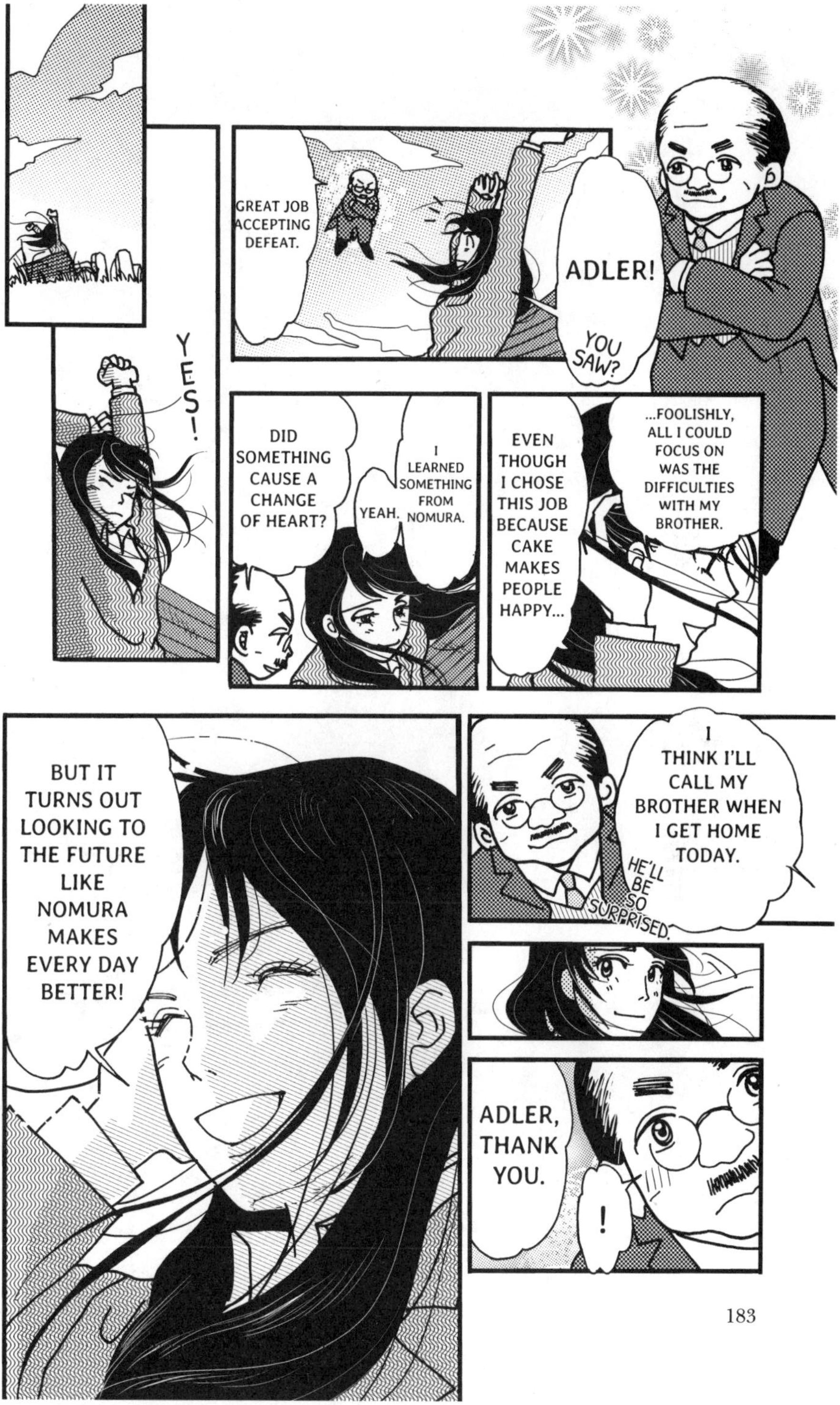
ADLER!
YOU SAW?
GREAT JOB ACCEPTING DEFEAT.
YES!
DID SOMETHING CAUSE A CHANGE OF HEART?
YEAH.
I LEARNED SOMETHING FROM NOMURA.
EVEN THOUGH I CHOSE THIS JOB BECAUSE CAKE MAKES PEOPLE HAPPY...
...FOOLISHLY, ALL I COULD FOCUS ON WAS THE DIFFICULTIES WITH MY BROTHER.
BUT IT TURNS OUT LOOKING TO THE FUTURE LIKE NOMURA MAKES EVERY DAY BETTER!
I THINK I'LL CALL MY BROTHER WHEN I GET HOME TODAY.
HE'LL BE SO SURPRISED.
ADLER, THANK YOU.
!

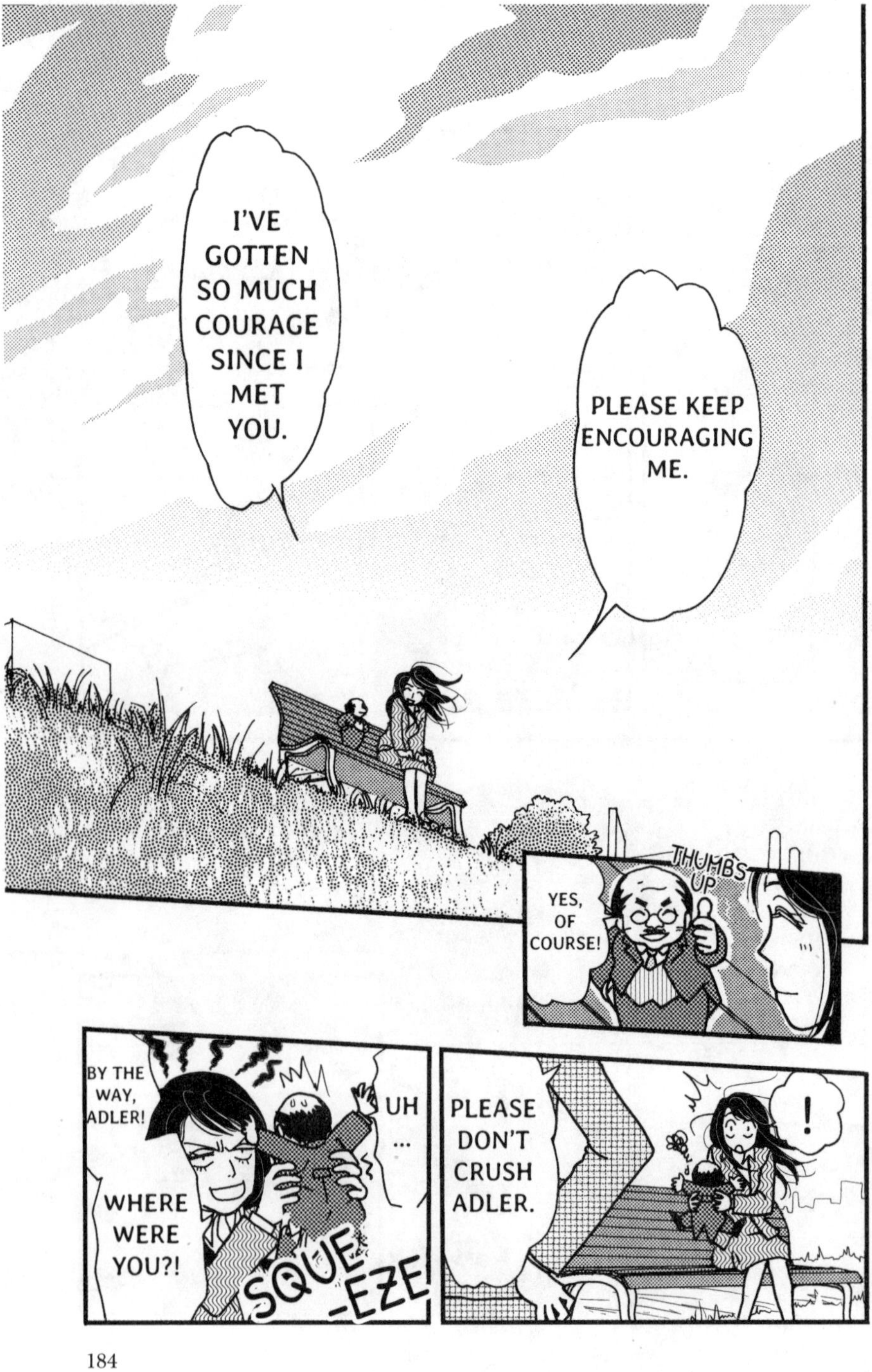
I'VE GOTTEN SO MUCH COURAGE SINCE I MET YOU.
PLEASE KEEP ENCOURAGING ME.
YES, OF COURSE!
THUMBS UP
BY THE WAY, ADLER!
WHERE WERE YOU?!
UH ...
SQUE-EZE
PLEASE DON'T CRUSH ADLER.
!

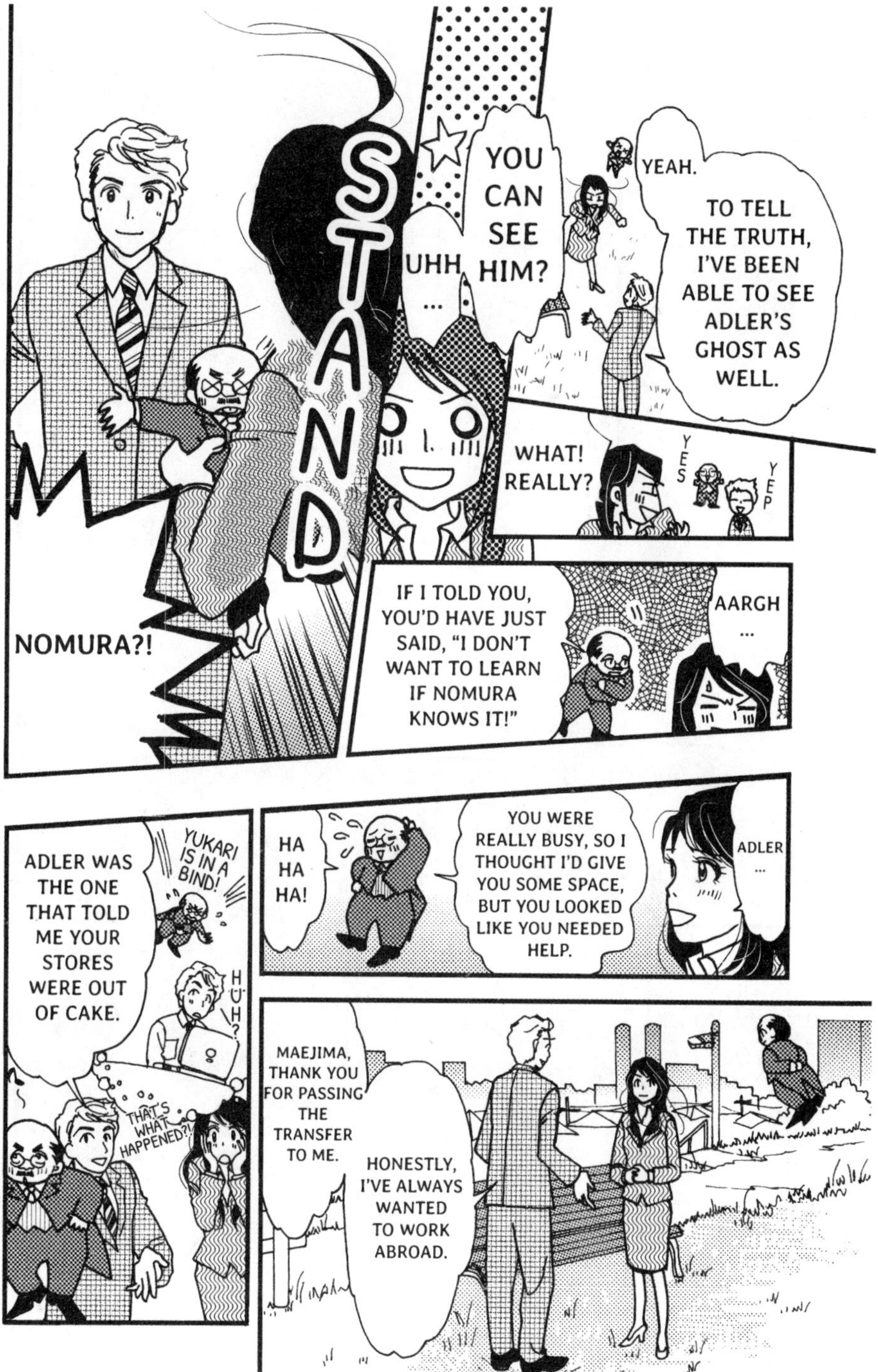
STAND
NOMURA?!
UHH ...
YOU CAN SEE HIM?
YEAH.
TO TELL THE TRUTH, I'VE BEEN ABLE TO SEE ADLER'S GHOST AS WELL.
WHAT! REALLY?
YES
YEP
IF I TOLD YOU, YOU'D HAVE JUST SAID, "I DON'T WANT TO LEARN IF NOMURA KNOWS IT!"
AARGH ...
ADLER ...
YOU WERE REALLY BUSY, SO I THOUGHT I'D GIVE YOU SOME SPACE, BUT YOU LOOKED LIKE YOU NEEDED HELP.
HA HA HA!
ADLER WAS THE ONE THAT TOLD ME YOUR STORES WERE OUT OF CAKE.
YUKARI IS IN A BIND!
HUH?
THAT'S WHAT HAPPENED?!
MAEJIMA, THANK YOU FOR PASSING THE TRANSFER TO ME.
HONESTLY, I'VE ALWAYS WANTED TO WORK ABROAD.

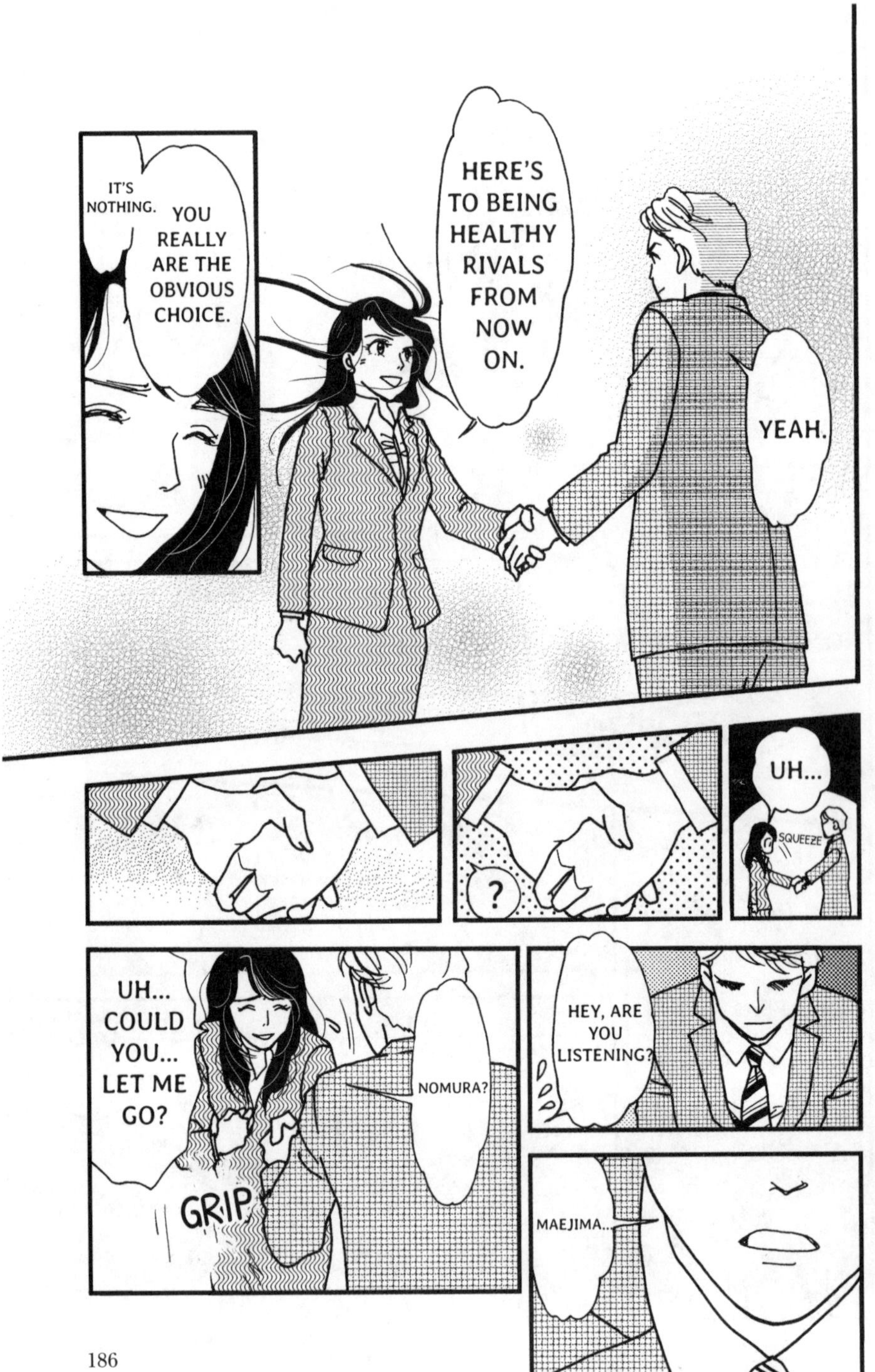
IT'S NOTHING.
YOU REALLY ARE THE OBVIOUS CHOICE.
HERE'S TO BEING HEALTHY RIVALS FROM NOW ON.
YEAH.
?
UH...
SQUEEZE
UH... COULD YOU... LET ME GO?
GRIP
NOMURA?
HEY, ARE YOU LISTENING?
MAEJIMA...

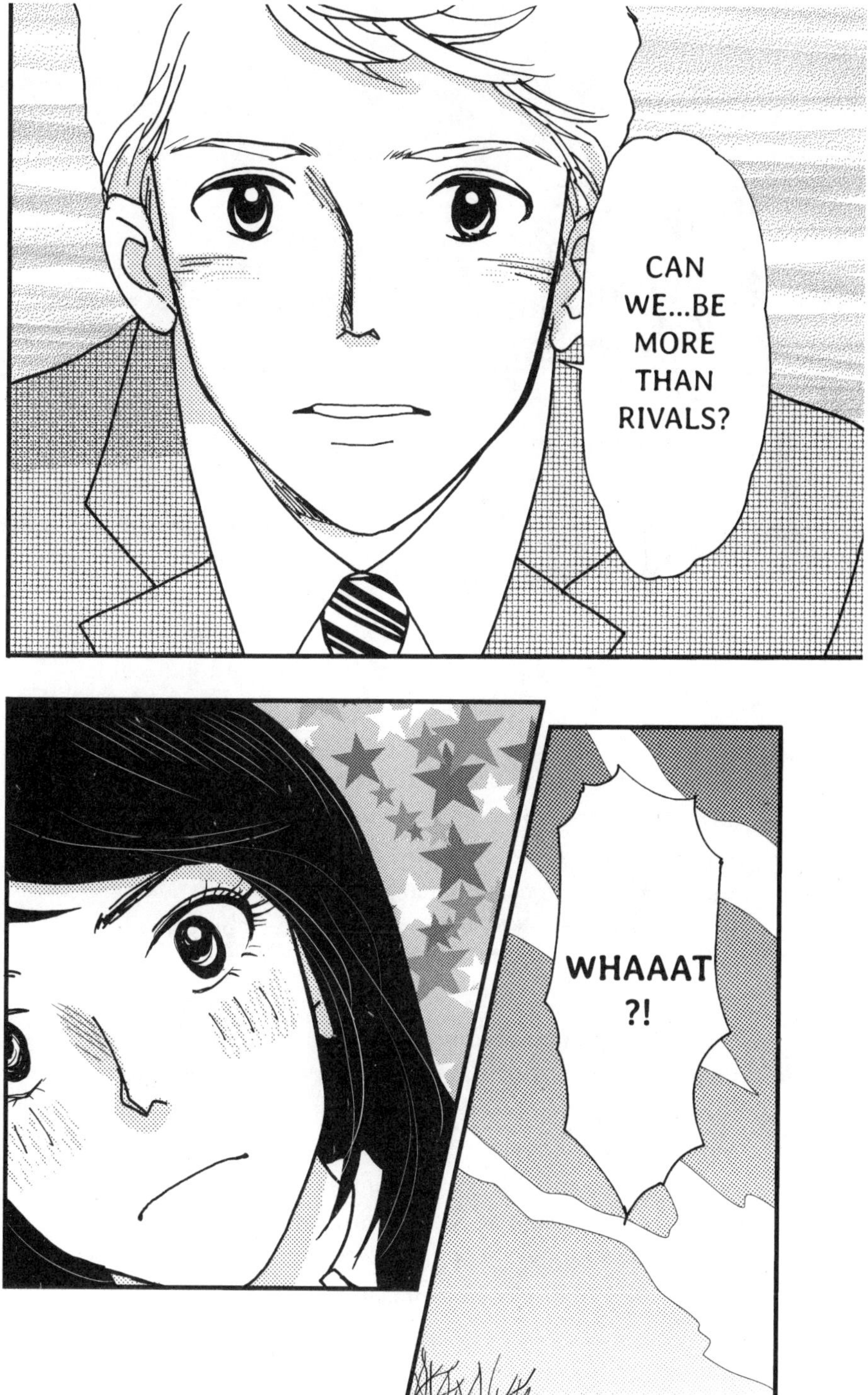
CAN WE...BE MORE THAN RIVALS?
WHAAAT ?!

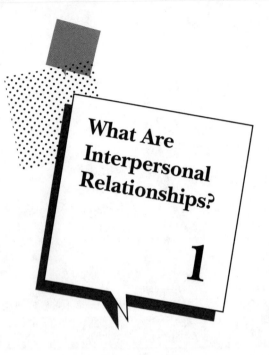

What Are Interpersonal Relationships?

1

⇒ Every Action Needs a Partner

In the Prologue, we touched on interpersonal relationship theory when I wrote, "Every action is interpersonal and requires a partner." We also learned that observing interpersonal patterns is a shortcut to understanding people.

Take, for example, a superior verbally abusing a subordinate, turning unreasonable anger on them. Then someone comes and taps them on the shoulder. It's their direct supervisor. Suddenly, their demeanor changes and they begin talking about their round of golf the other day with a big grin on their face.

Have you experienced something like that? To the superior, their subordinate and supervisor are completely different partners. A partner is someone who influences us with their actions, makes us feel specific emotions, and elicits certain responses. A partner is not only limited to someone else; there are times when we are our own partners. It is thought in Adlerian psychology that removing the idea of partners makes it impossible to discuss human activities.

Interpersonal Relationships and Emotions

We learned in Part 3 that our previous patterns of action toward our partners continue to have a warped influence on our current interpersonal relationships. In this way, when our partner is another person, things can go smoothly and be understood. But what does it mean when you yourself are the partner in the interpersonal relationship?

Let me explain using myself as I write this book as an illustration. I am considering what to write in Part 4. I've decided on the outline, but occasionally sit concentrating with my arms crossed, wondering about the specifics. I am talking to myself within myself, so to speak (this is called *self-talk*). To tell the truth, at this moment, I'm actually thinking of whether to use myself or another example.

Returning to Yukari's story, whenever she fails or things don't go her way and she gets discouraged, she starts thinking, "I need to try harder!" or "I don't want to lose!" and that is always accompanied by "I'm not good enough!" This internal dialog repeats itself.

This internal dialog with oneself as the partner is connected to the idea of self-concept that we learned about in Part 1's explanation of lifestyle on page 64 and is connected with one's self-acceptance as well as self-denial. For Yukari, she also repeated that "men are the enemy" over and over as an internal dialog and created a sense of rivalry with Rui Nomura.

⇒ Four Guidelines to Building Good Relationships

Now then, as we dip our toes into lifestyle, I'll also introduce you to these four guidelines for better relationships:

1) **Respect:** Treat everyone courteously. While people have many differences, including age, gender, occupation, role, interests, and so on, you need to accept that there aren't any differences when it comes to dignity.

2) **Trust:** Always search for the positive intention behind people's actions and believe them without looking for proof.

3) **Effort:** Try to agree and face the goal together with your partner while making an effort to solve problems.

4) **Empathy:** Have an open heart for your partner's thoughts, emotions, and conditions.

We touched lightly on empathy in Part 2. Then we learned more about it in Part 3. So next, I'll explain respect, trust, and effort in more detail.

In Japanese, respect has the connotation of looking up to someone above you. But in English, the word *respect* breaks into *re-*, meaning "again" or "backward," and *-spect*, meaning "to look at." In this way, it has the connotation of taking a step back from your partner and looking at them again with some distance, and then dealing with them with a cool head.

Trust means unconditionally believing your partner regardless of their tendencies or actions. This is different from *confidence*, which has conditions. Confidence requires determination and occasionally patience as well. Once you've decided to trust in someone, even if you are occasionally disappointed by their actions, it means continuing to recognize their character. Note that *mutual* is often used with these two words, as in mutual respect and mutual trust.

For *effort*, we saw Rui Nomura go around to the stores in his area and collect cake for the stores in Yukari's area at the peak of the Christmas sales battle. Nomura didn't see Yukari as an opponent, but rather as a member of the same company, so he helped her with her dilemma. He was putting the company and the customers ahead of winning or losing.

Emotions That Pull Us Apart and Bring Us Together

2

⇨ The Definition of Emotion

In Part 2, Chapter 1, "Reason and Emotion" on page 108, we learned that anger employs illogical circuits in order to bypass reason in the fulfillment of a goal. We learned that this anger has four goals (control, winning a struggle for leadership, protecting one's rights, and displaying a sense of injustice) and that, as a secondary emotion, it has as its base the primary emotions of loneliness, sadness, worry, and disappointment.

In this chapter, we'll introduce a general theory of emotion and Adler's view of the role of emotion in an individual's life. First, emotion can be broken down into three parts:

1) **Sensory Feelings:** A comfortable or uncomfortable state of consciousness created by your five senses

2)   **Mood:** A relatively continuous feeling, including exhilaration or depression, that is strongly linked with physiological function

3)   **Emotion:** A relatively more intense but shorter-lasting feeling that arises suddenly in regard to your partner

Adler divided emotions into two categories: those that pull us apart and those that bring us together. The former causes anger, and the latter causes happiness. However, the opposite is also possible. For example, happiness is usually a feeling that brings us together, but feeling happiness at another's misfortune, like when a fellow coworker you consider a rival makes a mistake and their suffering brings a smile to your face, turns that same emotion into one that pulls us apart.

⇨ Can you control your emotions?

Do our emotions control us, or do we control our emotions? Adlerian psychology believes it is the latter. Emotion has a partner and a purpose in the following way. Emotion doesn't cause people to act; people use emotion to achieve some purpose. Through Adlerian psychology, I have come to the following conclusions about the control of emotions:

1) Emotion is used in certain situations with certain people (partners) for a certain purpose (intention).
2) Emotions can be controlled. In other words, you hold the key to whether you react constructively or unconstructively to them.
3) Emotions (even jealousy or feelings of inferiority) are our partners.

Let's give an example. A mother is angry that her child in junior high school won't do their homework. Then the phone rings. The caller is her mother-in-law. The mother speaks on the phone in a sweet voice. When the child looks at her face, the mother's expression is no longer monstrous; it is smiling. As soon as the phone call is over, the mother is right back to shouting, "Do your homework!" at the child.

When the mother's partner was the child, she was showing her anger clearly, but then on the phone, she was a totally different person. Moreover, when taking the call from her mother-in-law, she spoke in a gentle voice. But then, the instant the call ended, she was right back to her previous anger. In this example, on one side, the mother is using the emotion of anger to try and get her child to do their homework—the purpose of the emotion being control. However, the mother doesn't need to use anger with her mother-in-law. As this example illustrates, you are the one who decides whether to use emotion with specific partners and whether to use it constructively or unconstructively.

Next, let's learn about the final point, "Emotions (even jealousy or feelings of inferiority) are our partners," by examining the feelings of jealousy and inferiority.

Jealousy's True Identity

3

⇨ **Jealousy Arises from a Certain Relationship**

I define *jealousy* as the emotion that causes us to try to bring down or get rid of others (a third person) or close relations (or, in the case of close relations, hold on to them) through suspicion when they make us feel like we are in danger of losing something of great personal value, including our relations, rights, possessions, or status. As seen in Yukari's story, the emotion of jealousy isn't only for romantic relationships—it's born from sibling rivalries and other rivalries from early childhood (including with parents). When compared to other emotions, it proves the most difficult to deal with. Suspicion accompanies jealousy. The French author François de la Rochefoucauld wrote in *Maximes*, "Jealousy lives in suspicion. As soon as it becomes a conviction, it either ends or turns into anger."

Envy is an emotion similar to jealousy, but they are not the same and you should not confuse them. The biggest difference between them, for our purposes, is that jealousy applies to three-way relationships and envy applies to two-way relationships.

In addition, while jealousy accompanies suspicion and is capable of developing into hatred, envy involves the feeling of wanting to be in someone else's shoes.

If we guess at the emotions that Yukari feels toward Rui Nomura from Adler's opinion on jealousy—that is, "Jealousy is based on a deep, powerful sense of inferiority"—we can see that she is envious of him and feels inferior to him in her rivalry with him over their boss. There might also be more complex feelings there, but that is something to look forward to in the story.

What Is Jealousy?

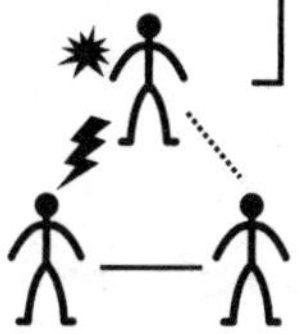

Definition The feeling that you have as you try to get rid of someone (a third person) when this suspicious person exposes you to the risk of losing what is important to you.

Differences with Envy

Jealousy	Envy
Three-Way Relationship	Two-Way Relationship
Many negative factors color your relationship with your partner and your feelings may develop into hatred.	You recognize the positive factors in your partner and you want to be like them.

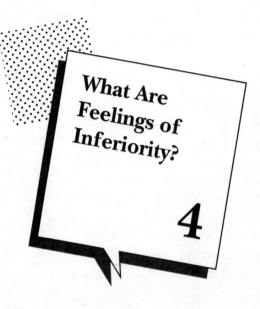

What Are Feelings of Inferiority?

4

⇨ Feelings of Inferiority to Oneself and Others

Feelings of inferiority were discussed on page 80 and defined as "a sense of deficiency based on a subjective opinion." In Adlerian psychology, this is less of a comparison with others and more of a negative feeling caused by how you are compared to your ideal self. Pity, frustration, irritation, envy, panic, disquiet, disappointment, anger, and so on are all collectively feelings of inferiority.

The origin of Yukari's feelings of inferiority begin with her one-year-older brother. But at some point, she developed her own goals and started making an effort to move herself toward them. Generally, feelings of inferiority are not good, but, according to Adler, "They can be a stimulant for healthy growth and effort. Everyone has feelings of inferiority. They cause us to pursue success and superiority. Exactly this constitutes our psychological life."

Feelings of inferiority serve at least two purposes:

1) They are the emotion that accompanies trying to live a better life.
2) They are an irreplaceable friend. If you look at all you have today, a lot of that has feelings of inferiority to *thank.*

If you are someone looking to grow, like Yukari, you should embrace these feelings because they "can be a stimulant for healthy growth and effort." These feelings are proof that you have a purpose, and they tell the tale of how you tried to live a better life. Feelings of inferiority (both toward others and ourselves) are not our enemies, but rather one of our best allies. Whenever we have accomplished something, they have been there, making us feel frustration, which becomes thoughts of "What if?" and urges us to better ourselves.

⇒ Healthy Reactions to Feelings of Inferiority

Feelings of inferiority are not a problem, but how we use them is very important. According to Adler, "What is important is not what a person has, but how they use what they were given." Keeping this in mind, it is extremely important how we respond to our feelings of inferiority with self-determination (page 78).

199

There are generally three ways we tend to respond unconstructively (occasionally destructively) to feelings of inferiority: we try to smother them, we use them as fuel for self-pity, or we try to involve others in our misery. Trying to smother them can have negative effects on your health: you may not be able to emerge from the morass of self-pity, and in the end, you may involve others and cause an uproar.

Have you ever had an experience such as breaking off a friendship in anger, losing your patience for something and not showing your best, making unreasonable demands of someone you have a grudge against, sabotaging someone else for whatever reason, and so on? Unconstructive responses to feelings of inferiority tend to create secondary feelings of inferiority about ourselves. In other words, unconstructive or destructive responses end up being directed not only toward others but also toward ourselves. For example, if you cut contact with a friend out of anger, once that anger recedes, it will be replaced by regret. You think to yourself, "Why did I do something so stupid?" and eventually, you experience sadness at losing an important friend.

If you are like most people, however, you have probably reacted constructively to most feelings of inferiority. They have been a part of the process of getting you here whenever you thought about how you felt, what you did, and what the outcome of an action was regardless of success or failure. You tried to get into a top-tier school, kept participating in a club despite not being good enough to compete, hit on someone out of your league, or struggled with a difficult job—the examples are endless. Feelings of inferiority were probably behind these actions, trying to bridge the gap between our objectives and our present situations. Feelings of inferiority probably spurred you into action, making you think things like, "I have to do something" or "I need to do more." Just like Yukari, feelings of inferiority have been your supporter and companion as you have grown to where you are today. That's why I say you should be grateful for these feelings.

Adler and America

Adler first visited America in 1926. He liked the country and the people welcomed him in return. After publishing *Understanding Human Nature* in 1927, he released one book after another.

In the beginning, Adler couldn't speak English, but he felt the need to master the language. There is a video of him speaking quite fluently with no translations in 1929, when he was already in his 50s. To master a second language later in life must have required serious effort on his part. He continued to work hard at achieving new goals, and he obtained his driver's license in the United States at the age of 60.

In the summer of 1929, Adler decided that he wanted to move to America, but he had trouble convincing his wife, Raissa. She categorically refused. From her perspective, it made no sense to give up her job in politics, her friends, and her family to move to a country where she didn't speak the language and did not agree with the politics. Consequently, Adler moved to the United States in 1929 without his family, reuniting with them only in 1935, when the Nazi's rise to power forced them to leave Vienna for the United States.

Among the three great minds of psychology, Adler alone is not rumored to have had any affairs, despite his separation from his family. Freud and Jung purportedly had many.

Part 5

What Is Encouragement?

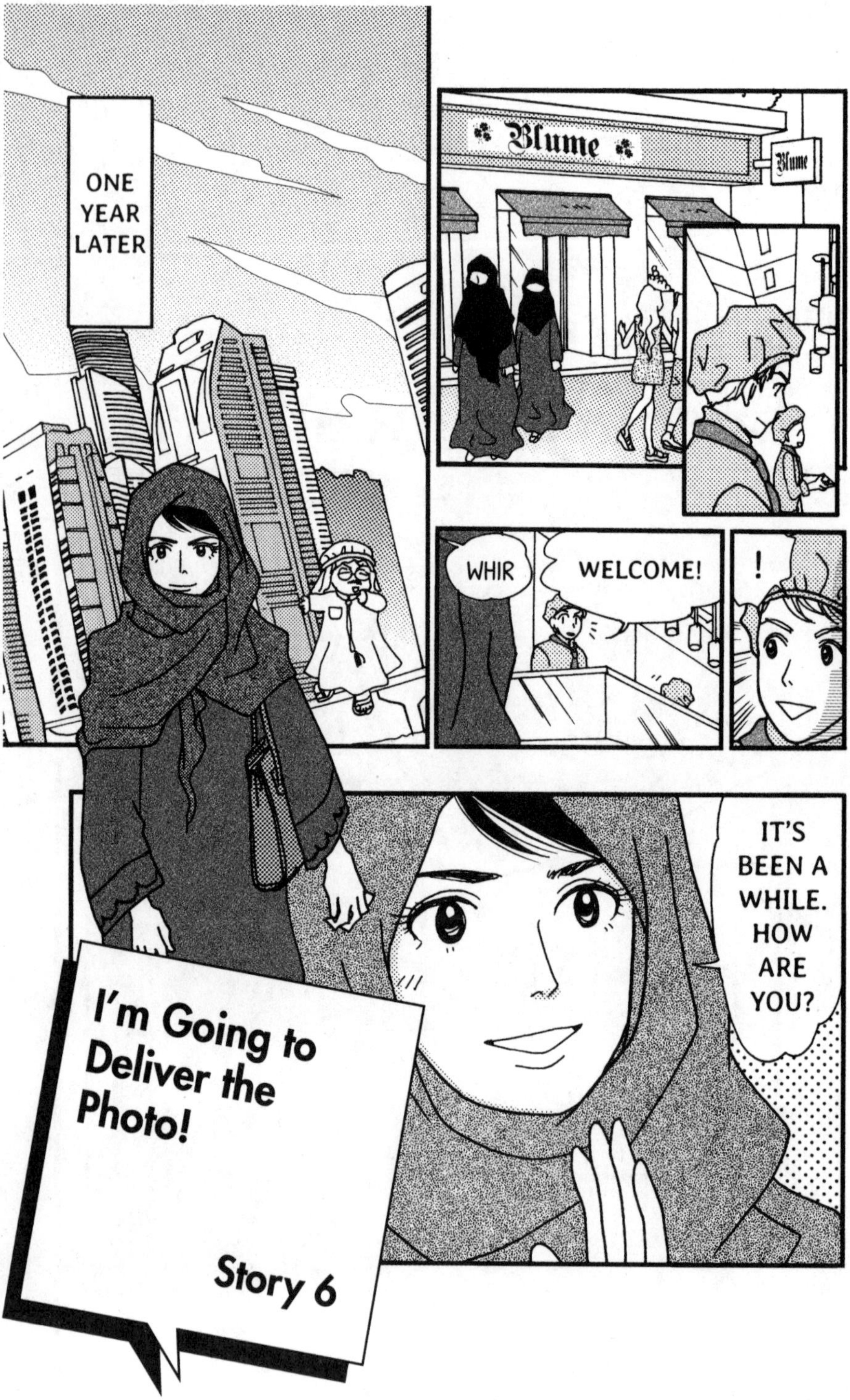
ONE YEAR LATER
Blume
Blume
WHIR
WELCOME!
!
IT'S BEEN A WHILE. HOW ARE YOU?
I'm Going to Deliver the Photo!
Story 6

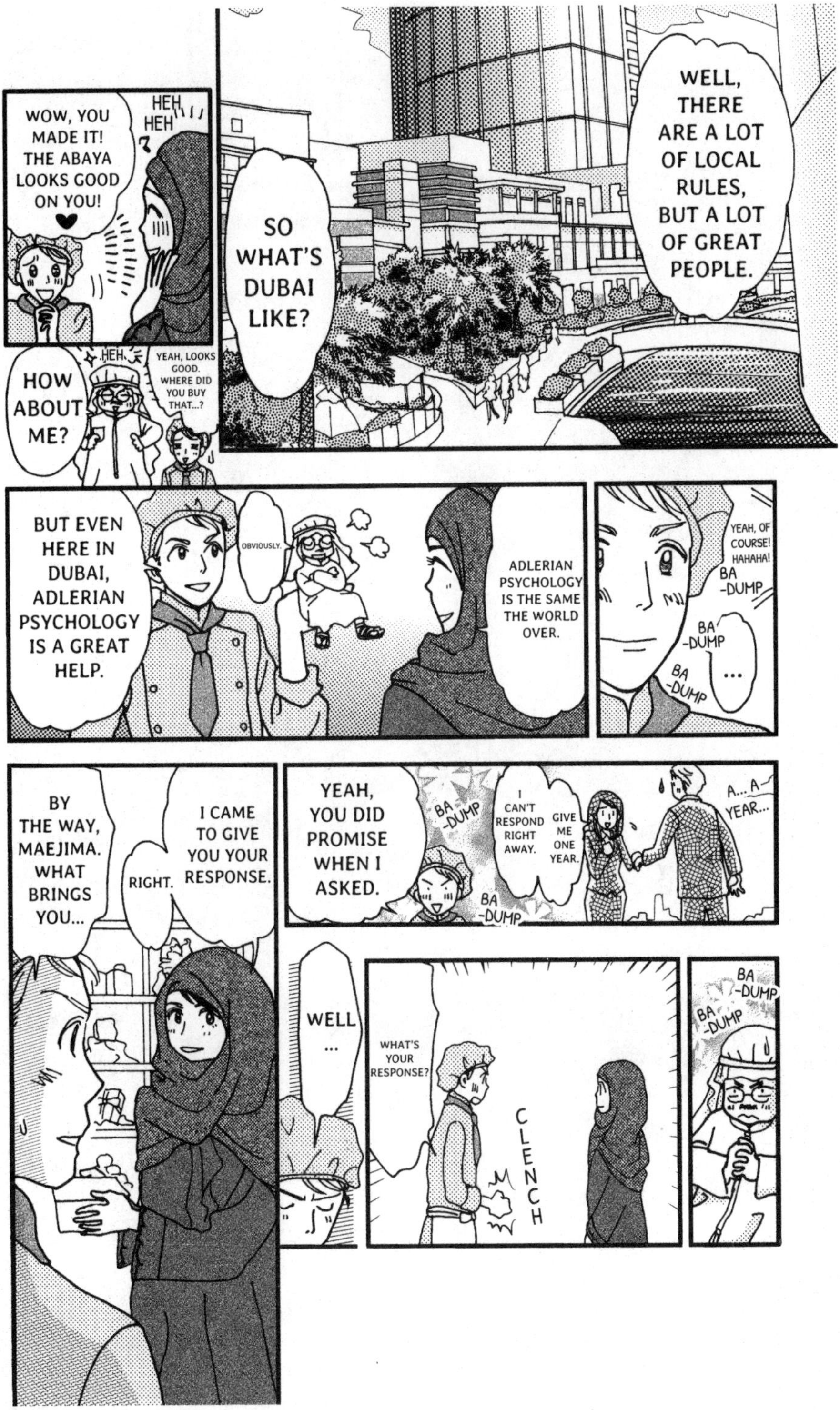
WOW, YOU MADE IT! THE ABAYA LOOKS GOOD ON YOU!
HEH HEH
HOW ABOUT ME?
HEH
YEAH, LOOKS GOOD. WHERE DID YOU BUY THAT...?
SO WHAT'S DUBAI LIKE?
WELL, THERE ARE A LOT OF LOCAL RULES, BUT A LOT OF GREAT PEOPLE.
BUT EVEN HERE IN DUBAI, ADLERIAN PSYCHOLOGY IS A GREAT HELP.
OBVIOUSLY.
ADLERIAN PSYCHOLOGY IS THE SAME THE WORLD OVER.
YEAH, OF COURSE! HAHAHA!
BA -DUMP
BA -DUMP
BA -DUMP
...
BY THE WAY, MAEJIMA. WHAT BRINGS YOU...
RIGHT.
I CAME TO GIVE YOU YOUR RESPONSE.
YEAH, YOU DID PROMISE WHEN I ASKED.
BA -DUMP
I CAN'T RESPOND RIGHT AWAY.
GIVE ME ONE YEAR.
A... A YEAR...
BA -DUMP
WELL ...
WHAT'S YOUR RESPONSE?
CLENCH
BA -DUMP
BA -DUMP

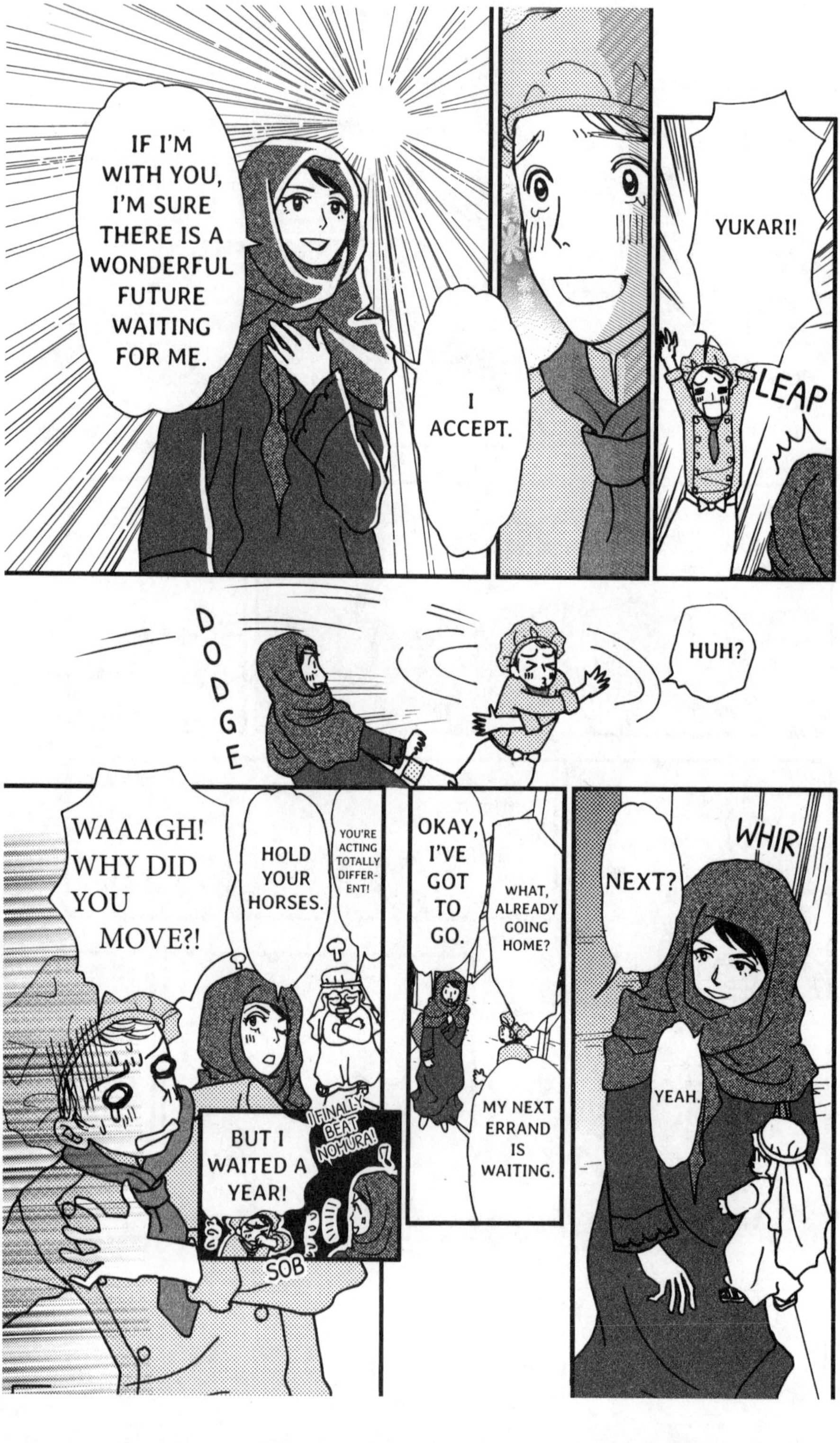
IF I'M WITH YOU, I'M SURE THERE IS A WONDERFUL FUTURE WAITING FOR ME.
I ACCEPT.
YUKARI!
LEAP
DODGE
HUH?
WAAAGH! WHY DID YOU MOVE?!
HOLD YOUR HORSES.
YOU'RE ACTING TOTALLY DIFFER-ENT!
BUT I WAITED A YEAR!
I FINALLY BEAT NOMURA!
SOB
OKAY, I'VE GOT TO GO.
WHAT, ALREADY GOING HOME?
MY NEXT ERRAND IS WAITING.
WHIR
NEXT?
YEAH.

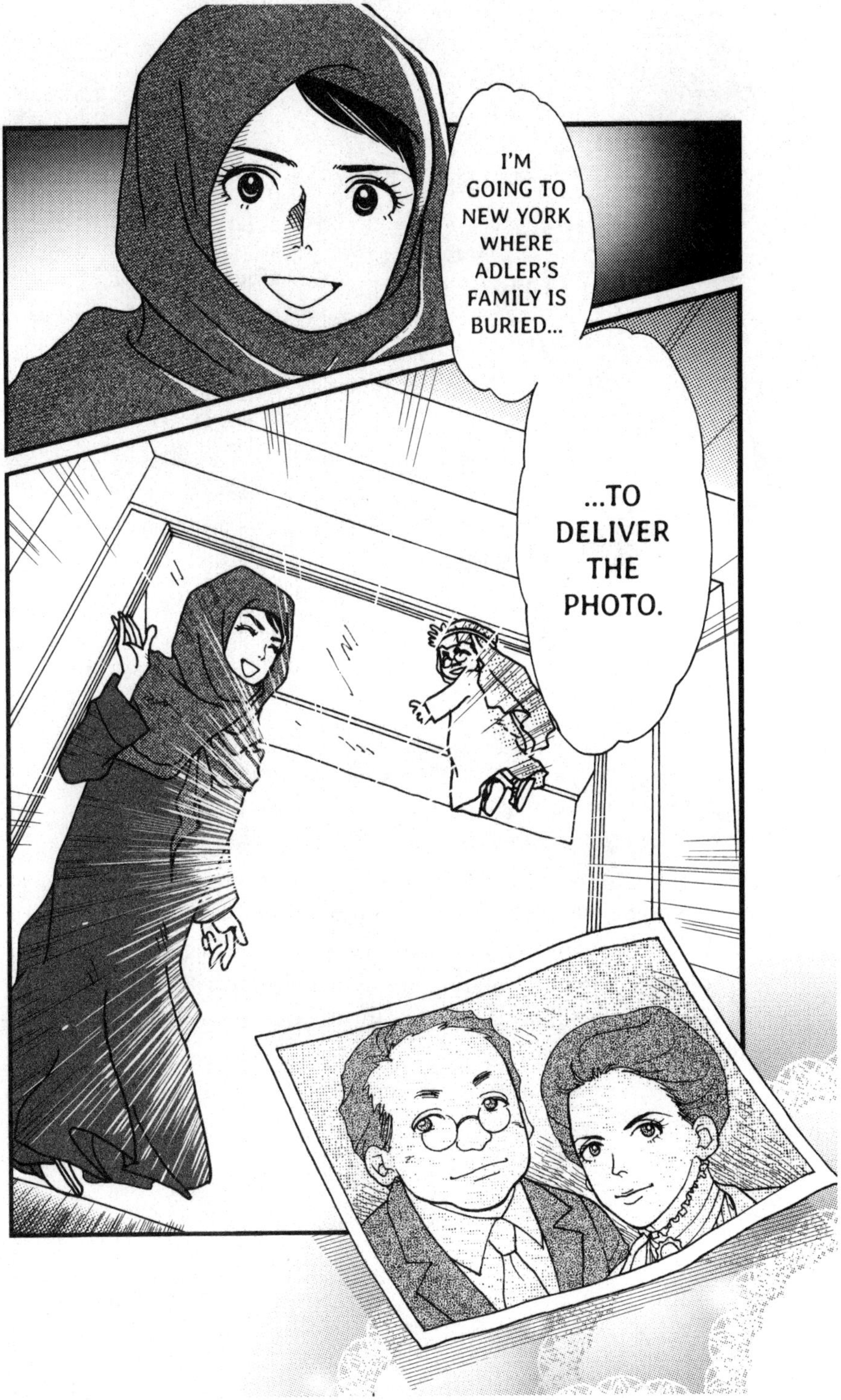
I'M GOING TO NEW YORK WHERE ADLER'S FAMILY IS BURIED...
...TO DELIVER THE PHOTO.

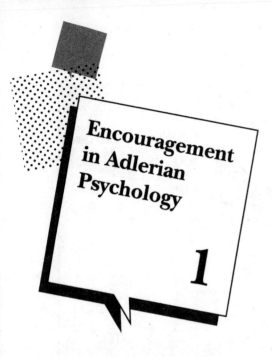

Encouragement in Adlerian Psychology

1

⇒ **The Basics of Encouragement**

Now, let's look back at Yukari's story. While having difficulties in her work as an area manager, she was able to encourage herself with Adler's help. She was able to manage only herself in the beginning, but she grew and began to encourage those around her as well.

As was touched on in the Prologue, *encouragement* is what gives people the strength to overcome difficulties. It is also completely dependent on having empathy and relationships built on mutual respect and trust. Part 2 introduced the opposite of encouragement, the strength-stealing discouragement. We also introduced the three stages of discouragement: (1) setting unreasonable goals, (2) focusing on areas of weakness, and (3) denying your self-worth.

In Part 2, we also introduced how even a timid person can start developing courage:

1)   Begin with relationships built on respect and trust.

2)   Recognize differences in personality.

3)   See weaknesses as strengths.

4)   Occasionally confront the other party.

These four steps are how to develop courage. Do you remember them?

In Part 5, we look at three more points: (1) the difference between praising and encouraging, (2) self-encouragement, and (3) encouraging others. Once you learn these, you will truly come to feel that Adlerian psychology is made exactly to encourage you and those around you.

⇨ The Difference Between Praise and Encouragement

Encouragement and praise are often mixed up. They share a similarity in that they are looking at the positives, but they are different things at their root. Let's break their differences into three points. The first difference is that while encouragement is giving the strength to overcome difficulties, praise is intended to make someone else feel good.

Next, encouragement is based on the respect, trust, and empathy that we learned about in Part 4. Praise, on the other hand, is a way to evaluate someone's good points; it can also have an undertone of manipulation.

There is another root difference between the two: while praise requires oversight and supervision to ensure results as a manager might utilize it in the workplace, encouragement builds someone up to be able to act on their own without the need for micromanagement. Encouragement is different from praising someone or inspiring them through cheers—it gives one the strength to overcome difficulties. Not only does this make people in a positive state (for example, happy) more positive, but it also offers people in a negative or depressed state a stable base of trust and respect that can be used for self-empowerment.

Keep in mind, however, that psychological techniques that increase motivation are considered dangerous to people in a negative state because the techniques become a form of manipulation.

What Is Encouragement?

The Differences Between Praise and Encouragement

Praise	Encouragement
Evaluates good points and celebrates Judgmental, superior-subordinate relationship	Gives one strength to overcome difficulties Empathic, equal relationship

| Makes One Partner-Dependent | Makes One Partner-Independent |

Carrot and Stick → Praise | Encourage ← Encourages your partner to be able to encourage themself

The Outcome of Encouragement

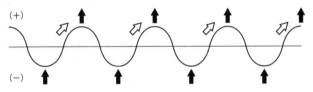

(+)

(−)

⬈ The outcome of making happy people happier (positives are enhanced)

⬆ The outcome of encouragement (not only for positive but also for negative states)

Self-Encouragement

2

⇒ **The Three Keys to Encouraging Yourself**

Discouraging pressures are all around us. It is important that we do not slip into a negative state. *Self-encouragement* is a tool that we can use to help ourselves and subsequently help others.

In environments that are full of discouraging pressures, how do we go about encouraging ourselves? These three are the key: (1) finding a feeling of belonging, (2) developing a feeling of trust, and (3) nurturing a sense of contribution.

The first, a feeling of belonging, is when you have somewhere you can be comfortable. Whether at work, at home, or in the area where you live, you feel like "I am supposed to be here."

212

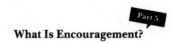

The second, a feeling of trust, means trusting in the people around you. If this feeling is present and there is a shared goal, then cooperating with the people around you becomes possible.

The third, a sense of contribution, is the feeling that you are valued by the people and world around you. It is believing that people are counting on you for your contributions to their lives.

Out of these three, Adlerian psychology considers a sense of contribution to be the most important. Contributing is the route to the most happiness. Your wealth, status, age, or experience do not matter. As long as you have the will to contribute, you can.

⇛ How Do I Encourage Myself?

The quickest way to encourage yourself is to fill your words, image, and actions with encouragement. The first step is to use clear, positive words with yourself and those around you. You do this through *affirmation*. Words exert an influence on us from our emotional selves deep in our hearts to our physical body. Even when you are in a tough spot, you encourage yourself by saying, "I won't get discouraged."

When your words become positive, your image of yourself will become positive as well. It's important to make so definite and positive an image that there is no room for any negativity— *stray thoughts*—to creep in.

While turning your words and image positive, the next step is to spread it to your actions. Occasionally, you need to just go for it as well. This is *decisive action*. Affirmation, stray thoughts, and decisive action—the important thing about these three is to use them affirmatively as if you've already achieved them.

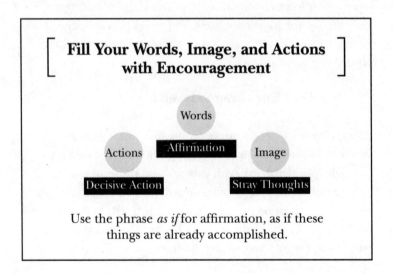

Fill Your Words, Image, and Actions with Encouragement

Words

Actions Affirmation Image

Decisive Action Stray Thoughts

Use the phrase *as if* for affirmation, as if these things are already accomplished.

Dr. Joseph Pellegrino, an Adlerian psychology researcher and head of the Montreal Individual Psychology Research Center (and also a former teacher of mine), recommends reciting the following sentences, which are a connection of affirmation, stray thoughts, and decisive action, in order to encourage yourself:

- I am a unique and competent person. I decide what I do with my life.
- I have personal characteristics (skills, abilities, and strengths) and other positive aspects, and I can use them in my environment.
- I will face life's difficulties and accept the challenge of overcoming them.
- I will regard my errors and mistakes as opportunities for learning and growth.
- I will focus less on completion and perfection and more on effort and progress.
- In this world, my life has a purpose and a meaning.
- I am more than what I or others see me as.
- I conduct myself as the person I truly want to be.

Encouraging Others

3

⇨ The Three Levels of Encouragement

People with the courage to overcome their difficulties don't do things that would discourage others and are able to encourage others smoothly. Keep the following three levels in mind:

1) Encourage others within the bounds of mutual respect and trust.
2) Encourage others in a way that they can encourage themselves.
3) Encourage others in a way that is useful to the community.

Starting with a relationship built on mutual respect and trust, your partner should not just be waiting for your encouragement while acting, but rather should be able to spontaneously encourage themselves. Ideally, this will result in them not thinking "I only need to take care of myself," but instead encouraging those around them as well.

Using the manga as an example, Yukari saw Rui Nomura as a rival, but he always acted with mutual respect and trust, and so he saved her when her mistake caused a dilemma.

Seeing Nomura's consistent demeanor not only changed the way she saw him but also changed the combative relationship she had with men in general. This changed the way she acted to her subordinates and expanded her viewpoint away from tending to think about herself first to considering what was best for the office or the company as a whole. This is precisely the outcome of encouragement.

⇨ How to Encourage Others

You can use five methods to encourage others:

1) Focus on the positives.
2) Change from a subtracting points system to an adding points system.
3) Emphasize the process.
4) Accept mistakes.
5) Convey appreciation.

The first method of encouraging others is to focus on the positives rather than the negatives. We are all absolute masters at searching for mistakes and focusing on negative areas. We have had our negatives focused on for years at school and home, and even at work there is ten times more focus on the negatives than the positives.

What is the outcome of all of this negative focus? We unconsciously focus on the negatives and overlook the positives all around us. Instead, self-determined people should change their focus from the negative to the positive, which will have the effect of bringing people together.

The second method of encouraging others is to switch from a system of subtracting points from people to a system of adding points. Subtracting points means looking at someone below you, emphasizing deviations from some expected standard. The more knowledgeable and experienced the person, the more likely they are to use subtraction. But if you want to understand the people around you, you should use empathy to lower yourself to their level, see with their eyes, hear with their ears, and feel with their heart. If that is how you deal with people, you'll remember to appreciate their effort.

The third method of encouraging others is strongly linked to the previous two. It is not only looking at the outcome, but emphasizing the process. The productivity mindset "Make it fast and good" places all of the emphasis on the end product, but some people are inspired by the blood, sweat, and tears of the process. It's necessary to recognize all of the effort and the little victories as well.

The fourth method of encouraging others is accepting mistakes. In Adlerian psychology, failure is seen as proof that you tried and had a chance to learn. And this applies not only

to yourself but to others as well. Yukari learned a lot from the mistakes she made over her subordinates' failures and the trouble that followed.

The fifth method of encouraging others is to convey appreciation. Be sure to reply to contributions made on your behalf by others with words of gratitude such as "Thank you" or "That's a great help." If it's embarrassing to say words of thanks, an email, memo, or a heartfelt letter will do as well. The story ended with Yukari visiting Nomura in Dubai and then setting off to New York to visit the resting place of Adler's family to return his photo. She is really trying to convey her heartfelt gratitude to Nomura and Adler.

Yukari's story is at an end, but your encouragement tale is just beginning. Good luck!

Column

Adler's Twilight Years and Passing

Adler became friends with American billionaire Charles Henry Davis. For treating his daughter's depression, Davis donated large sums to Columbia University, where Adler was lecturing, found him a job at Long Island College of Medicine, and worked as his academic and professional agent. Partly because of this, Adler became the best paid lecturer in the United States at that time and was able to visit the whole country with his personal driver.

Adler the workaholic, who had such a hectic lecture schedule that he couldn't find time to write his books, loved Hollywood movies. In Adler's *Case Seminar*, which I translated into Japanese, there are many stories of movies and actresses between the counseling and the case studies.

Even after reuniting with his family in 1935, Adler didn't change his pace and continued working, even planning a lecture and conference circuit in the spring of 1937. At the end of May, he made a side-trip to Scotland. On May 28, while in Aberdeen for a morning lecture, he was taking a walk near his hotel when he had a heart attack and collapsed. While being taken to the hospital in an ambulance, he drew his last breath. He was 67 years old. He left this world without seeing the completion of his work.

Freud, being in exile in London, read of Adler's death in the newspaper and left this note addressed to his friend (you can feel Freud's jealousy toward Adler): "For a young Jewish boy born outside of Vienna, dying in Aberdeen, Scotland itself is unprecedented, and evidence of how successful he truly was."

Author's Profile

Toshinori Iwai

Toshinori Iwai was born in Ibaraki prefecture in Japan in 1947. He graduated from Waseda University in 1970. He worked in management for several foreign companies, then created the Human Guild LLC in April 1985. He participated in Adlerian psychology counseling, counselor education and enrichment, and research. Since April 2021, he has worked as a visiting professor at the Hollywood Graduate School of Beauty Business. He is known for writing a number of books on the subject of Adlerian psychology and its applications.